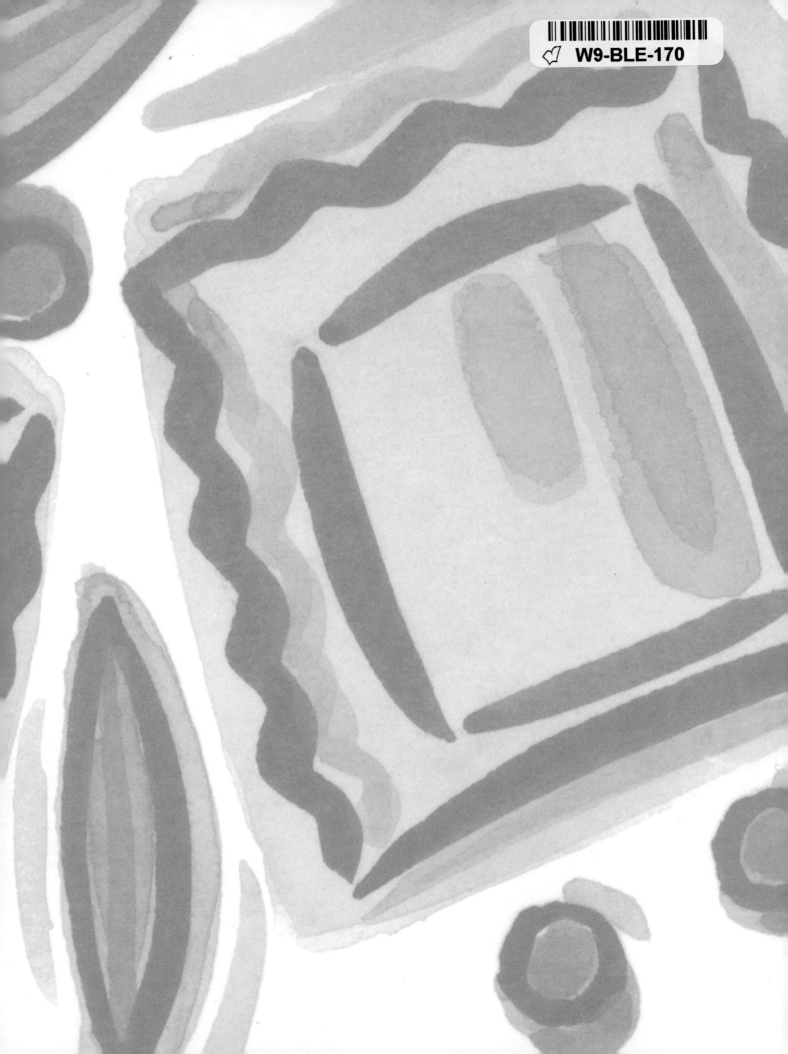

The Encyclopedia
of
Pasta

Bridget Jones

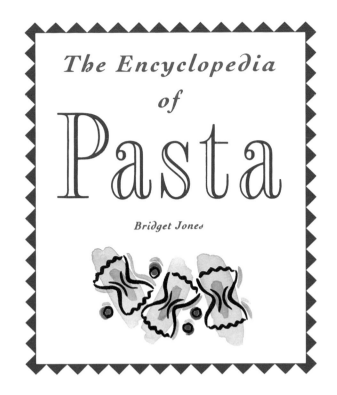

The Encyclopedia
of
Pasta

Bridget Jones

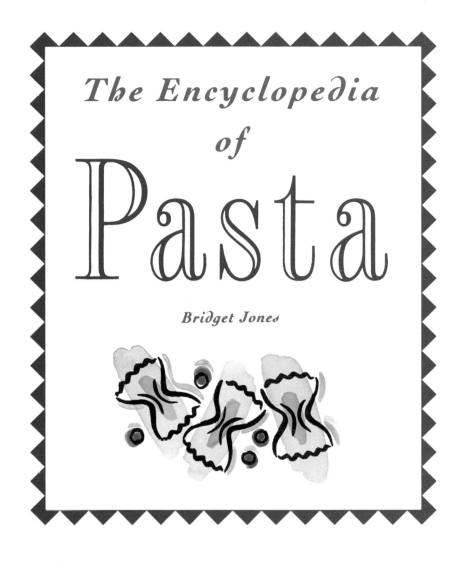

THUNDER BAY
P·R·E·S·S

A Quintet Book

Copyright © 1994 Quintet Publishing Limited.

All rights reserved under the Pan American and International Copyright
Conventions. First published in the United States of America in 1994 by
Thunder Bay Press.

Library of Congress Cataloging-in-Publication Data

Jones, Bridget.
    The encyclopedia of pasta / Bridget Jones.
        p.   cm.
    ISBN 1-57145-005-X: $29.95
    1. Cookery (Pasta) 2. Pasta products. I. Title.
TX809, M17J654 1994
641.8'22--dc20

                                                                94-14139
                                                                DIP

This book was designed and produced by
Quintet Publishing Limited
6 Blundell Street
London N7 9BH

Creative Director: Richard Dewing
Designer: Peter Laws
Project Editors: Katie Preston and Claire Tennant-Scull
Editor: Michelle Clark
Photographer: Andrew Sydenham
Home Economists: Samantha Dobson and Nicola Fowler

Typeset in Great Britain by
Central Southern Typesetters, Eastbourne
Manufactured in Singapore by Star Standard Pte. Ltd.
Printed in Singapore by Eray Scan Pte. Ltd.

Thunder Bay Press
5880 Oberlin Drive, Suite 400
San Diego, California 92121

Acknowledgements
Picture on page 7 courtesy of the Pasta Information Bureau. Picture on
page 8 courtesy of the Italian Trade Center. Picture on page 6 courtesy of
the Mansell Collection. Pasta making equipment for photography supplied
by Lakeland Plastics and Debenhams – Le Vrai Gourmet.

CONTENTS

An Historic Food

(49)-2013-Macaroni drying in the dirty streets of Naples, Italy.
Copyright Underwood & Underwood.

Pasta – the practical food for today's busy cook – has a long tradition, set in the history of many nations, and steeped in the controversy of international culinary claims. Pasta goes so far back in the history of food that it is talked of as one of the first palatable forms of using grain and ways of preserving the milled grain. It is undoubtedly the continued popularity of pasta that has brought about discussion of its origins.

The Italians have to be thanked for making pasta the varied and multi-national product it has become, but whether or not it is fair to say that they invented pasta dough is unclear. From research into writings on the topic, it seems that pasta is a food that has evolved in different corners of the world in parallel, rather than stemming from one particular source.

THE ORIGINS OF PASTA – SOME ANCIENT STORIES OF ART AND TRAVEL

One popular theory is that the explorer Marco Polo discovered pasta on his travels to China during the 13th century, and took the idea home to Venice. The Chinese were making noodles long before Marco Polo visited their country, but there is also evidence that the Italians were producing an equivalent food. References to pasta-making equipment date back before Marco Polo's travels, and there were recipes for vermicelli and filled pasta in a 13th-century publication that also preceded his return from the Orient. The Etruscan art of early Italian civilization includes cooking equipment that could well have been used for making pasta. It is suggested that the first Italian experiments may have been along the lines of a Greek dough.

Apart from these two popularly discussed sources of pasta, Indians and Arabs were also making pasta by (if not before) the 13th century, so either could well have introduced the idea to Europe. The names *sev* or *seviyan*, for Indian vermicelli, have evolved from *sevika*, an early name for pasta, meaning thread. Other names for the first pastas indicated that it was long and thread-like, and *spaghetti* is derived from *spago*, meaning string. Later, *macaroni* was to become the generic term for pasta. By the 18th century, the same term was used for young men who travelled to Italy with the fashionable intention of improving their cultural outlook, but who, instead, indulged in the pleasures of consuming pasta – dandy *macaronis* indeed.

A DIFFERENT PLACE, A DIFFERENT FORM

It is interesting to look at the shapes and types of pasta and similar doughs that have developed in Europe. The Italian-like filled pasta of Poland, for example, was brought to the country as a result of a marriage with Italian royalty, and then there are the robust noodles of Germany. Potato, cheese and flour are all used as bases for pasta doughs that range from dumpling-like gnocchi to curly spätzle and noodles similar to tagliatelle.

Oriental forms of pasta are distinctly different from these, having a lighter texture. As well as doughs based on wheat flour, rice flour and flour made from mung beans are used to make rice sticks or clear, cellophane noodles. Oriental methods used to shape pasta also differ from those of other countries, with noodles being formed by a technique of twirling and stretching the dough. Swinging the dough around rather like a short skipping rope extends it rapidly and makes exciting entertainment for a hungry audience in restaurants. As the dough flies, it thins, and it is folded and swung time and time again to create the long, slim noodles that everyone eagerly awaits.

IDEAL FOR TODAY'S BUSY COOK

One of the first forms of convenience food, pasta still provides an excellent variety of culinary opportunities: there are instant forms, ready meals, quick-cook mixtures and fresh doughs. Thankfully, there are good-quality dried pastas (which have to be boiled for the traditional 10–20 minutes) and these still predominate. With specialist Italian, Oriental and Indian stores in most large towns and cities, the supermarket supply of familiar pasta shapes and noodles

Commercial Pasta production, Italian style

can be readily supplemented by the more unusual forms. High-quality fresh pasta is now mass-produced and widely marketed, and inexpensive hand-turned pasta machines are sold in most good cookware stores, so it is not difficult to make a batch of noodles at home.

The exciting aspect of pasta is that it can provide whatever you need, be it a really tasty, satisfying family meal, a romantic dinner for two or a stunning dinner party dish. It is all things to all people, from inexpensive novelty shapes for the under-fives to a gourmet topic of conversation for devotees of unusual ingredients.

The Italians still dominate the world in terms of the quantity of pasta that they produce – 2.203 million tons in 1991, with a capacity for an even higher figure of 2.7 million tons. Italian pasta finds its way all over the world, but it is still as popular as ever at home, with an average annual consumption of 55 pounds per person in Italy – that is over 1 pound pasta per person, per week. The rest of us have a way to go before we catch up. Switzerland is leading, at the 20 pounds per person mark, the USA clocks in at around 17½ pounds, and Greece manages 17 pounds. The Canadians may be hot on the trail at 14 pounds, but the United Kingdom has still got some way to go, with an average consumption of just 5 pounds per head.

Enough facts and figures, controversy and history, though, and on to the real business of pasta: buying, cooking and eating it. The ever-increasing choice makes pasta cookery a real pleasure, and I hope you will enjoy exploring the diverse world of pasta.

THE WORLD OF PASTA
◆

THIS SECTION PROVIDES AN OVERVIEW OF THE DIFFERENT GROUPS OF PASTA
THAT ARE AVAILABLE WORLD-WIDE BUT, FIRST, A FEW USEFUL NOTES.

USING THE PASTA GLOSSARIES

Italy is by far the most prolific producer, so it makes sense to begin by listing and illustrating the many shapes and styles of pasta *alla Italiana.* You will also find information on oriental pasta and the better-known types from other countries. In addition, there is a section on flavored pastas with tasting notes.

There are also tips on an equally important group of specialist items: whole wheat, gluten-free, egg-free and even low-protein pasta, or alternative grain pastas.

SELECTING THE RIGHT PASTA FOR THE MEAL

Suggestions for which pasta to serve with a particular sauce are included throughout the recipes. There are some traditional partnerships, with the long thin pastas being served with thin sauces, while the chunky pastas and those in shapes to catch juices would be offered with meatier or more substantial mixtures, but there are some unusual combinations to try, too.

I also make comments occasionally about the appearance or the substance of the pasta. This is because they may vary when cooked. You may have come across advice on selecting pasta that suggests that the bright yellow-colored products are superior to the paler more opaque types. If you extend your view of pasta beyond the narrow confines of the one or two most commonly found Italian sauces by shopping, tasting and testing, you will find that this is nonsense. There are many traditional, rather murky looking pale pastas that are more starchy – dare I say it, stodgy – when cooked, but they are ideal for rich, meaty sauces and not at all inferior to the clearer, more yellow shapes. As a general rule, the only pastas I sometimes felt could be called inferior were some of the really speedy quick-cook types that resembled traditional Italian pasta in shape, but failed miserably in achieving the right texture or flavor.

INGREDIENTS USED TO MAKE PASTA

Pasta is generally made from wheat flour (but see also Specialist Pastas, page 14–15), usually durum wheat or hard wheat with a high gluten content. Water, eggs, salt and oil or butter may be added. Most dried pastas are made of flour and water, without any egg added, but tagliatelle and pappardelle, among others, do contain egg. The best way to check this is to read the ingredients list.

SOME ITALIAN PASTA TERMS

COTTURA
This term indicates the cooking time. For example, "Cottura: 5–6 minuti," means to cook the pasta for 5–6 minutes.

PASTA ALL'UOVO
This is pasta with egg added.

PASTA ASCIUTTA
This is pasta that is cooked and drained, then served with a sauce, as opposed to a stuffed or baked pasta, such as cannelloni or lasagne.

PASTA FRESCA
This is fresh pasta that has not been dried.

GLOSSARY OF
ITALIAN PASTA

AGNELLOTTI, AGNOLLOTTI OR AGNOLOTTI (1)
Cushions of stuffed pasta, round or semi-circular, attributed to Piedmont region.

AGNOLINI (Not shown)
Small ravioli.

BIGOLI (Not shown)
A type of spaghetti.

BUCATINI (3)
Thick, hollow spaghetti.

CAMPANELLE (4)
Bells. Small cones of pasta with frilly edges. Good for trapping sauce.

CANNERONI (6)
Larger than canneroncini, these are short pasta tubes.

CANNERONCINI (7)
Short lengths (about ½ inch) of narrow pipes.

CAPELLINI (8)
Thin hairs. Very fine spaghetti.

CICATELLI DI SAN SEVERO (12)
One of a range of handmade pasta from the Puglia region. These opaque, white, curled shaves of pasta are made from wheat flour and water, but no egg. They swell significantly on cooking, and are recommended for serving with long-cooked meat sauces. They remind me (slightly) of the spätzle that I made.

1

3

2a

5

7

6

12

13

8

14

2b

11

15

9

4

10

16

17

AMORI/AMORINI (2a & b)
Knots. They do not resemble knots, but are hollow spirals that may be ridged.

ANELLINI (Not shown)
Tiny rings, for use in soups.

BAVETTE (Not shown)
Oval spaghetti.

BIGNI (Not shown)
Local name for spaghetti.

CANDELE (5)
Meaning candles, the pasta shapes are, in fact, pipes, about ½–¾ inch in diameter.

CANNELLE (Not shown)
Meaning pipes, and including cannellini, cannolicchi, cannelloni and canneroni.

CANNELLONI (Not shown)
Popular pipe shapes, used for stuffing, coating with sauce and baking.

CAPELLINI SPEZZIATI (9)
Short, broken lengths of capellini.

CAPPELLETTI (10)
Little hats. Small circles of pasta indented in the center or with a pinched pleat, which forms their hat shape.

CASARECCIA (11)
Slightly twisted lengths of "S"-shaped pasta.

CASONSEI (Not shown)
Stuffed rings of pasta from Bergamo.

CONCHIGLIE (13 & 15)
Shells. They come in many sizes, from conchigliette, for soup, to large conchiglioni, for stuffing.

CONCHIGLIE RIGATE (14)
Large shells with a ridged texture. Ideal for boiling, draining, stuffing and baking or broiling with a gratiné topping.

CORALLINI (16)
Tiny soup pasta that look like little slices of hollow spaghetti.

DITALI (17)

Meaning thimbles, these are short lengths of hollow tube, slightly smaller than the end of your little finger. Good for salads and for a chunkier pasta in soup.

DITALINI (19)

Smaller than ditali both in length and diameter, with proportionally thicker pasta.

FETTUCCINE (22a & b)

Flat noodles. This is the alternative Roman name for tagliatelle. Readily available fresh.

FISCHIETTI (18)

Little whistles. Thin macaroni.

FRESINE (23)

Straight noodles, slightly narrower than tagliatelle and in similar lengths to short spaghetti.

GENOVESINI (26)

Presumably attributed in origin to Genoa, these are short, diagonally cut lengths of fairly thick tube pasta. Rather like short, plump penne.

GLI STROZZAPRETI (27)

The basic shape as casareccia, but the cut lengths are curled around into "C" or "S" shapes.

GNOCCHETTI SARDI (28)

Small versions of gnocchi, they are ridged, opaque and pale in color. Good with meaty sauces.

GOMITI (Not shown)

Hollow corners of pasta, like elbows, lumache (small) or pipe.

GRAMIGNA (Not shown)

Couch grass. Pasta shaped like grass.

I GARGANELLI ROMAGNOLI (31)

Squares of pasta rolled diagonally to make slim rolls with pointed ends.

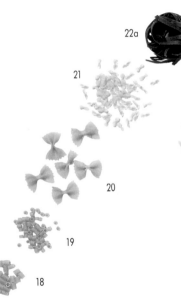

FARFALLE (20)

Butterflies. The term "bows" is also sometimes used for the same pasta shape. Made from thin, flat pasta, these shapes tend to cook quickly for their size. Good for adding to hotpots or layered (moist) dishes in which the pasta is cooked from raw.

FARFALLINI (21)

Wonderful, tiny farfalle, for soups or when small shapes are required. Very decorative.

FUSILLI (24)

Spirals, which may be long or short depending on the region of origin. Apparently, they were originally made by wrapping spaghetti around knitting needles, which gives some indication of the size and thickness of the pasta.

FUSILLIER COL BUCO (25)

Long, slim spirals (about the same length as short spaghetti).

GNOCCHETTO (29)

More yellow in color than gnocchetti, ridged and semi-tubular in shape. Look more like an average pasta shape than the more gnocchi-like types of dried pasta.

GNOCCHI (30)

Little dumplings. The dried pastas are shaped to resemble gnocchi which are marked with a fork. There are many types of fresh gnocchi (*see* pages 46–49).

IS MALLOREDDUS LUNGHI (32)

Like small, pale (creamy white), distinctively ridged gnocchetti but tightly curled.

LASAGNE (Not shown)

Wide strips or squares of pasta. Available fresh or dried.

LASAGNETTE (33)

Small lasagne. The same as malfade, this is a type of wide ribbon noodle with frilly edges.

LE EMILIANE (Not shown)
A name for nests of pappardelle.

LINGUINE (Not shown)
Little tongues. Narrow noodles or flat spaghetti, readily available fresh.

LUNETTE (Not shown)
A term used on some brands of semi-circular stuffed pasta.

MACARONI OR MACCHERONI (36)
Hollow tubes of pasta, larger than spaghetti. Originally sold in long lengths, wrapped in blue paper packages, and still available as such from better delis. Quick-cook, short-cut macaroni and elbow macaroni (another term for elbows or slightly longer right angles) are the most popular and readily available types. This was once the generic name for a limited range of early pasta types, especially those used by the British.

MALFATTINI (Not shown)
Finely chopped.

MISTA PASTA (38)
Mixed pasta. Mixed shapes sold together.

MISTO CORTO (39)
Mis-shapen. A mixture of tubes, spaghetti and broken pieces of similar length.

ORECCHIETTE (41)
Little ears. Opaque pasta, paler than usual shapes and slightly thicker than some. With a slightly softer texture when cooked, ideal for rich sauces (vegetable ragoûts or meaty sauces). Look as though they have been formed as the result of someone pressing their thumb into a piece of pasta.

36

37

41

35

38

42a

34b

40

42b

34a

39

43

LUMACHE (34a & b)
Snails. Available in different sizes, the large ones are ideal for stuffing. I also found this name attributed to ridged shell shapes – presumably snail shells!

LUMANCHINE (35)
Small snail shapes as above, but not as distinctive in shape. For salads, stuffing vegetables (bell peppers) or when a reasonably chunky soup is required.

MACCHERONCINI (Not shown)
Very small macaroni.

MACCHERONI RIGATI (Not shown)
Ribbed macaroni.

MAFALDE (37)
Wide, flat noodles with fluted or ruffled edges.

MAFALDINE (Not shown)
Flat noodles with fluted or ruffled edges, narrower than mafalde.

NIDI (40)
Nests. Small, rounded bundles of tagliatelle or fettuccine, these unravel when cooked. Pasta nests as a base for serving a sauce are created by arranging the cooked pasta in a nest shape on the plate.

OFFELLE (Not shown)
Stuffed pasta of ravioli type from Trieste.

PAGLIA E FIENO (42a & b)
Straw and hay. Green and white linguine or very narrow flat noodles mixed together. Also available as pink and white, flavored with tomato and plain.

PANSOTTI (Not shown)
Stuffed pasta of Ligurian origins, usually triangular.

PAPPARDELLE (43)
Wide, ribbon egg noodles. Traditionally an accompaniment for rich meat or game sauces, such as hare or meat sauces.

PASTA A RISO (44)
Pasta in the shape of small grains of rice. This cooks quickly and may be used instead of the Greek equivalent, known as orzo or minestra.

PASTINE (Not shown)
Small pasta shapes; soup pasta.

PENNE (45)
Quills. Hollow pasta cut into short lengths, at a slant.

QUADRETTI (Not shown)
Small squares of pasta for soup.

RADIATORI (48)
Radiators. Deeply ridged, pale pasta like old-fashioned radiators.

RAVIOLI (Not shown)
Small, stuffed pasta shapes. May be square or round, depending on their region of origin.

SPAGHETTI (52)
Long, slim, solid pasta. The majority is now shorter than it used to be, but it is still available in long, blue packages.

SPIGANARDA (53)
Similar to pasta a riso, but consists of longer grains.

STELLINE (54)
Tiny stars. Soup pasta.

TORTIGLIONI (58)
Ridged tubes, like rigatoni, but curved, with the ridges forming a slight spiral on the pasta.

TRENETTE (Not shown)
Finer than linguine or similar to flattened spaghetti.

TUBETTI (59)
Small tubes. Small, short lengths of hollow pasta.

PENNE, MEZZANI (46)
Small penne, slimmer and slightly shorter.

PENNE, MEZZANINE (47)
Yet smaller penne, shorter and slimmer than both the above.

PERCIATELLI (Not shown)
Thick, hollow spaghetti, thicker than bucatini.

PERLINE (Not shown)
Little pearls. Small soup pasta.

RIGATONI (49)
Ridged tubes, like large ridged macaroni. Good with meat sauces and for baked dishes.

RUOTI (50)
Wheels. Cartwheel shapes.

SEDANI (Not shown)
Ridged, curved tubes of macaroni type, resembling celery stalks.

SPAGELLINI (51)
Short, thin pieces of spaghetti.

TAGLIATELLE (55)
Familiar ribbon noodles. *See also* Fettuccine.

TORCHIETTI (56)
Small torches. Slightly swirled lengths of ridged pasta.

TORTELLINI (57a & b)
Stuffed pasta, formed from squares or circles, filled and folded in half, then pinched together into rings.

VERMICELLI (Not shown)
Thin worms. The Neapolitan term for spaghetti, which is slightly thicker than the familiar form. However, on an international basis, this is the term ascribed to fine spaghetti.

ZITI (60)
Spinsters or batchelors. Thick macaroni.

ZITONI (61)
Thicker than ziti.

SPECIALTY PASTAS

◆

THE FAMILIAR WHEAT FLOUR PASTAS ARE ALSO AVAILABLE IN ORGANIC FORMS AND AS WHOLE WHEAT TYPES FROM LARGER SUPERMARKETS AS WELL AS DELIS AND HEALTHFOOD STORES. HOWEVER, THOSE WHO MAY SUFFER FROM AN ALLERGIC REACTION TO THE PROTEIN CONTENT OF WHEAT AND SOME OTHER GRAINS WILL BE PLEASED TO KNOW THAT THERE IS A GOOD CHOICE OF WHEAT-FREE PASTA PRODUCTS. THEY ALSO PROVIDE AN EXCITING RANGE OF INGREDIENTS FOR ANY INTERESTED COOK. THE FOLLOWING IS A SAMPLE OF THE RANGE I LOCATED, BUT THERE ARE MANY SMALL STORES OFFERING A VARIETY OF DIFFERENT PRODUCTS, SO SEE WHAT YOU CAN FIND.

GLOSSARY OF SPECIALTY PASTAS

RICE PASTA (1)
There is a variety of rice pastas, including **VEGETABLE RICE PASTA, RICE** (1a), **RICE, TOMATO AND BASIL PASTA** (1b), and garlic and parsley rice pasta. They are gluten-free and made without eggs, and are available in a number of shapes, refined and stoneground.

The flavor of rice comes through clearly (especially in plain rice pasta), and this makes a pleasant change. Good with thin sauces as the texture is rather stodgy compared to traditional pasta. Take care with the cooking process as undercooking gives the pasta an unpleasant grainy "bite," while overcooking quickly makes it soft. Use the largest available pan for cooking.

LOW-PROTEIN PASTA (2)
Made from blended vegetable starches, including potato and maize. Unusual in appearance

for its white color and a real surprise in terms of texture and flavor. The texture was firm with a good bite (this was a product that suffered very slightly if the timing was not exact, either under or over, when cooking). Apart from its usefulness for those on a special diet, it is an interesting ingredient that looks and tastes good. The lack of salt is noticeable, but this is not a problem if the pasta is tossed with butter or seasoned olive oil before serving.

BARLEY PASTA (3)
A stoneground product produced from barley, it is wheat-free and without eggs. Check the details on the packages as differences may occur between brands. This has a nutty flavor and a slightly soft texture, with the whole grain adding interest to the texture. Take care not to overcook this pasta.

SPELT PASTA (4)
Spelt is a registered trade name for this American pasta. Organic and wholegrain, and made from a wheat-related grain. It is not necessarily suitable for those following a gluten-free diet, but more information is available from the Coeliac support groups.

The Spelt Elbows I tried had a smoothness to their texture that is not usually associated with whole wheat pasta. Lovers of Italian pasta would find the texture and flavor disappointing, and anyone used to whole wheat products may find it lacking in bite.

ORGANIC PASTA (5)
Prepared using organic ingredients, a wide choice of refined and whole wheat pastas, as well as products prepared from other grains are available.

CORN AND VEGETABLE PASTA (6a)
Colorful pasta shapes made from cornmeal with spinach, beets, tomato, celery and onion. Attractive and gluten-free, without eggs either. Lighter than stoneground and whole wheat types, these are a good choice for serving when catering for "traditionalists" and those who may be

COOKING NOTE

I found that some of the cooking times suggested by manufacturers of specialist pastas were quite inaccurate. In particular, some of the very short cooking times were too short, and the pasta was just not cooked. When using a new product, it is worth checking the pasta at different stages during boiling. Also, you will need a large pan for some specialist pastas as they make the water starchy.

avoiding gluten or eggs. The pasta I cooked was good, with excellent texture and a tasty flavor that was not too strong, but justified the pasta being labeled as "vegetable." Spinach varieties are always a good test of the quality of a pasta, and I could taste the spinach in these, as well as the onion and other vegetables of the other varieties.

CORN PASTA (6c & d)

Pure corn pasta, made only from maize without any added starch and binders, is gluten-free and made without eggs. Available in a variety of flavors, including:

CORN AND PARSLEY (6b)

Corn, chili and tomato, and corn and spinach. Shells, spaghetti, twists and rigatoni. I was delighted with the results from the various corn pastas I tried. The texture was good in all cases, and it compared very well with Italian wheat pasta. Also, the flavor was delicate and pleasing, and would go well with any pasta sauce. The types I tried were not temperamental in the cooking, so a couple of minutes too little or long did not spoil them.

WHOLE WHEAT PASTA (7)

There is a wide variety of whole wheat pasta products available, from supermarkets as well as specialty stores.

RICE AND MILLET PASTA (8)

Stoneground, whole-grain pasta that is wheat- and gluten-free. It is also made without eggs.

KAMUT PASTA (9 a & b)

Kamut is a registered trade name for a range of Italian pasta products. Marketed as whole-grain and organic, the information on the package provides promotional information on the ingredients without giving details of exactly what goes into the pasta product, other than a reference to *Triticum polonicum* after the trade name. *Triticum* is the Latin name for a wild species of grain from which wheat developed (the Latin name of durum wheat is *Triticum durum* for this reason). It should not be eaten by those following a gluten-free diet.

When cooked, the pasta I tried became quite pale. It was firm and *al dente* in texture. Anyone used to eating a high-fiber whole wheat pasta would probably find the texture too smooth, light, soft or plain, and it cannot be compared directly with whole wheat pastas in terms of texture. I found it to be similar to white bread with fiber added.

BUCKWHEAT PASTA

(Not shown)

Made without wheat flour, this is suitable for those following a gluten-free diet. Note, though, that Japanese soba noodles are also made from buckwheat flour, but are often combined with wheat flour, so, if you are allergic to wheat, take care when selecting Japanese-style noodles as some oriental labeling suffers badly from translation difficulties.

FLAVORED PASTAS

♦

THERE IS A WIDE CHOICE OF FLAVORED PASTA PRODUCTS, AND THE QUALITY IS EQUALLY VARIED, BUT THEN THIS IS TRUE OF ALL FOOD PRODUCTS. THE INFORMATION THAT FOLLOWS APPLIES TO THE DRIED PASTAS THAT I TRIED. SOME OF THE FLAVORED FRESH PASTAS, PARTICULARLY THE LESS EXPENSIVE BRANDS, CAN BE RATHER COARSE AND RAW IN TASTE. BY WAY OF CONTRAST, SOME OF THE BEST FRESH PASTAS REALLY ARE A TREAT.

GLOSSARY OF FLAVORED PASTAS

PORCINI PASTA (1)
Delicious pasta flavored with dried ceps or porcini. A distinctly flavored pasta that will stand alone if dressed with a little butter, oil, cream or other very simple sauce. Clever mushroom shapes enhanced the image. Would be terrific in a hearty mushroom soup (it was a shame to drain away their cooking water), or in hotpots and moist stews. The expensive Italian brand I tried really was worth it.

CORN AND SPINACH PASTA (2)
See Specialty Pastas. The combination of corn and spinach were good in flavor and color. Good spinach color.

BLACK SQUID (3a & b)
Cuttlefish or squid ink is used to enrich rather than strongly flavor the pasta. Although squid ink pastas do not have a "fishy" flavor, they are tinged with seafood, and I would not serve them with a poultry sauce or meat. Best for seafood or vegetable-based sauces.

ASPARAGUS (4)
At first taste, a bit "grassy," but better when tossed with melted butter. Serve with a light, creamy or milk sauce.

SMOKED SALMON (5)
The pasta smelled strongly of smoked salmon, but the flavor had diminished markedly after boiling. For the price, I recommend buying plain pasta, and spending the price difference on fresh smoked salmon to toss into it.

CORN, TOMATO AND CHILI (6)
See Corn pasta in the Glossary of Specialist Pastas. Quite distinctly tasted of chili, but the tomato does not come through. Good in flavor and texture.

CHAMPIGNON (7)
From a French range, the "pâtes aux oeufs frais aromatisées" that I tried were flavored with dried "trompettes de mort" mushrooms. A good flavor, milder than porcini pasta. Serve plain with butter, oil or cream and cheese. Toss with sautéed mushrooms to accentuate the flavor, or toss with butter, and serve as a base for creamy chicken mixtures or milk-based seafood sauces. Take care not to drown the delicate mushroom pasta.

BASIL (8)
Quality is important when buying herb-flavored pasta. I tried a French-made brand of tagliatelle that had a good, mild basil flavor. Good tossed with oil or butter as a base for a topping or simply with cheese.

SPINACH (9)
Qualities vary widely, but expensive types are worth the extra for a good spinach flavor.

GARLIC AND CHILI (10)
The Italian brand I tried was good (spaghetti), with a pronounced pep coming from the chili.

CHIANTI SPECIALITY (11)
Novelty pasta in the shapes of red grapes (beet), white grapes (plain) and leaves (spinach). This was very good, and the spinach flavor was the best of all the spinach pastas that I tried specifically for this chapter. Looks terrific!

BLACK AND WHITE SPAGHETTI (12)
Flavored with black squid ink and plain. A good combination that makes an elegant base for seafood. A smart option for appearance rather than flavor.

BLACK OLIVE SPAGHETTI (13)
This is good! A light flavor of black olives that is just sufficient to assert itself. Ideal for tossing with olive oil and garlic, and topping with pecorino. Would be lost with a strong (meat-type) sauce, milk or cream. Diced fresh tomatoes or sun-dried tomatoes would go well, especially with fresh basil or parsley.

TOMATO (14)
As for spinach, the quality varies significantly, and some pink pasta tastes rather bland.

GARLIC AND TOMATO (15)
The garlic tends to overpower the tomato, so the latter contributes color rather than flavor.

FASTA PASTA

There is a wide range of quick-cook pasta, instant noodles and sauced pasta. Here are just a few of them.

BOIL-IN-THE-BAG PASTA
Perforated boiling bags containing slim pasta spirals (or other shapes) that cook in about 7–8 minutes. Easy to drain, but the texture is not as good as "proper" pasta.

INSTANT CHINESE NOODLES
These are soaked in freshly boiled water instead of having to be boiled. They are great; a real boon for a-meal-in-a-hurry dishes.

INSTANT OR VERY SPEEDY PASTAS
These are usually in cake form, like Chinese dried noodles, and vary considerably in quality and flavor. In general, I find that the more they offer in the way of flavoring, the less like real food they tend to be.

QUICK-COOK PASTAS
Spaghetti in a major Italian range cooks in 3 minutes to give excellent results, but some larger shapes tend to have a slightly slimy texture. Quick-cook macaronis vary: some are ready in 3 minutes, others in 7 minutes. I found the latter to be excellent.

SAUCED DRIED PASTA
There is an ever-increasing and changing range of dehydrated sauce and pasta mixes, rather like flavored rice mixes. Frankly, with fresh pasta so readily available, I would opt for a bowl of pasta topped with a little oil or butter and some grated cheese.

SWEET PASTAS

◆

I HAVE NOT EXPLORED SWEET PASTA HERE BEYOND INCLUDING SOME EXAMPLES OF FILLED PASTAS WITH SWEET FILLINGS AS THERE WERE SO MANY SAVORY RECIPES I WANTED TO INCLUDE, BUT THERE ARE TRADITIONAL SWEET PASTA DISHES.

GLOSSARY OF SWEET PASTAS

Plum and Blackberry Compote

FRUIT COMPOTES FOR PASTA

Stewed fruits may be served with noodles and plain pasta. Cherries, plums, apricots and other full-flavored fruits should be used. There are Eastern European and Italian dishes of this type.

FRUIT-FILLED PASTAS

Pasta shapes filled with whole cherries, plums, apricots or other fruit, boiled and served with butter, sugar and sour cream are popular in many Eastern European cuisines.

LOKSHEN PUDDING

A Jewish pudding of noodles (tagliatelle or ribbon noodles) in which boiled noodles are baked with eggs, dried fruit, cinnamon and sugar.

MACARONI MILK PUDDING

A British pudding. Macaroni is baked in milk and sugar until the milk has been absorbed, and the pasta is tender and creamy. Vanilla, lemon rind or a cinnamon stick may be added.

Cherry Pierozki

MOHN NUDELN

Austrian dessert of noodles tossed with butter, sugar and poppy seeds.

SUESSEN NUDELAUF

An Austrian dessert of noodles layered with apples or plums and sugar, then baked. Fried bread crumbs form a crisp topping, and sour cream is served with the pudding.

POLISH POPPY SEED PUDDING

A traditional Christmas Eve pudding. The cooked ribbon noodles are tossed with butter, sugar and poppy seeds. Noodles with poppy seeds is also a popular combination for sweet puddings in other Eastern European countries.

SEVYIAN

An Indian milk pudding with vermicelli (vermicelli being known as *sev*, or *sevyian*). The vermicelli is broken into small pieces, and simmered in milk. Green cardamoms, raisins or golden raisins, pistachio nuts and almonds are added. Rose water is used, and cloves may be added. The sweet mixture is cooked until the milk has been absorbed, and the pasta is thick and creamy – delicious warm or cold.

SWEET-FLAVORED PASTAS

A popular American concept, pasta may be flavored with chocolate, fruit or other foods, and served with sweet sauces or with butter and sugar or cream.

Chocolate Bows with Chocolate Sauce

ORIENTAL PASTAS

◆

CHINESE EGG NOODLES ARE READILY AVAILABLE FROM MOST SUPERMARKETS
AND MANY WHOLEFOOD OR HEALTHFOOD STORES SELL A VARIETY OF
ORIENTAL PASTA, NOTABLY JAPANESE NOODLES. SPECIALIST CHINESE OR
ORIENTAL SUPERMARKETS ARE THE PLACES TO FIND A LARGE RANGE OF
DIFFERENT RICE STICKS AS WELL AS FRESH EGG NOODLES AND WON TON
WRAPPERS.

Japanese Rice Sticks

The following is a guide to some of the main types. Inconsistencies in terms of translations and local names, as well as the general similarity between some types of noodles in Chinese, Thai, Malaysian and Singaporean cooking, make this a difficult subject on which to offer a definitive list, but the following glossary provides a good starting-point for discovering the delights of oriental pasta. If you make a new discovery, study the package as there are often diagrams showing how to cook the pasta. Also, I find that the store-keepers are always keen to help by explaining how they cook the product. The fun part of shopping this way and pleading ignorance is that most of the other customers in smaller stores readily join in to contribute ideas and anecdotes about their cooking.

A note about cooking times: most packages give instructions, and they should be followed as the products vary enormously. I have given some indication of the times I have used or come across, and they may be of help in the absence of other guidance. As a general rule, though, the finer and less dense the noodles, the shorter the cooking time (with the exception of egg noodles). Generally, the Japanese method of cooking noodles is to soak or boil them, then to rinse them in cold water before using. Personally, unless I am serving the noodles cold, I find that they do not have to be rinsed if they are used immediately. If there is any delay after cooking though, rinse in cold water to arrest the cooking process.

GLOSSARY OF ORIENTAL PASTAS

SAIFUN NOODLES (1)
Japanese dried, very fine, opaque white noodles, made from sweet potato starch and potato starch. An alternative to shirataki, these can be served in dishes such as sukiyaki, or they can be served cold. They are cooked for 3–4 minutes in boiling water, or soaked in hot water for 2–3 minutes before adding to a hotpot.

MUNG BEAN THREAD OR TRANSPARENT NOODLES (2)
Clear, shiny noodles. The Chinese type are usually made from mung bean flour. Various other cellophane noodles, particularly Japanese varieties, are made with buckwheat flour, yam flour and wheat starch.

CHOW MEIN NOODLES (3)
Cakes of dried, yellow noodles, made from wheat flour, possibly with egg (check ingredients listed on package) or with coloring; *see* Egg noodles.

SANUKI SOMEN (4)
Soumen, or somen, noodles. Dried, white and made from wheat starch, these are round and fine, as for marufuji somen and somen. They should be cooked in boiling water for 4–5 minutes, or until tender.

NAENG MYUN (5a & b)
Fine, vermicelli-like, Japanese noodles for adding to nang myun soup. Made from wheat flour, buckwheat flour and sweet potato starch. The noodles themselves are fine, round and shiny and light brown.

DRIED WHEAT FLOUR NOODLES (6)
Long, white, narrow noodles.

SHIRATAKI (7)
Japanese white noodles prepared from a plant known as the devil's tongue plant, a root vegetable similar to yam. The root is used to make a flour that is formed into a cake or loaf known as konnyaku. The same dried flour is used to make the noodles. Sold canned or in sausage-shaped plastic tubes, the noodles are kept in water. They are ready cooked for adding to dishes, such as sukiyaki.

SOBA (8)
Japanese pasta, made from buckwheat flour, with or without wheat flour, possibly with yam flour added. There are many types, some containing a larger proportion of buckwheat flour than others.

NAI YAU MEIN (9)
Chinese dried, flat, narrow white noodles with milk powder added.

EGG NOODLES (10a, b, c, d l)
The most popular type of oriental noodles, used in Chinese, Japanese, Singaporean (Hokkien); Malaysian (Mee); and Thai (Ba Mee) cooking. Available fresh and dried, they may be thin or fine, thread noodles or medium. There are also slightly thicker fresh noodles (comparable to linguine of Italian origin). In general, the noodles seem to vary slightly in thickness. They are packed in cakes or bundles, and cook quickly. Some dried types are simply soaked in boiling water for about 15 minutes, while others may be boiled for just 2–3 minutes.

FRESH EGG NOODLES
(Not shown)
Larger Chinese supermarkets sell two or three types, of different widths. They may be rounded or thin and slightly flattened, slightly thicker than spaghetti, or wider and more like narrow Italian noodles. The noodles are folded in small bundles, dusted with cornstarch. They keep well in the refrigerator for about a week, or they freeze well and may be cooked from frozen. They cook quickly (in 2–3 minutes) when added to boiling water.

TOMOSHIRAGA SOMEN (11)
Dried, white somen noodles.

RICE STICKS AND RICE VERMICELLI (12a, b, c, d & e)
Noodles made from rice flour, available in a variety of widths from fine vermicelli (yinsi rice vermicelli) to wide ribbon noodles. Sometimes sold cut flat, but more often formed into large or small bundles, rather like skeins of wool. Also known as Singaporean or Malaysian BEE HOON or MEE HOON or Thai SEN MEE, or Indian SEV.

BEE HOON OR MEE HOON
Singaporean and Malaysian names for Chinese rice vermicelli, *see* Rice sticks.

SEN MEE (Not shown)
Thai term for rice vermicelli. Thin and semi-transparent.

SEV (Not shown)
Indian rice vermicelli.

HO FUN, HOR FUN, KUA TEAW OR KWAY TEOW (13)
Chinese noodles made from wheat flour and cornstarch or rice flour. White and quite wide, they are similar to short tagliatelle or ribbon noodles.

UDON (14)
Japanese white noodles, thicker than somen. Also available in form of whole wheat udon (dried) in healthfood stores. Fresh noodles are most common in Japanese supermarkets – find them in chilled vacuum packs, possibly cooked ready for serving with soup.

ISHIGURO YAHAIMO SOBA (15)
A variety of Japanese dried, fine noodles made from wheat flour, buckwheat flour and yam flour.

MARUFUJI SOMEN (16)
Fine, round, white Japanese noodles made from wheat flour. *See* Sanuki Somen.

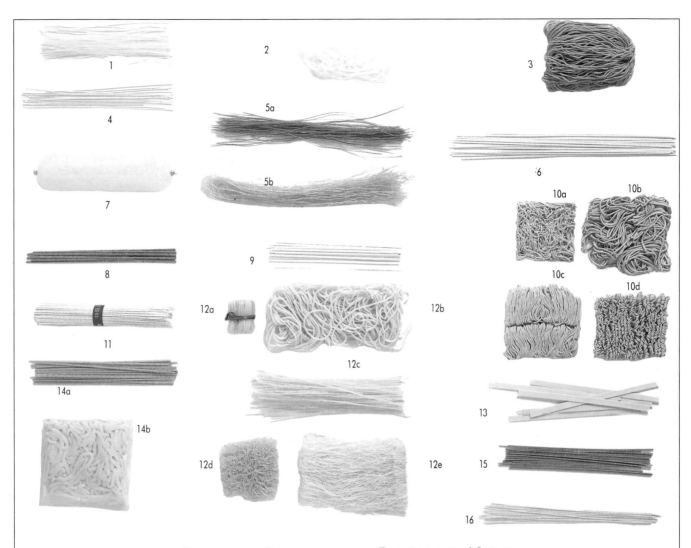

OTHER ORIENTAL PASTAS NOT ILLUSTRATED

ARROWROOT VERMICELLI
Fine white noodles made from arrowroot.

LAKSA NOODLES
Fresh rice noodles, these are white and slightly thicker than spaghetti (Malaysian/ Singaporean).

HARUSAME
Japanese bean starch noodles.

HIYAMUGI
Japanese, medium-thick white noodles that are usually served cold in the dish of the same name. They are cooked for about 7–8 minutes until softened.

RAMEN NOODLES
Fine, white Japanese wheat noodles, served in a soup.

SEN LEK
Thai rice flour noodles, slightly thicker than sen mee.

SEN YAI
Thai term for white rice flour noodles that are thicker than sen mee and sen lek.

WON TONS
Fine, egg noodle-like dough, stuffed and boiled or deep-fried. Won ton wrappers are small, square wrappers, sold fresh. They freeze well. Won ton wrappers may also be used for making dim sum.

WOON SEN
Thai term for fine bean thread vermicelli.

EXAMPLES OF PASTA FROM OTHER COUNTRIES

◆

What Follows is Just a Sample of the Pasta-type Foods That are Popular in Countries Other Than Italy and the Orient. In Eastern and Northern Europe, There are Many Dumplings That are Similar to Filled Pasta and Indeed, it can be Difficult to Decide Where to Draw the Line Between Pasta and Dumpling. I Have not Included the Many German Dumplings, but Have Restricted the Examples to Smaller Shapes.

GLOSSARY OF PASTA FROM OTHER COUNTRIES

Savory Noodle Kugel

CSIPETKE
Tiny flour, egg and water dumplings from Hungary. The dough is rolled out to a ½-inch thickness, and cut into narrow ½-inch wide strips. Then tiny pieces are pinched off, and rolled into small balls, the size of little beans. These are boiled or cooked in a stew. Served with goulash.

FIDEOS
Spanish version of vermicelli, available in different thicknesses; used in soups and sometimes for a variation on paella.

GALUSKA
Hungarian dumplings made from a soft dough of flour, eggs and milk. The mixture is placed on a wetted board, and small pieces cut into a pan of boiling water, a method similar to making spätzle.

KASNUDLN
Austrian filled pasta or noodles, shaped as squares, folded and stuffed with different fillings, such as meat, ham, mushrooms, cottage cheese or leftovers. Eaten as a main dish, tossed with butter and served with salad. Similar to uska or tortellini. Also made with sweet fillings, such as ground poppy seeds or dried fruit and dusted with sugar.

KNEDLE
A potato and flour dough is used to make these stuffed pasta-like dumplings. The stuffing may be savory or sweet.

KNEDLIKY
Small, Austrian dumplings that may be based on a dough with bread or potatoes, these are similar to knedle, which may be compared with potato gnocchi of Italian cooking. Czechoslovakian cooking also includes its own version.

KNEIDLECH
Jewish matzo balls, made from matzo meal enriched with chicken fat and egg, and rolled into tiny balls.

KOPYTKA
Polish equivalent of Italian potato gnocchi.

KREPLACH
Triangular, filled pasta or dumplings (see page 227).

LASANKI
Polish pasta squares. An egg pasta dough, cut into tiny squares. Good with cabbage, sauerkraut, butter, garlic and onion. These are a lunch dish or may be served as a side dish with stewed meats.

LENIWE PIEROGI
Lazy pierogi. A Polish quick alternative to cheese-filled pierogi (*see* Pierogi), a dough of potatoes, cottage cheese, bread and flour is shaped into short sausages.

Kreplach

LOKSHEN
Jewish name for egg noodles, the same as tagliatelle.

LOKSHYNA
Russian name for egg noodles.

MATZO MEAL NOODLES
Jewish soup noodles, made from a batter of matzo meal cooked in the form of a pancake, then cut into ¼-inch wide strips.

NOKY
Czechoslovakian noodles, made in the same way as galuska.

ORZO
Also known as minestra, orzo is similar to pasta a riso. It is added to braised dishes and hootpots.

PELMENI
A Siberian filled pasta, made from a dough of flour and eggs and filled with ham, pork or game to make semicircular shapes. Served with butter, or lemon juice and parsley.

PIEROGI
Polish filled dumplings that are similar to ravioli. Pierogi are semicircular, and may be filled with meat, cheese or other fillings, such as sauerkraut.

SCHLICK KRAPFEN
Austrian filled pasta similar to ravioli, served in soup or with butter and cheese.

SPÄTZLE
German noodles, made from a thick batter of potatoes, flour, eggs and water. The batter is cut into short strips, and these are slid off a board into boiling water. Alternatively, the batter may be piped into the water, and short lengths cut off. Good with meaty stews. The spätzle may be flavored with herbs or other seasonings, and vegetables may be used in the batter. I have also seen reference to stiffer spätzle from a dough, but the batter is the original and lighter form (see pages 50–51). Sold fresh and chilled in vacuum packs in some delis.

TARHONYA
Hungarian noodle dough that is dried and coarsely grated into pellets. Said to be one of the oldest of noodle doughs and an early way of preserving food, the noodles take the name of barley noodles for their grain-like shape. The nomadic Magyar tribes originally made the dough, and tarhonya is still popular today. The pellets can be cooked by simmering and then frying (they can simply be cooked until the liquid has evaporated, with butter added to start the frying process), or

they can be boiled and drained as for ordinary pasta. Served with goulash.

TRAHANA
Grated noodle dough, as for tarhonya.

USZKA
Polish dumplings filled with dried mushroom stuffing (see page 224). Similar to tiny tortellini.

VARENYKY, OR VARIENIKI
Russian filled dumplings, semicircular in shape and filled with sauerkraut or cheese.

Similar to ravioli in texture. May be filled with sweet cheese mixture, and served with fruit or filled with fruit. There are several variations on these, both savory and sweet. Lithuanian varenyky are filled with meat, and old recipes call for large amounts of kidney fat or suet.

ZACIERKI
Polish homemade pasta formed from a fairly standard flour, egg and water dough. The zacierki are shaped by pinching off bits of dough, or by cutting it up roughly. The dough may also be coarsely grated.

Top, Lasanki with Cabbage   Above, Pierogi

PASTA ON THE PLATE

◆

Linguini with Green Peppers and Pesto

WHAT SORT OF IMAGE DOES PASTA HAVE IN YOUR HOUSEHOLD AND WHEN DOES PASTA IMMEDIATELY SPRING TO MIND AS THE IDEAL INGREDIENT FOR A MEAL?

THE POPULAR IMAGE OF PASTA IS ITALIAN, QUICK, EASY, NUTRITIOUS, SLIMMING AND . . . CREATIVE.

LET US PAUSE TO TAKE A LONGER LOOK AT SOME OF THESE IDEAS. 🍎 DOES OUR EXPERIENCE OF COOKING AND EATING PASTA REINFORCE OR DISPEL THESE POPULAR IDEAS?

I THINK PASTA IS A TERRIFIC, VERSATILE INGREDIENT; BETTER STILL, IT CAN BE DELICIOUS AND DIFFERENT TO EAT IN VERY MANY WAYS. 🍎 I HOPE THAT THE FOLLOWING PAGES EXPAND YOUR REPERTOIRE.

THE IMPORTANT FACTOR TO REMEMBER ABOUT PASTA IS THAT IT IS NOT EATEN ON ITS OWN. 🍎 THEREFORE, ITS TRUE FOOD VALUE IN THE DIET IS SUBJECT TO THE ACCOMPANIMENTS OFFERED WITH IT, OR THE DISHES FOR WHICH IT IS AN ASIDE. 🍎 THIS IS VERY IMPORTANT.

IF YOU HAVE A SERIOUS INTEREST IN THE FOOD VALUE OF PASTA, THEN YOU WILL APPRECIATE THAT THIS VARIES ACCORDING TO THE PRODUCT. 🍎 APART FROM THE COMPLETELY SEPARATE TYPES OF PASTA – CHINESE, JAPANESE, ITALIAN – THERE ARE REGIONAL SPECIALTIES, FOREIGN INTERPRETATIONS, FAST FOODS AND MANY BRANDS.

THE INFORMATION MANUFACTURERS PUT ON THEIR PACKAGING IS ERRATIC IN THE DETAIL IT PROVIDES, AND IT IS NOT POSSIBLE TO PROVIDE ACCURATE INFORMATION TO COVER ALL PASTA. 🍎 HOWEVER, IT IS HELPFUL TO OFFER GENERAL GUIDANCE.

Pasta in the Diet
PUTTING IT INTO PERSPECTIVE

First, I ought to stress that the word "diet" is used here in the nutritional sense, that is, to refer to all food that is eaten, regardless of any specific characteristics relating to individuals and specific types of diet. I do not use it to indicate a "reduced-calorie" or "calorie-controlled" diet. Also, this information is based on Italian-type pasta rather than oriental pasta, such as rice sticks or won ton dough.

A WELL-BALANCED DIET

Advertisements bombard the public with information about "healthy" foods, but, in fact, there is no such thing as an unhealthy food. Butter, cream and other high-fat products are all relevant in a balanced diet, provided they are eaten as a *small* proportion of a varied total food intake. On an everyday basis, we should all consume significantly more starch and fresh fruit and vegetables than protein and fat; and we should consume regular and frequent supplies of dietary fiber or non-starch polysaccharides. Variety is probably the most useful key to a well-balanced diet.

PASTA: A USEFUL FOOD FOR SENSIBLE EATING

Pasta is a useful food to include in a well-balanced diet. In itself, it does not have a high fat content, it provides starch for energy, and it may include a small, but useful, source of protein. Egg pasta can make a valuable contribution of protein to a vegetarian diet where many different sources make up the total intake, unlike a diet based on fish, poultry or meat where concentrated sources of animal protein are eaten regularly.

As pasta is often eaten with substantial salads, it can be a useful food for promoting healthy eating.

There are many excellent sauces and accompaniments that substantiate the image of pasta as a well-balanced, healthy food. However, there is also a distinct tendency to smother pasta with olive oil, butter, cream and cheese, so it is up to us whether we eat it in a healthy or less healthy way.

PASTA FOR ENERGY: A CARBOHYDRATE FOOD

Primarily, pasta is a carbohydrate food, usually based on wheat. Its main contribution to diet is starch. Depending on the type, as we have seen, the pasta may also make a contribution of protein (not that protein is a nutrient lacking in the Western diet). It also provides some minerals and contributes a small amount of certain vitamins.

To put this into context, pasta is similar to potatoes or rice in its role in our diet. Starches should be the main source of energy in the diet (as opposed to sugars and fats). The body breaks down food to obtain energy. Simple sugars are most easily broken down, and starch, which does not have a high fiber content, is digested more quickly than foods that contain a significant amount of fibre.

ALL-IMPORTANT FIBER

Fiber is essential in the diet. White pasta is *not* a valuable source of fiber, but whole wheat pasta does provide a useful supply of dietary fiber, or non-starch polysaccharides. as the experts would like it termed.

PASTA AND FAT: COMPARISONS WITH ALTERNATIVES

Pasta is often promoted as a low-fat food. It does have a low fat content in itself and, when olive oil is used in its manufacture, the greater percentage of the fat it does have, may be monounsaturated. Potatoes, rice, couscous and wheat are also low-fat foods, and they may contain less fat than pasta.

Tagliatelle with Grated Carrot and Scallion

For example, 4 ounces raw macaroni contains about 1.8 grammes fat; a similar weight of raw potato contains 0.2 grammes fat. As 4 ounces raw potato is hardly a representative portion, and 4 ounces macaroni is a generous portion, a better comparison is between 4 ounces raw macaroni with 1.8 grammes fat and 12 ounces raw potato with 0.7 grammes fat: the macaroni has more than double the quantity of fat in the potato.

This comparison can be made between egg noodles and various other types of pasta with similar indications. It is also interesting to compare pasta with rice. Rice has a higher fat content than potatoes, but it is lower than pasta.

I am adopting a pedantic approach and splitting hairs simply to put pasta into context, but pasta, potatoes and rice are *all* carbohydrate-rich foods which have a low fat content. The actual fat content of pasta depends on the ingredients used to make it – it is a product, not produce.

PASTA AND CALORIE-CONTROLLED DIETS

Pasta is a useful food to eat when following a reduced-calorie or calorie-controlled diet because it provides reasonable bulk for its calorie content. The same is true of any food that has a high starch and low fat content, such as potatoes and rice.

One of the difficulties of promoting pasta as useful in low-calorie diets and when slimming is in distinguishing the low-calorie dishes with pasta from the others, which are calorific. For example, a hearty bowl of boiled pasta with steamed zucchini, tossed with fresh basil and topped with 2 tablespoons of grated Parmesan cheese, plenty of black pepper and 1 tablespoon of fromage frais is every slimmer's dream meal. However, the simpler alternative of pasta tossed with olive oil and garlic, and served with a bowl of Parmesan or pecorino to taste will provide a far higher calorie intake, quite out of the realms of the target for a low-calorie meal. So, it is all down to what you serve it with.

TEN CALORIE-COUNTED TOPPINGS

The calorie counts for the following are a guide for the ingredients given, excluding the pasta. Each idea provides a single serving.

1 Thinly slice 4 ounces young zucchini. Steam them over boiling water for 5 minutes, cook them in the microwave for about 1 minute, or blanch them in boiling water for 1 minute. Toss with pasta, 1 finely chopped scallion, a few shredded basil leaves and plenty of freshly ground black pepper. Add 2 tablespoons grated Parmesan cheese. *Kilocalories 66*

2 Grate 4 ounces carrot, and mix with 2 tablespoons orange juice. Add 1 chopped scallion, and toss this with the pasta. Serve with ¼ cup grated mild Cheddar cheese. *Kilocalories 151*

3 Hard-cook and roughly chop 1 egg. Press ¼ cup cottage cheese through a strainer, and toss with the pasta. Add the egg, 3 tablespoons snipped chives and 3 table-spoons chopped fresh parsley. Season with a little grated nutmeg and freshly ground black pepper. *Kilocalories 137*

4 Melt 1 tablespoon butter in a pan, and lightly scramble 1 egg until beginning to set. Toss with the pasta. Serve topped with 4 ounces cooked fresh spinach. Sprinkle with freshly ground black pepper. *Kilocalories 218*

5 Peel, de-seed and roughly chop 4 ounces tomatoes. Hard-cook and roughly chop 1 egg. Toss the egg and tomatoes with the pasta, and season with freshly ground black pepper. *Kilocalories 105*

6 Dice 3 ounces cooked chicken breast (without skin), and mix with 2 tablespoons fromage frais. Add freshly ground black pepper and 2 tablespoons snipped chives. Toss with the hot pasta. *Kilocalories 140*

7 Flake 2 ounces canned tuna in brine (drained), and toss with the pasta. Add a little grated lemon rind, 2 tablespoons chopped fresh parsley and a squeeze of lemon juice. Serve on a generous green salad. *Kilocalories 50*

8 Mix 3 tablespoons dry white wine, 4 ounces sliced leek, 1 sliced celery stalk, 1 diced carrot and 4 ounces shredded green cabbage in a saucepan. Cover and cook, shaking the pan often, for 15 minutes. Add 4 ounces tomatoes, peeled and chopped, and plenty of salt and pepper, and cook, covered, for a further 15 minutes. Toss with the pasta, and serve with 1 tablespoon grated Parmesan cheese. *Kilocalories 139*

9 Chop 1 garlic clove, and mix with 1 teaspoon chopped fresh oregano and ¼ cup chopped walnuts. Press ¼ cup cottage cheese through a strainer. Toss the garlic, oregano, walnuts and cottage cheese with the hot pasta. *Kilocalories 231*

10 Dice 2 ounces lean cooked ham. Thinly slice 4 ounces zucchini, and toss with 1 teaspoon olive oil in a small saucepan. Cover and cook over a low heat for 5 minutes. Toss the zucchini and ham with the pasta. *Kilocalories 200*

LIGHT PASTA AND LOW CALORIE COUNTS: SOME SERVING IDEAS

Here are a few suggestions for serving calorie-controlled dishes that taste as good as they look.

- First, check the calorie content of the brand of pasta you are cooking.
- Always weigh the amount of pasta you are cooking per portion (check the package or table for details of this), so you can serve an amount for which the above calculation is easy.

SERVING STYLES

◆

*O*N THE WHOLE, PASTA HAS A RATHER EVERYDAY IMAGE – THE IDEAL FOOD
FOR FAMILY MEALS, A SAFE OPTION FOR MOST CHILDREN, A QUICK MEAL FOR
BUSY WORKING PEOPLE, AND A GOOD STAPLE INGREDIENT TO HAVE, BUT
THERE IS SOME CHEESE IN THE REFRIGERATOR. IT MAY ALSO BE BOTH MODERN
AND FASHIONABLE, BUT IT IS OFTEN OVERLOOKED AS A MAIN INGREDIENT FOR
DINNER PARTIES, A SOPHISTICATED LUNCH OR A CELEBRATION FAMILY MEAL.

PASTA EFFECTS: SIMPLE WAYS WITH VERSATILE PRODUCTS

The recipes in the chapters that follow highlight a variety
of ways in which pasta can be used, apart from the familiar
boiling or baking, then serving. If you know some of the
alternatives, then these can be adapted to suit a range of
recipes. The following examples may inspire you to
experiment with some of your favorite dishes.

COLORFUL PRESENTATIONS

This must be the most obvious example of how to make
plain pasta look more interesting. Instead of serving pasta
of just one color, combine two or more different colors.
Also, rather than mix the different pastas when cooking,
so that they are simply tossed together when served,
cook them separately, and arrange them in a serving dish.

For results that make a real impact at a sophisticated
meal, avoid the usual red, green and white novelty
shapes. The longer pastas colored with squid ink, tomato,
tumeric, saffron, herbs and so on are ideal choices for
such occasions. Fresh pastas are perfect for cooking
separately as they cook quickly, so you can even use the
same saucepan provided you have a kettle of boiling
water at the ready to avoid a cold start each time. Try
the following ideas.

- Arrange different colors of pasta in lines on a large
  rectangular or oval dish. This works particularly well
  for tagliatelle, malfadine, spaghetti and other long
  shapes.

- Spoon short shapes into wedges of different colors in
  a round dish, or alternate two colors. Arrange sprigs
  of fresh herbs, or spoon a sauce in the middle.

- Arrange concentric rings of spaghetti of different
  colors on a large platter.

- Layer pasta of different colors in a deep, straight-
  sided glass serving bowl or soufflé dish.

- Use two or more colors of lasagne when layering
  baked dishes.

- Use two colors of pasta when making ravioli, tortellini and other filled shapes. Place the filling on one
  color, then lay a sheet of a second color on top.

A DIFFERENT APPROACH TO SHAPE

Why is lasagne *always* rectangular or square? Whether
you make your own pasta or not, there is no reason
always to make rectangular or square layered pasta bakes.
As it is often difficult to find a suitable rectangular dish
for many bakes anyway, simply adopt a different approach,
and cut the pasta to fit dishes you have.

- If you make your own pasta, then roll it out into a
  circle, and cut it to fit the chosen dish before boiling
  it. You may have to trim the pasta after cooking, at
  least for a neat top layer.

- If you buy lasagne, simply lay the pasta in a round
  dish, as you would in a square or rectangular one. For
  a neat top layer, arrange strips of lasagne from the

middle outward, leaving a circle with a diameter of about 2 inches uncovered in the middle. Overlap the strips all around the remainder of the dish, and trim their edges; then cut out a circle of pasta to neaten the middle.

- Make individual portions of baked pasta by layering pasta in ramekin dishes, individual casseroles or soufflé dishes. Large squares of fresh lasagne are ideal for trimming to fit small dishes.

- Instead of serving a thick sauce or vegetables on a bed of cooked pasta, when the sauce is cooked, cook squares of fresh lasagne in boiling water, and layer them in the middle of individual plates with the sauce. Add a gratin topping, and broil to brown. This is also an excellent way of making an attractive presentation of sautéed vegetables and pasta as a side dish for broiled fish, poultry or meat. For successful results, do not spoon too much sauce or too many ingredients between the pieces of pasta; otherwise they will run out from between the layers, and look unattractive.

- Homemade stuffed pastas do not have to conform to the traditions of round or square shapes for ravioli or neatly twisted tortellini. For special occasions allow your imagination a little freedom, and use cookie cutters to make differently shaped stuffed pasta.

- For Valentine's Day ravioli, encase scallops or oysters between two layers of heart-shaped pasta. Serve on a White Wine Sauce (see page 60), tinted pink with a little tomato paste, and garnish with fronds of fresh dill. Make just two or three for a first course if you do not want to spend too long shaping them. Shapes that look a little wrinkled when cooked can be beautified by topping with a little grated Parmesan and broiling for a few seconds – this hides the creases that would otherwise spoil the heart shape.

- Christmas pasta is a fun idea for a festive dinner party appetizer. Cut Christmas trees out of green pasta and stars out of turmeric pasta; then fill them with the stuffing of your choice, and sandwich them in pairs. Serve on a simple sauce, such as Béchamel or White Wine Sauce (see page 60).

RINGS, SWIRLS, MOLDS AND LOAVES

Once it has been boiled and drained, pasta can be used in the same way as pastry dough for some dishes, or it can be baked into a shape. Here are a few pointers.

- Layer circles of pasta in ramekins or small soufflé dishes with mixtures that set when baked; then unmold them when cooked.

- Line a ring mold with cooked lasagne, alternating colors for best effect; then fill with a mixture which sets when baked. Fold over the ends of the pasta to neaten the shape, and unmold when cooked.

- Layer cooked lasagne with meatloaf mixture in a loaf pan, lining the bottom with non-stick baking parchment first. Start with a layer of lasagne, cut to fit the base of the pan; then build up with layers of meat, and end with a layer of lasagne. Cover with foil, and bake as usual. Use lasagne verde for good effect, and serve on a plate flooded with tomato sauce.

- Jelly-roll style swirls of pasta are attractive. For simple impact, cook strips of lasagne until tender; then spread with a finely ground, well-seasoned mixture of fish, poultry or meat. Roll up, and place in a baking dish; then add stock, wine or a sauce, cover, and braise until cooked through.

A TOPPING SAUCE

- Instead of smothering stuffed pasta shapes with a sauce, ladle the sauce on to the plate; then arrange the pasta on top. This is ideal for strong-colored sauces, such as tomato. Add a herb garnish to the pasta, which can look a little anemic otherwise.

- An alternative method of serving pasta and sauces is to put half the pasta in a warmed dish, top with the sauce, and add the remaining pasta. Add a garnish of herbs or other suitable ingredients (tomato slices, avocado slices, bell pepper slices and so on), then take the dish to the table. This works well with attractive pasta shapes, such as porcini-flavored pasta or the attractive grape shapes mentioned on page 16.

Making More of Pasta Menus

A SLIGHTLY DIFFERENT IMAGE

I WOULD NOT WANT TO LOSE PASTA AS A FAST FOOD, BUT IT IS FAR MORE VERSATILE THAN THIS, AND I HOPE THE RECIPE SECTIONS HIGHLIGHT JUST HOW ADAPTABLE IT IS. FIRST, THOUGH, HERE ARE A FEW IDEAS FOR SCENE SETTING FOR A DIFFERENT PASTA MEAL.

SEAFOOD EXTRAVAGANZA

Share a seafood extravaganza with friends, and prepare a serve-yourself meal. Offer crudités of vegetables instead of a first course, so that appetites are highly tuned for a main event. Arrange a selection of prepared seafood on a large platter. There are a few ideas for this next, but you can make it as simple or as interesting as you wish, and as the market permits. Keep cooking methods simple, either presenting dressed ingredients (cold) or broiling and poaching them, such as:

- dressed crab
- peeled, cooked, large shrimp sprinkled with lemon juice and snipped chives
- scallops, dotted with butter and broiled on their shells
- freshly cooked mussels in their shells
- cooked lobster, halved, cleaned and topped with fresh bread crumbs and a little finely chopped mozzarella, then broiled.

Cook a large bowl of paglia e fieno as the centerpiece for the table, toss a little butter with it, and shred basil into the bowl. Have a large bowl of freshly grated Parmesan cheese and a dish of sour cream with chives. Encourage diners to create their own combination of pasta and seafood. Provide finger bowls and dishes for redundant shells.

ORIENTAL-STYLE FONDUE

Serve a pasta hotpot meal, Japanese style. Arrange all the foods, have a spirit burner with a pot of stock simmering on it, and provide guests with individual bowls and chopsticks. Small metal baskets may be used to lower the food into the pot. Your guests then cook some rice sticks or noodles and the chosen seafood accompaniments in the stock as they require them.

- Make a large pot of dashi (see Japanese Stock, page 57) and of Chicken Stock (also see page 57), and combine them.
- Soften a selection of rice sticks and oriental egg noodles, then drain, and arrange them on platters for heating at the table.
- Prepare a platter with cubes of firm bean curd and button mushrooms.
- Arrange shredded Chinese leaves, carrot flowers (see page 255) and fine green beans on a platter.
- Prepare a seafood platter, with peeled, cooked, large shrimp, neat chunks of skinned white fish fillet and halved, shelled scallops.
- Provide a small bowl of dipping sauce for each diner. This could be, for example, garlic with soy sauce, or sake with soy sauce and chopped scallion, or sliced red chilis with soy sauce.

Pasta As You Wish

PASTA AS YOU WISH

Select or make three or four types of fresh pasta. For example, meat-filled tortellini, porcini-flavored shapes, fresh tagliatelle flavored with garlic, spinach gnocchi and so on.

- Prepare a tomato sauce (see pages 58 and 59 for options) ahead, make a large bowl of Pesto (see page 67), and prepare a pot of either olive oil with chopped garlic or butter, placing it over a candle warmer.

- Grate some Parmesan and pecorino.

- Have a bowl full of fresh herbs to mix in, such as shredded basil, chopped parsley and snipped chives.

- Cut some ripe avocados, and arrange them on a dish; sprinkle with lemon or lime juice.

- Have bowls of lemon and lime wedges, olives and pitted fresh dates to decorate the table.

Arrange the pastas in a decorative wheel of color on a large serving dish. Uncork a bottle of good red wine, and pour it into large-bowled glasses to savor the color and bouquet. Serve warmed crusty French bread as an accompaniment.

FORMAL DINNER PARTIES

I hope you will be inspired by the recipes in the chapters that follow, but, even so, it can be difficult to decide on the complete menu. There are a few golden rules to consider.

- Select foods that complement each other when you add all the courses together.

- Try to introduce complementary flavors, with contrasting textures and colors to make an interesting menu.

- Always plan a menu that you can prepare with confidence and without having to spend hours in the kitchen after your guests have arrived or (worse) between courses.

- Try to balance the number of courses and the bulk of the food. For example, do not fill everyone up with a hearty first course, then follow with a substantial main dish and a heavy pudding, as this will leave them feeling desperately uncomfortable. If you are planning to serve a multi-course menu, then make them all light.

MENUS FOR ALL OCCASIONS

COOK-AHEAD SUPPER

Dispense with the dessert, and offer fruit with cheese for this simple, mid-week meal to share with friends.

Zucchini and Basil Salad
(see page 314)
Warmed pitta bread

◆

Mediterranean Medley
(see page 108 and Note below)
Chicory with Dates and Olives
(see page 316)

◆

Fresh fruit and cheese

NOTE
*Cook the chicken in the sauce; then let it cool and chill until ready to reheat.
Cook the pasta in boiling salted water for two-thirds of the suggested time, let cool, and this may also be covered and chilled overnight if liked. Bring the chicken mixture back to a boil, add the pasta, and complete the cooking just before serving.*

GAME DINNER PARTY

Smoked salmon
Light rye bread and butter

◆

Pheasant Cappelletti with Dried
Morels and Oyster Mushrooms
(see page 210)
Leeks with Spinach (see page 314)

◆

Lime mousse *or* Chocolate roulade

◆

Stilton cheese
Warmed water biscuits

DIM SUM SUPPER PARTY

Practice your dim sum skills before preparing them for a dinner party as they can be a little fiddly. Then make a collection of individual dim sum, and keep them hot over candle warmers. A dish of stir-fried vegetables provides a palate-cleansing side dish.

Crispy Won Ton Parcels
(see page 259)
Shrimp Har Kow (see page 256)
Beef Shiu My with Chili Dipping
Sauce (see page 262)
Pan Stickers (see page 268)
Stir-fried vegetables
(see Note below)

◆

Green fruit salad *or* Fruit sorbet

NOTE
For the stir-fried vegetables, cut all the vegetables finely, and combine a good selection of perfectly fresh produce. Matchstick strips of celery, carrot, green and red bell pepper and leek make a good combination. Then tiny florets of broccoli, baby corn and sliced button mushrooms may be added. Let the vegetables cook briefly in their own cooking juices in the covered pan before serving. Season them lightly with a little soy sauce or salt and freshly ground black pepper.

HEARTY WINTER WEEKEND LUNCH

This is the ideal menu for Saturday lunch with friends or visiting relatives. It will provide fuel for a long afternoon walk or a visit to the store, and keep everyone happy until supper time.

Minestrone (see page 96 and
Note below)
Walnut and Olive Rolls
(see page 309)

◆

Fresh fruit and cheese

NOTE
The soup can be made the day before, and chilled overnight, but remember not to add the pasta until the soup is reheated; otherwise it will swell too much.

PASTA FOR BRUNCH

A great feast for a late morning breakfast or early lunch all rolled into one!

Smoked trout with lemon wedges
with Melba toast *or* hot bagels

◆

Pink grapefruit halves and melon
wedges

◆

Poached Eggs with Creamed
Watercress (see page 160)
served in nests of fresh linguine verde
or paglia e fieno

◆

American muffins *or* Danish pastries

SIMPLY SPICY SUPPER

A really tasty supper that combines Indian and Chinese influences. The first course can be omitted, and a platter of poppadoms with yogurt and grated cucumber served instead.

Avocados with tomatoes in oil and vinegar
Crisp poppadoms

◆

Curry Mee (see page 284)

◆

Fresh mango, papaya and pineapple with lime wedges

LIGHT, INFORMAL LUNCH OR SUPPER

Cucumber and Shrimp Sauce (see page 134)
Squid ink or spinach tagliatelle
Good Green Salad (see page 312)

◆

Brandied oranges (see Note below)
Whipped cream or fromage frais

NOTE
For a quick dessert, peel juicy oranges, removing all the pith, and cut them into slices. Navel or navelina oranges are ideal as they do not have seeds. Arrange the slices in a shallow, glass dish, and sprinkle them with superfine sugar. Trickle some brandy over them, cover and chill for a couple of hours before serving topped with toasted slivered almonds.

VEGETARIAN DINNER PARTY

This will delight any food enthusiast, vegetarian or not.

Stuffed Baby Eggplants
(see page 315)

◆

Patty Pan and Avocado Topping
(see page 185)
Paglia e fieno, fresh spirals (mixed white and verde) or porcini mushroom shapes
Good Green Salad (see page 312)

◆

Chocolate mousse or Ice-cream bombe (see Note below)

◆

Coffee and mints

NOTE
With the excellent range of good-quality purchased ice-creams now available, making a "cheat's" bombe can be a quick and delicious answer to the question of what to have for dessert. A domed metal bombe mold is the ideal freezing vessel, but do not despair if you do not have one, use a freezer-proof pudding basin instead. Chill the basin thoroughly, then line it with a layer of slightly softened ice-cream, smoothing it around the sides until you have evenly coated the basin. Freeze the ice-cream for a couple of hours, then add another layer of slightly softened ice-cream, and freeze again. Fill the middle before freezing the bombe overnight. Instead of using three different flavors of purchased ice-cream, you may wish to use a vanilla ice-cream, and add your own interesting ingredients for each layer, such as chopped, toasted hazelnuts, grated chocolate, dried fruits soaked in brandy, or liqueur, or mashed bananas. Unmold the bombe by dipping the mold in hot water up to the brim for a moment or two. Decorate with fruit and whipped cream.

JAPANESE-STYLE VEGETARIAN MEAL

For atmosphere, serve the food on low tables, and provide cushions for guests to sit on the floor. Keep table decorations minimal. Provide chopsticks and bowls. Offer Japanese rice crackers with pre-dinner drinks.

Hiyumagi (see page 276 and Note below)
Soba with Bean Curd and Nori (see page 278)
Fried Shiitake and Snow Peas with Crispy Noodles (see page 270)
Shredded vegetable salad (see Note below)

◆

Chopped fresh lemon jelly with exotic fruit (see Note below)

◆

Warmed sake

NOTE
Serve squares of egg omelet with the Hiyumagi instead of the shrimp, and omit the bonito fish from the dipping sauce. To make an attractive vegetable salad, coarsely grate a white radish, and toss it in rice vinegar. Coarsely grate or shred 2 carrots, and toss in a little Japanese soy sauce. Cut half a cucumber into fine matchstick strips, and toss in a little rice vinegar. Arrange the vegetables in neat piles on a large platter just before serving. For the dessert, make a fresh lemon jelly by boiling the rind and juice of 2 lemons in 2½ cups water; then strain the liquid. Set the jelly with agar agar (the vegetarian alternative to gelatin), and cut it into cubes. Arrange the jelly cubes on a platter or shallow bowl with prepared exotic fruit, such as lychees, star fruit, mango, halved passion fruit and so on.

PASTA KNOW-HOW
◆

*U*NLIKE DELICATE PASTRIES, PASTA DOUGH WITHSTANDS THE TOUCH OF AN
INEXPERIENCED HANDLER, SO DO NOT SHY AWAY FROM TEMPTING ITALIAN-STYLE
STUFFED PASTAS OR HOMEMADE LASAGNE BECAUSE YOU HAVE NEVER MADE ANY
BEFORE. ❦ ONCE YOU ARE FAMILIAR WITH THE DOUGH, YOU WILL PROBABLY FEEL
INCLINED TO EXPERIMENT WITH FLAVORS – AND THIS IS WHEN IT
REALLY DOES BECOME WORTHWHILE BECAUSE THE BETTER-QUALITY
PURCHASED PASTA OF THIS TYPE IS EXPENSIVE.

APART FROM ITALIAN EGG PASTA, YOU WILL FIND GNOCCHI AND
ORIENTAL-STYLE PASTA IN THIS CHAPTER. ❦ REMEMBER THAT THEY ALL FREEZE
WELL, SO YOU CAN HAVE A MAMMOTH COOKING SESSION AND STORE ENOUGH FOR
SEVERAL MEALS.
HAVE FUN EXPERIMENTING AND, IN THE PROCESS, DEVELOPING YOUR PASTA
REPERTOIRE.

Making Pasta at Home

Freshly made Italian pasta dough, quickly boiled and tossed with lots of melted butter or warmed olive oil, pepper, a little garlic and, perhaps, some chopped parsley or shredded basil, is delicious and simple to make. However, even though it is *possible* to make delicate Chinese-style won ton dough, the technique for making long oriental egg noodles is not one that is practical for the home cook to learn. The information that follows on mixing, kneading and boiling, therefore, applies to the Italian-style doughs, and specific notes and information are included with the various other basic pasta recipes.

Pasta is not difficult to make, but it does take a bit of kneading. Unlike delicate pastry, the dough is firm and glutinous, so some muscle power is required rather than the delicate touch practiced by pastrycooks. Bread flour is used for its gluten content, giving the dough its characteristic strength and texture, and letting it be rolled quite thinly with smooth results.

EQUIPMENT

If you already have a reasonably well-equipped kitchen, then you will not have to buy anything special for making pasta. However, if you have never tried making pasta before, you may find the following points helpful.

A LARGE COUNTER
This is something you do need for rolling out pasta dough. Make sure it is thoroughly clean and dry before you start. Unlike pastry making, you do want the pasta to "adhere" to the surface slightly as you roll it, so it will pick up any grime!

ROLLING PIN
A rolling pin without knobs on the end is essential; otherwise you will end up with infuriating grooves running down the length of the pasta after you have rolled it out beyond a certain size.

Useful equipment: slotted spoon; pasta boiler and colander; pasta machine, and metal rolling pin.

Look out for rolling pins that have a central section that rotates on thin handles. As well as wooden ones, marble and stainless steel pins are good, as they are easier to clean, and they do not stick quite as easily.

Specialist cookware stores sell extra-long pasta rolling pins, but an average-length simpler implement is fine.

PASTRY WHEEL OR LARGE KNIFE

A pastry wheel is useful for cutting between filled and covered ravioli, and it will give the pasta shapes an attractive fluted edge. However, a long-bladed cook's knife will do the job efficiently.

RAVIOLI TRAY OR TIN

This is a small tray with indentations rather like a shallow bun or muffin pan, and a raised, serrated cutting edge between the indentations. The rolled-out pasta dough is laid over the pan, and lightly pressed into the indentations; then the filling is added to these, and the pasta is brushed with beaten egg between the dots of filling. A second sheet of pasta is applied on top, and rolled with a rolling pin to separate the individual ravioli.

PASTA MACHINES

The most common and useful one for the average household is a hand-turned rolling machine. Small but heavy, the machine clamps to a counter. The rollers may be set apart at different widths, so that the dough can be rolled and folded several times instead of being kneaded by hand.

Cutting rollers can be fitted for making tagliatelle or linguine. A ravioli filler can also be attached. With this, folded sheets of pasta and the filling are fed in through a hopper; then the rollers do the job of filling and separating the individual pasta shapes. This is useful if you want to make very small pasta shapes, which are fiddly to manufacture by hand.

LARGE SAUCEPAN OR PASTA BOILER

It is worth investing in a very large saucepan that will have dozens of culinary uses apart from cooking pasta. Look out for a deep saucepan, complete with an integral strainer that fits snuggly inside the pan to make maximum use of its capacity. Then, when the pasta is cooked, you simply lift out the perforated lining. This also prevents pasta sticking to the bottom of the pan.

LARGE COLANDER

A deep colander is essential for draining pasta well. A stainless steel colander can be placed back on top of the saucepan, which is extremely useful when you are juggling a colander of pasta and trying to add the finishing touches to a sauce.

Kneading the pasta dough by hand

Kneading the dough by machine

MIXING PASTA DOUGH

Put the flour and salt in a bowl, and make a well in the middle, then add the liquid ingredients to the well. Gradually stir the flour into the eggs until the mixture clumps together – a fairly flat, sturdy plastic or wooden mixing spoon is best for this. Then abandon the mixing spoon, and use your hands to bring the dough together, scraping the dough from the spoon and the sides of the bowl with a flexible spatula. Press the dough together into a ball, rolling it around the bowl. Depending on the recipe, the dough may seem either slightly too dry for comfortable kneading or slightly too sticky at this stage, but the kneading process is important for achieving the right texture, ready for rolling out the dough.

KNEADING PASTA DOUGH BY HAND

Turn the dough out on to a lightly floured counter, and knead it well until it is smooth. Sprinkle a little flour over the counter during this time if necessary, but try to avoid adding too much flour as this will make the dough too dry.

The secret is to keep the dough moving all the time as you knead it firmly by grasping the front of the dough with your fingers, folding it back and pressing it down with the heel of your hand. This creates a sort of "rocking" movement.

Turn the dough around and over occasionally, keeping it moving, so that it is evenly kneaded. Pasta dough is quite tough and, if it is not moved, then it is easy to end up kneading it from one side only.

When the dough is smooth and warm, put it in a plastic bag, and let sit for 15–30 minutes. Do not chill the dough at this stage.

KNEADING PASTA DOUGH BY MACHINE

If you have an electric pasta-maker, then follow the manufacturer's instructions. The most popular type of pasta machine is the compact, hand-turned rolling machine that is supplied with different rollers and attachments for cutting noodles and filling ravioli as well as rolling pasta dough.

First, knead the dough by hand until it comes together in a fairly smooth ball. Then put this through the rollers, set to the widest setting. Fold the dough, press it together, and roll it on the widest setting again. Repeat this process several times until the dough is smooth. This, clearly, is less tiring than kneading by hand, and gives good results.

Once the dough is smooth, fold it, and press it together into a neat lump; then put in a plastic bag, and let sit for 15–30 minutes.

ROLLING OUT PASTA DOUGH

You can either roll the dough out by hand with a rolling pin or by machine. If you have a machine, then this stage is quick and easy. Simply pass the dough through the rollers, reducing the gap between them each time.

Work with a quantity of dough that you can handle easily. Unless you have a large kitchen table or counter and a long pasta rolling pin, cut the complete batch of dough in half or quarters for rolling out. Keep the rest covered to prevent it drying out.

Press the dough into the shape required, and lightly flour the counter before rolling it out. Try to keep the dough in the shape you want to end up with, pulling the corners out slightly as you work to make a square or rectangular shape, or turning the dough to make a round.

Lift and turn the dough occasionally to prevent it sticking, and keep the counter lightly floured. Do not dredge the counter heavily with flour as this will dry the dough, and make it more difficult to roll. Ideally, the dough should just cling to the counter as it is rolled. After the dough is part-rolled, and has been turned a couple of times, it becomes smooth and less likely to stick, so it is not necessary to flour the counter further. Lifting and shaking the dough slightly helps it keep its texture.

As you roll the dough – particularly if you are rolling it out with a rolling pin – look out for thick areas, and concentrate on rolling them out to achieve an even result. It is easy to continue rolling in one direction, so that the edges or one area of dough becomes far thinner than the middle or another area. Gently smoothing the dough with your hands occasionally helps, and this is a good way of thinning any thick patches.

Pasta dough can be rolled out very thinly until you can see your hands through it, but this is not necessary. However, do not leave the dough thick, as it makes noodles chewy and disappointingly stodgy. You should have to work fairly hard at rolling and stretching the dough without breaking its smooth surface; otherwise the chances are that it is too thick. For noodles, the dough should be like thick brown paper or a thin French crêpe after rolling.

If the time allows, leave the dough to rest for 10 minutes after rolling and before cutting. This relaxes the dough, and helps to prevent it shrinking when cut, but it is not an essential process. If you do leave it to relax, make sure the counter underneath is dusted lightly with flour, and cover with plastic wrap.

CUTTING PASTA

CUTTING NOODLES BY MACHINE

This is a simple matter of changing the rollers to cut noodles. If you have rolled the pasta by hand, then the dough must be floured before cutting.

CUTTING NOODLES BY HAND

Sift a little flour over the dough, and smooth it very lightly with the palm of your hand. Roll the dough up loosely; then cut it into strips as wide or as narrow as you want to make the noodles. Cut fine strips for linguine, ½-inch wide strips for tagliatelle or fettuccine, and 1-inch wide strips for pappardelle.

As soon as you have cut the strips, shake out the pasta dough, and put it on a plate dusted with flour.

CUTTING LARGE SHAPES

Lasagne may be cut into squares measuring about 4 inches, or into rectangular shapes measuring about 6 × 4 inches. However, when you make your own pasta, you do not have to comply with the convention of always making square or rectangular lasagne.

The only point to consider when cutting large pieces of pasta is the size of the cooking container available.

CUTTING DECORATIVE SHAPES

Cookie cutters and aspic cutters are ideal for stamping out decorative shapes. Flour the cutter occasionally to prevent the pasta sticking to it.

LASANKI

Lasanki are small pasta squares of Polish origin.

To make them, first cut the pasta dough into strips, then cut them across into squares – they should measure about ¼–½ inch.

HAND-MADE BOWS

Cut strips of pasta, then cut these into short lengths, and pinch them together in the middle to make bows. It is worth mentioning that although they are very good when homemade, honestly, it is a time-consuming process, and the pasta tastes just as good in easier-to-make squares or diamond shapes!

Cooking Pasta

There are all sorts of amusing stories associated with cooking pasta, particularly when it comes to testing whether or not the pasta is cooked. It is difficult to forget the kitchen in one particular male's residence at college where there was spaghetti stuck firmly to the sloping ceiling. The spaghetti was flung at the ceiling as a test of its tenderness. I would imagine, though, that if the pasta was soft enough to stick to the ceiling, it was overcooked!

Some recommend pinching a piece of spaghetti or pasta between the fingers, but the most hygienic, and satisfactory, method is to lift a piece on a slotted spoon, and taste it. When it is ready, the pasta should be tender without there being any taste of uncooked flour. You should also be able to bite the pasta: it must not be soft, but tender, the ideal being *al dente*, meaning "to the tooth," that is, still slightly firm when you bite it.

GREAT PANS OF WATER

Pasta should be added to plenty of boiling salted water, and, indeed, Italian cookbooks and packages of good-quality purchased pasta quote a vast volume that is beyond the capacity of most domestic saucepans. It is worth investing in one very large pan, stockpot or a special pasta pan that has an integral strainer. Alternatively, a pressure cooker (without its lid and weights) is often large enough to cook pasta.

To be perfectly practical, you can usually get away with using a large saucepan (about 6-pint capacity) for cooking 12–16 oz pasta, but it does not allow enough room to boil the pasta rapidly. The other alternative is to use more than one pan or, with fresh pasta, to have a back-up kettle of boiling water ready, and cook the pasta in two or more batches.

SALT AND OIL

Add salt to the cooking water, for flavor, and a little oil. The oil helps to stop the water from frothing up and over the edge of the pan as it boils. I have read elsewhere that oil helps to prevent pasta sticking together, but I have never found that this problem has arisen, because the only time I have had pasta stick is when I have attempted to cook it in too small a pan with too little water.

DRIED PASTA

Follow the instructions on the packet as the different shapes and ingredients do result in variations in the cooking time required. When adding long pasta to a pan, hold the pasta, and lower it into the water as it softens.

As a guide, allow 12–15 minutes cooking time for the majority of pasta. Some shapes and spaghetti take 15–20

minutes; then there are quick-cook varieties that are ready in a few minutes. However, I find the texture of some of the quick-cook Italian-style stypes is slimy and generally unacceptable. The majority of macaroni is now short cut and quick to cook, requiring about 7 minutes. Long macaroni, in bright blue packages, is still to be found in better delis and Italian stores. It is worth getting even if you intend breaking it up into small pieces for cooking and adding to cheese sauce because the taste is so much better.

DRIED ORIENTAL PASTA

Chinese egg noodles do not need to be boiled at all. You simply cover them with boiling water, and let them sit for about 15 minutes; then drain.

The cooking time for rice sticks varies, but it is usually about 2 minutes in boiling water. Again, it is important to read the instructions on the packages, as these products can become soft and soggy quite quickly after the quoted cooking time.

PASTA PORTIONS

The quantity of pasta to allow per portion depends on how it is served and on individual appetites, which seem to vary more widely with pasta than with many other foods. The following is a guide to the uncooked weight of pasta to allow per portion.

- Pasta starter: 2–3 ounces per person
- Pasta aside (as an accompaniment for a substantial sauce): 4 ounces
- Pasta main course (with a light main sauce): 6 ounces
- Pasta main course (for a hearty portion, with oil or melted butter and cheese, or equally light dressing or topping): 8 ounces

Fresh Pasta Shapes

FRESH PASTA

Fresh pasta cooks in about 3 minutes. It also swells more than some types of dried pasta. Filled pasta shapes can take longer, depending on the filling, which may need cooking or heating through thoroughly. Read the instructions on the package carefully when buying filled pasta shapes. The information in the chapter on Stuffed and Filled Pasta (page 191) provides further advice on cooking these shapes.

COOKING PASTA SHEETS

Lasagne and large pieces of pasta really do have to be cooked in a large volume of water, and with plenty of room for the water to boil rapidly. If the sheets are allowed to stay still in a small pan of water, they stick together and cook unevenly. If you do not have a very large saucepan, cook pasta sheets in batches.

DRAINING AND SERVING

Have a warmed serving dish ready to hold the cooked pasta. If the pasta is to be served plain, then you should have butter or warmed oil ready for dressing it. Freshly ground black pepper or grated Parmesan cheese may also be added.

Drain the pasta as soon as it is cooked, as a few extra minutes can ruin its texture, particularly in the case of fresh pasta.

Pasta sheets and tubes (cannelloni) should be rinsed under cold running water immediately they are drained to prevent them cooking further. Then they should be laid out on clean dish cloths ready for use. If they are left folded in a colander, stacked or closed, they will stick together and become difficult to use.

Storing and Freezing Pasta

DRIED PASTA

Keep dried pasta in its sealed bag or in an airtight container, and use within the recommended period given on the package. Because of its long shelf-life, the pasta will not suddenly go off or endanger health if the "use by" date on the package has expired by a couple of weeks, but the flavor and texture will gradually deteriorate with prolonged storage past this date.

FRESH PASTA

This should be kept chilled, and used within a couple of days of making. Always observe the recommended "use by" date on packages of purchased fresh pasta.

COOKED PASTA

Plain cooked pasta or cooked pasta dishes keep reasonably well, depending on the other ingredients used in them. Leftover cooked pasta or pasta that is cooked ahead for salads should be covered tightly to prevent it drying out; then kept in the refrigerator as soon as it has cooled.

The best method of reheating plain, cooked pasta is to do this in a microwave. It heats very quickly, and any significant quantity should be stirred after 2 minutes to ensure even heating. Alternatively, place the covered dish of pasta over a saucepan of boiling water.

Sauced pasta can be reheated in a microwave, over a saucepan of boiling water, or in the oven. When reheating pasta dishes in the oven, take care not to overcook them, or to dry out the surface before the pasta is thoroughly reheated. As with any other food, when reheating pasta dishes, make sure the whole batch of food is heated throughout before serving. Never reheat food more than once.

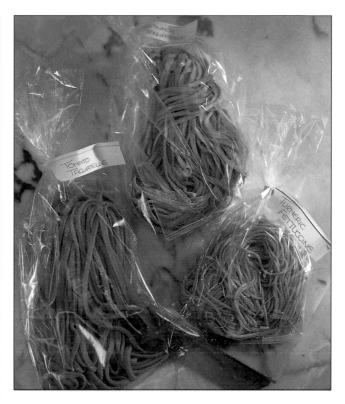

Storing Fresh Pasta

FREEZING PASTA

Uncooked fresh pasta freezes extremely well, and it can be cooked straight from frozen, allowing a nominal extra amount of time for tagliatelle and shapes, and slightly longer than this for filled pasta.

Ordinary cooked pasta does not freeze well. Although it is acceptable as a short-term measure for leftovers, which can be turned into a useful lunch dish another time, it is not to be recommended as a method of cooking ahead for dinner parties and so on. This is also true of soups, hotpots or other very moist dishes (unthickened, stock-based sauces) that contain separate pieces of pasta. On thawing, the pasta is too soft and it breaks up easily.

Macaroni cheese and similar pasta dishes in which the pasta is protected by a fairly thick sauce have slightly better freezing qualities, however. Also, baked dishes containing sheets or similar large areas of pasta, such as lasagne or cannelloni, freeze very well.

THE RECIPES

♦

THE DOUGHS

Rich Egg Pasta Dough   *Spinach*   *Beet*   *Turmeric*

Eggless Pasta Dough

Use virgin olive oil for a pronounced flavor or a lighter oil if you prefer. Walnut oil may be used instead of olive oil to give the dough a distinct, delicious, walnut flavor. Melted butter may be substituted for some of the oil, if liked. Use up to 4 tablespoons of butter with 2 tablespoons olive oil.

MAKES ABOUT 1¼ POUNDS PASTA

- *3 cups white bread flour*
- *1 teaspoon salt*
- *6 tablespoons olive oil*
- *scant ⅔ cup water*

Mix the flour and salt together in a bowl, making a well in the middle. Add the oil and two-thirds of the water, then mix well with a spoon until the flour clumps together.

Use your hand to continue mixing, and add a little more of the water, if necessary, to bind the ingredients into a dough. This pasta dough is slightly softer than the dough made with eggs. Knead the pasta until it is smooth and let it rest until required (page 36).

Pasta Dough

MAKES ABOUT 1¼ POUNDS PASTA

- *3 cups white bread flour*
- *1 teaspoon salt*
- *3 eggs*
- *4 tablespoons olive oil*
- *1 tablespoon water*

Mix the flour and salt together in a bowl, making a well in the middle. Beat the eggs with the olive oil and water, then pour the mixture into the well in the flour.

Gradually stir the flour into the eggs, first using a spoon, then your hands, following the advice for mixing pasta on page 36. Knead the pasta until it is smooth, then let it rest until required (also see page 36).

♦

Rich Egg Pasta Dough

MAKES A GENEROUS 1½ POUNDS PASTA

- *4 cups white bread flour*
- *1 teaspoon salt*
- *4–5 large eggs*

Mix the flour and salt in a bowl, making a well in the middle. Beat the eggs, then pour two-thirds into the well in the flour.

Gradually mix in the flour, adding more egg until the mixture clumps together (I actually used 4½ large eggs to get the right consistency for a firm, manageable dough, but the dough may need all 5 eggs depending on slight variations in the absorbency of the flour and the size of the eggs).

Mix and knead the dough following the instructions on page 36 and let sit before using.

FLAVORED PASTA DOUGH

◆

BEET
Use the Pasta Dough recipe on page 44. Purée ⅓ cup peeled, cooked beets with 2 of the eggs, then press the purée through a fine strainer (if the mixture is *not* strained, the pasta will be slightly speckled). Add the beet purée with the remaining eggs, then omit the olive oil.

This dough is slightly softer and requires slightly more flour for kneading and rolling.

CARDAMOM-SPICED
Split 10 green cardamom pods and scrape the tiny black seeds from the pods into a mortar. Grind the seeds to a powder with a pestle, then add the powder to the flour when making either the Pasta Dough or the Rich Egg Pasta Dough on page 44.

This pasta has a distinct, but delicate, cardamom flavor that goes well with fish, vegetables and chicken.

CARROT
Use the Pasta Dough recipe on page 44. Peel and boil 4 ounces carrot until tender. Drain, mash and strain the carrot, then let cool until it is warm. Add the purée to the eggs, and omit the oil and water from the dough.

CUMIN-SPICED
Add 1 tablespoon white cumin seeds to the flour.

This may be combined with the cardamom-spiced (above) or Turmeric (below) flavored pastas, or both. Cumin-spiced pasta is good with some egg- or cheese-based dairy sauces, meat, poultry and vegetables.

CURRY-SPICED
Split 4 cardamom pods, scrape the tiny black seeds from inside into a mortar, and grind them to a powder with a pestle. Heat 2 tablespoons ghee *or* butter in a small saucepan. Add 1 finely chopped garlic clove, 1 tablespoon finely chopped onion, 1 tablespoon ground cumin, 1 tablespoon ground coriander, 1 teaspoon turmeric and the ground cardamom seeds. Cook, stirring, for 2–3 minutes; then set aside to cool. Beat the spice paste with the eggs for either of the Pasta Dough or Rich Egg Pasta Dough recipes on page 44.

HERB
Add 4 tablespoons chopped mixed fresh herbs to the Pasta Dough (see page 44) or 5 tablespoons if making the Rich Egg Pasta Dough (also see page 44).

Parsley, chervil, thyme, sage, marjoram, oregano, savory, tarragon, chives and fennel are all suitable.

Balance the mixture by using more of the mild herbs, like parsley, chives and chervil, with strong flavors, such as oregano, thyme and rosemary.

Tarragon, parsley and chives are a good combination. Use 1 tablespoon of tarragon to 2 of each of the others if you want a mild tarragon flavor.

For oregano with parsley and sage, use 2 tablespoons parsley and 1 tablespoon of each of the others.

LEMON
Add the grated rind of 2 lemons to the eggs of either of the pasta dough recipes (see page 44), and chopped parsley or snipped chives if liked.

OLIVE, OLIVE AND GARLIC, OR OLIVE, OREGANO AND GARLIC
Finely chop ⅔ cup pitted black olives, and add to the flour of either of the pasta dough recipes (see page 44). Finely chop 2 garlic cloves, and add them to the eggs if liked. Mix 2 tablespoons chopped fresh oregano with the flour.

SPINACH
Wash and trim 8 ounces fresh spinach, and place the wet leaves in a saucepan. Cover tightly, and cook over a high heat, shaking the pan often, for 5 minutes, or until the leaves have wilted and are tender. Spoon the leaves into a strainer placed over a basin. Use the back of a mixing spoon to press the liquid from the spinach. Then squeeze the leaves with your hand until they are as dry as possible. Stir the liquid drained from the spinach. Add 6 tablespoons of the spinach liquid to the Pasta Dough (see page 44) in place of the olive oil and water. If making the Rich Egg Pasta Dough (also see page 44) add the same quantity of spinach liquid, and use just 4 eggs.

TOMATO
Beat 1 tablespoon concentrated tomato paste into the eggs for either of the pasta dough recipes (see page 44). Chopped herbs, such as oregano or parsley, may be added, too, if liked.

TURMERIC
Add 1 teaspoon ground turmeric to the flour for either of the pasta dough recipes (see page 44).

Turmeric pasta has a mild, slightly peppery flavor.

WALNUT
Use walnut oil instead of olive oil in the Pasta Dough recipe (see page 44).

Potato Gnocchi

Potato gnocchi may be served on their own as a light lunch dish – good with a crisp side salad of mixed leaves – or they may be offered as a base for rich, meaty sauces. I have given melted butter, Parmesan and pepper as the dressing here, but lightly sautéed, chopped fresh garlic in plenty of hot olive oil is a delicious alternative.

SERVES 4

FOR THE GNOCCHI
- *1 pound potatoes*
- *2 tablespoons butter, melted*
- *1 teaspoon salt*
- *1 egg, beaten*
- *1½ cups white bread flour*

TO SERVE
- *⅓ cup melted butter*
- *freshly ground black pepper or nutmeg*
- *freshly grated Parmesan cheese*

To make the gnocchi, boil the potatoes in their skins until tender (about 20 minutes), then drain and peel them under cold running water. Mash the potatoes, and press them through a fine strainer.

Beat the butter, salt and egg into the potatoes; then gradually stir in the flour. Use a spoon at first; then mix the dough together with your hand. Knead the dough lightly until smooth.

Knead a hand-sized lump of dough until smooth; then roll it into a long, thick sausage shape on a lightly floured surface, and cut off 1-inch lengths. Use a fork or one finger to make an indentation in each piece of gnocchi.

Place the gnocchi on a well-floured plate or tray, cover and keep cool until they are to be cooked. Bring a large saucepan of salted water to a boil. Drop in the gnocchi, and bring back to a boil. Boil the gnocchi for 4–5 minutes, keeping the water just bubbling, not boiling too rapidly or the gnocchi may break up.

Drain the gnocchi as soon as they are cooked, as they will become soft and watery if boiled for too long. Use a slotted spoon to remove the gnocchi from the pan if you have to cook them in batches.

Serve freshly cooked with hot melted butter, freshly ground black pepper or nutmeg and grated Parmesan cheese.

Spinach Gnocchi

Ricotta cheese and eggs combine with spinach and flour to make these gnocchi, which are lighter than those based on a potato dough. For sure success, it is best to chill this mixture overnight before shaping and cooking the gnocchi.

SERVES 4

FOR THE GNOCCHI
- *1⅓ cups cooked fresh or frozen spinach, drained and chopped*
- *2 cups ricotta cheese*
- *salt and freshly ground black pepper*
- *¼ cup freshly grated Parmesan cheese*
- *1 cup all-purpose flour*
- *2 eggs, beaten*

TO SERVE
- *⅓ cup melted butter*
- *freshly grated Parmesan cheese*

To make the gnocchi, first press all the liquid from the spinach. Press the ricotta through a fine strainer. Mix the ricotta, spinach, plenty of seasoning and Parmesan cheese. Stir in the flour and the eggs to make a soft dough. Chill the dough for several hours, or put it in the freezer until it is firm enough to shape.

Shape small ovals of dough, and place them on a floured tray or plate. Bring a large saucepan of salted water to a boil. Add the gnocchi in batches, and bring the water back to a boil. The water should only just boil, because if it bubbles too rapidly, the gnocchi will break up. Cook the gnocchi for 4–5 minutes; then remove them with a slotted spoon and drain well. Keep cooked gnocchi hot until all the batches are ready.

Serve piping hot, tossed in melted butter, seasoned with freshly ground black pepper, and sprinkled with Parmesan cheese.

FLAVORED POTATO GNOCCHI

◆

PARMESAN AND OREGANO

Add 1 tablespoon chopped fresh oregano and ¼ cup freshly grated Parmesan cheese to the potatoes. Stir in a little grated nutmeg with the flour. Serve with garlic sautéed in olive oil.

RICOTTA GNOCCHI

Omit the butter. Press 1 cup ricotta cheese through a fine strainer and beat it into the potatoes. Add 2 tablespoons finely chopped parsley and a little grated nutmeg. Serve with hot melted butter and shredded basil.

CLOCKWISE FROM TOP

1 Potato Gnocchi   2 Spinach Gnocchi   3 Parmesan and Oregano Gnocchi   4 Kopytka   5 Baked Semolina Gnocchi

Kopytka

This is the Polish equivalent of Italian potato gnocchi.

SERVES 4

FOR THE KOPYTKA	TO SERVE
• *1 pound potatoes*	• *1 cup fresh bread crumbs*
• *1 cup all-purpose flour*	• *⅓ cup butter*
• *½ teaspoon salt*	
• *1 egg, beaten*	

To make the kopytka, first boil the potatoes in their skins until tender (about 20 minutes). Then peel them under cold running water. Mash the cooked potatoes, and press them through a fine strainer into a bowl. Stir in the flour and salt; then mix in the egg to make a soft dough.

Next, prepare the bread crumbs for serving. Fry the bread crumbs in 2 tablespoons of the butter, stirring and turning them until they are crisp and golden. Set aside to cool.

Have a well-floured tray or plate ready, and prepare a small heap of flour, or have a dredger nearby, to dust your hands as you work. Roll small portions of the dough into balls slightly smaller than walnuts. Make an indentation in each ball with the tip of your finger.

When all the kopytka dough has been shaped, bring a large saucepan of salted water to a boil. Cook the kopytka in batches, bringing the water back to a boil, then keeping it just bubbling, for 4–5 minutes. Do not boil the water too rapidly or the kopytka will break up, but if it does not boil, they will simply sink and become soggy.

Drain the kopytka using a slotted spoon, and place them in a warmed serving dish. Keep hot while the remaining kopytka are cooked. Melt the remaining butter for serving, and pour it over the kopytka. Sprinkle with the fried bread crumbs and serve at once.

KOPYTKA WITH PORK FAT

This sounds awful but tastes very good! Traditionally, pork fat is diced, and gently cooked in a heavy-bottomed pan until it renders its fat and the pieces become small and crisp. A little of the hot cooking water from the kopytka is spooned over the cooked dumplings, then they are dressed with hot pork fat and the crispy remains of the fat.

As it is quite difficult to find chunks of pork fat these days, instead, skin a piece of salt pork and melt the fat from the skin, then finely dice the meat and fat and render this in a heavy-bottomed saucepan or by roasting in the oven. Only three or four tiny pieces should be scattered over each portion.

Baked Semolina Gnocchi

This is different to the other gnocchi recipes as it is cooked to a thick porridge in the saucepan before being chilled, cut up and baked. The shaped pieces freeze well. Rich Tomato Sauce or Light Tomato Sauce (see pages 58 and 59) may be served with these or the Parmesan Cheese Gnocchi variation. Pesto (see page 67) is also good with these lighter Baked Semolina Gnocchi.

SERVES 4

- 3¾ cups milk
- 1 bay leaf
- 1 blade of mace
- 1 onion, thickly sliced
- 3 cloves
- 1¾ cups semolina
- ½ cup butter
- 1 cup ricotta cheese
- freshly grated nutmeg
- salt and freshly ground black pepper
- 2 eggs, beaten
- olive oil, for greasing
- 3 tablespoons freshly grated Parmesan cheese

Heat the milk, bay leaf, mace, onion and cloves together, slowly, until just coming to a boil. Then remove the pan from the heat, cover and leave the milk until cold. Heat the milk until it is about to boil again; then strain it into a large, clean, heavy-bottomed saucepan.

Sprinkle the semolina into the milk, stirring all the time, and bring to a boil. Do not stop stirring, or the semolina will cook in lumps. The mixture becomes quite stiff as it cooks and thickens, but persist in cooking it

well, as this is important if the gnocchi are to be of the right consistency.

Remove the pan from the heat, and beat in half the butter. Then press the ricotta cheese through a strainer and mix it into the semolina with plenty of seasoning. Finally, beat in the eggs. Grease a baking pan (a roasting pan is ideal for this) with a little olive oil, and spread the mixture out in it to a thickness of about ½ inch. Keep the edges neat and of an even thickness.

Let the semolina mixture cool; then chill it thoroughly for at least 2 hours, until it is firm enough to be cut into squares.

Preheat the oven to 400°F. Melt the remaining butter, and use a little to grease a shallow, ovenproof dish. Use a sharp, wetted kitchen knife to cut the semolina mixture into small squares. Arrange the gnocchi, overlapping, in the dish, preferably in a single layer; then trickle the melted butter over them, and sprinkle with the Parmesan. Bake for about 20 minutes, or until crisp and golden on top. Serve at once.

PARMESAN CHEESE GNOCCHI

Prepare and cook the semolina as above, but omit the ricotta, and do not stir in the butter. Instead, beat 1 cup freshly grated Parmesan cheese into the hot semolina with the seasoning, nutmeg and eggs. Continue as above, coating the gnocchi with butter before baking.

Spätzle

This is an example of a pasta–dumpling cross from Eastern European culinary traditions. I took a deep breath before I attempted to make this thick mixture as I remember previous efforts involving much sloppy batter, great cauldrons of boiling water, wet chopping boards, a sticky stove and general disaster, but, with careful attention to the batter, just the right number of eggs and enough flour, these worked a treat! I was so delighted with the results that I went on to cook several batches with various flavorings, the best of which I have included here.

Spätzle may be treated as gnocchi, and served with butter or olive oil or other simple dressings, such as sour cream and chives or dill. However, they are also the ideal accompaniment for rich meat or game sauces and good in substantial meat and vegetable hotpots or soups.

SERVES 4

FOR THE SPÄTZLE
- 2 cups all-purpose flour
- ½ teaspoon salt
- 4 eggs, beaten
- about 3 tablespoons water

TO SERVE
- ¼ cup melted butter

To make the spätzle, first, mix the flour and salt in a bowl, making a well in the middle. Add the eggs; then gradually work in the flour, and beat hard until the batter is very thick and smooth. Add the water gradually, so that you can beat the batter without difficulty. However, the mixture should be thick, elastic and quite "stringy" in texture, not freely pouring.

Prepare a large saucepan of boiling salted water, and have a slotted spoon ready. Pour the melted butter for serving into a warmed dish, and keep this hot ready to receive the cooked spätzle. Rinse a small cutting board under cold running water, and wet a large, flat-bladed kitchen knife in the same way. Drop a large pat of the batter on the board. Regulate the heat under the pan of water so that the water is just boiling.

Use a cutting and sliding action to scrape thin, short lengths of the batter sideways into the pan of boiling water. Rinse the knife under running cold water every three or four cuts to prevent the batter sticking to it. The water must be boiling, otherwise the spätzle will stick to the bottom of the pan. Cook the batter in batches. Once the spätzle have been in the pan for about 30 seconds, gently ease them off the bottom with the slotted spoon.

Boil the spätzle for 2–3 minutes, until they are swollen and firm. Drain them well, and place them in the hot butter, toss them in it, and keep hot until all the batter has been cooked. Serve piping hot.

Using a plastic bag to cut and shape the Spätzle dough

COOK'S TIPS

- Beating the batter to achieve a smooth, elastic texture is important.
- If the batter feels slightly too runny, set it aside to sit for 30 minutes before adding more flour, as this will encourage the starch grains to swell and the batter to become slightly less runny. Adding too much extra flour may give a stodgy result.
- I used a small, laminated board with a smooth surface for holding the batter. I suspect some of the problems I had before when trying to shape spätzle, were partly due to the fact that I was using a wooden board to which the batter tended to cling.
- If you do not have a small board, the spätzle may be shaped by squeezing the batter out of a plastic bag and snipping it into short lengths. To do this, put some batter in a plastic bag (one that does not have a gusset), and rinse the blades of kitchen scissors under cold water. When the water is boiling, snip a small point off one corner of the bag, and support it while allowing the batter to flow out slowly. Snip off short lengths of batter. This is a speedy method of shaping spätzle, but they tend to be lumps rather than the finer, long, thin shapes achieved when using a board. Take care not to cut a chunk off the end of the bag when snipping the batter!

FLAVORED SPATZLE

GARLIC AND OREGANO
Add 1 tablespoon chopped fresh oregano *or* 2 teaspoons dried oregano and 2 finely chopped garlic cloves to the eggs.

HERB SPATZLE
Add 2 tablespoons each of chopped parsley and chives, and 1 tablespoon chopped fresh thyme *or* 1 teaspoon dried thyme to the flour.

CELERY LEAF SPATZLE
Finely chop the leafy tops of a head of celery and add to the eggs. Cook 2 tablespoons celery seeds in the butter for serving for a few minutes; then toss the cooked spätzle with this.

Dropping the Spätzle batter into boiling water

Won Ton Dough

This is not the easiest of doughs to roll, but I find these basic quantities work reasonably well, making a mixture that can be rolled out sufficiently thinly to make light boiled or puffy, crisp fried won tons. If you happen to visit an oriental supermarket, look out for ready-made won ton wrappers, cut in small squares and dusted with cornstarch. They are usually sold with the other chilled foods, such as fresh egg noodles, and often come in sizeable packages, but these may be split and frozen quite successfully.

MAKES 18 WON TONS

- ½ cup cornstarch
- ½ cup all-purpose flour
- ¼ teaspoon salt
- 1 egg, beaten
- 2 tablespoons water

Mix the cornstarch, all-purpose flour and salt in a bowl, making a well in the middle. Add the egg and water to the well; then gradually work in the flour with a mixing spoon to make a dry dough. Scrape all the cornstarch from around the bowl, and knead the dough by hand until it is smooth and soft.

Dust the counter with a little cornstarch. Keep the counter lightly dusted with cornstarch, but it is more important to keep the dough moving to prevent it sticking. If you dredge the cornstarch too thickly, the dough will become dry on the surface, and it will break easily.

Cut the dough in half for rolling out, and keep the portion that is not being worked covered with plastic wrap to prevent it drying out.

Dust the counter and rolling pin with cornstarch, and roll the dough out thinly, until it is about 10 inches square. Take care not to rip the dough, as it tends to stretch apart and will not rejoin easily. Trim the edges of the dough, and cut it into three strips, then across into three squares. Roll out each of the squares again until quite thin and measuring about 4 inches before filling.

The squares should be filled as soon as they have been rolled; then they should be placed on a baking sheet dredged with cornstarch to prevent them sticking.

PUFFY DEEP-FRIED WON TONS

Add 2 teaspoons baking powder to the flour for a dough that puffs up when deep-fried. Use it, for example, for making deep-fried Sweet-and-sour Won Tons (see page 258).

Homemade Won Ton Dough

Store-bought Won Ton Dough

Won Ton Soup

Dim Sum Dough

**This is a basic dough that may be used to make a
variety of steamed, filled dim sum.**

MAKES ABOUT 24 DIM SUM

- *1 cup white bread flour*
- *pinch of salt*
- *3 tablespoons boiling water*
- *2 tablespoons lard or white vegetable shortening*
- *cornstarch, for dusting*

Mix the flour and salt in a bowl. Pour the boiling water
over the lard in a heatproof jug, and stir until the fat
melts. Then stir the hot liquid into the flour to make a
smooth, fairly soft dough. Knead the dough until smooth
on a counter lightly dusted with cornstarch. Use the
dough as soon as it is made, keeping the portion not
being worked covered in plastic wrap to prevent it drying
out.

53

ESSENTIAL SAUCES AND CONTEMPORARY DRESSINGS

◆

*H*ERE, YOU WILL FIND A CLASSIC COLLECTION OF RECIPES ALONGSIDE THOSE THAT DEPART FROM TRADITION.

WHETHER YOU BOTHER TO MAKE YOUR OWN STOCK OR NOT IS ENTIRELY UP TO YOU. THERE ARE HIGH-QUALITY CHILLED STOCKS AVAILABLE, WHICH REALLY ARE GOOD, OR SOME BOUILLON CUBES THAT ARE NOT OVERSEASONED OR ARTIFICIAL IN FLAVOR, BUT AVOID THE STRONG-FLAVORED CUBES THAT ARE VERY HIGHLY SEASONED AND BRING AN ARTIFICIAL TASTE TO OTHERWISE GOOD INGREDIENTS.

YOU MAY WANT TO MAKE YOUR OWN STOCK FOR SOME SPECIAL DISHES, OR WHEN YOU HAVE A LEFTOVER CARCASS OR THE BONES FROM A PIECE OF MEAT. ❦ FOR MANY STEWS, POULTRY OR MEAT MIXTURE, I OFTEN RELY ON THE FLAVOR OF THE INGREDIENTS AND USE WATER WITH CAREFUL SEASONING. ❦ ONE POINT TO REMEMBER IS THAT YOU DO HAVE TO MAKE THE CHINESE STOCK TO GET THE RIGHT FLAVOR WHEN IT IS SUGGESTED IN A DISH.

I HOPE YOU FIND THESE RECIPES BOTH USEFUL AND INSPIRING FOR QUICK MEALS AS WELL AS THOSE OCCASIONS THAT DEMAND HOURS OF PREPARATION IN THE KITCHEN.

MANY OF THESE SAUCES FORM A USEFUL BASE FOR FISH, POULTRY, MEAT OR VEGETABLE TOPPINGS; OTHERS ARE ESSENTIAL "INGREDIENTS" IN BAKED PASTA DISHES. ❦ THE CHAPTER ALSO INCLUDES SIMPLE DRESSINGS WHICH CAN BE TOSSED WITH FRESHLY COOKED PASTA FOR A TASTY LUNCH OR SUPPER.

Fish Stock

If you have fish trimmings, such as skin and bones, then use them to make fish stock or ask the fish vendor, who will usually be able to provide suitable stock trimmings. Do not add gills as they make the stock bitter. However, with the ready availability of excellent-quality frozen fish, there are often times when trimmings are not available, so this recipe uses a small amount of fish fillet instead.

MAKES ABOUT 1½ QUARTS

- *8 ounces white fish fillet, such as grouper, flounder or haddock*
- *1 onion, thinly sliced*
- *1 large carrot, thinly sliced*
- *2 celery stalks, thinly sliced*
- *1 bay leaf*
- *4 sprigs of parsley or a handful of parsley stalks*
- *1 small sprig of thyme*
- *1 teaspoon black peppercorns*
- *1½ quarts water*

Put the fish in a saucepan. Add the onion, carrot, celery, bay leaf, parsley, thyme and peppercorns. Pour in the water, and bring to a boil very slowly. Reduce the heat so that the water simmers gently. Cover the pan, and simmer for 1 hour. Let cool; then strain the stock. The stock is not salted, so that salt may be added to the recipe in which it is used.

Beef Stock

If you buy from an independent butcher, then you will be able to get some beef bones cut into practical sizes for putting into a large saucepan. You will also need some meat to make a decent stock. This recipe is based on beef shank. If you can get any bones, roast them at 350°F for 1 hour before boiling, and boil some water in the roasting pan to get all the flavor from the cooking juices.

MAKES ABOUT 1½ QUARTS

- *1 pound cubed beef shank*
- *1 large onion, thinly sliced*
- *2 carrots, sliced*
- *2 celery stalks, sliced*
- *1 bay leaf*
- *1 blade of mace*
- *1 sprig of thyme*
- *6 sprigs of parsley or a handful of parsley stalks*
- *1 teaspoon coriander seeds*
- *1 teaspoon black peppercorns*
- *2 quarts water*

Put the beef, onion, carrots, celery, bay leaf, mace, thyme, parsley, coriander seeds and peppercorns in a large saucepan. Pour in the water, and bring slowly to a boil. Skim off any scum that rises to the surface of the water, then reduce the heat, and cover the pan. Simmer the stock gently for 3 hours. Strain the stock, and use as required. Salt is not added to the stock, so it can be added to the recipe in which the stock is used.

Vegetable Stock

You can vary this according to whatever is available and the strength of flavor required.

MAKES ABOUT 1½ QUARTS

- *2 large onions, thinly sliced*
- *2 large carrots, thinly sliced*
- *4 celery stalks, thinly sliced*
- *1 small turnip, diced*
- *1⅓ cups sliced small button mushrooms*
- *1 bay leaf*
- *4 sprigs of parsley or a handful of parsley stalks*
- *1 sprig of thyme*
- *1 garlic clove, peeled*
- *1½ quarts water*

Put the onions, carrots, celery, turnip, mushrooms, bay leaf, parsley, thyme and garlic in a saucepan. Pour in the water, and bring to a boil. Reduce the heat, cover the pan, and simmer gently for 1¼ hours. Pour the stock through a fine strainer. Salt is not added to the stock, so it can be added to the recipe in which the stock is used.

Chicken Stock

Chicken stock can be made from a meaty roast chicken carcass, from the uncooked carcass left after boning a bird, from a roast or by boiling a whole bird. Boiling a whole chicken gives by far the best stock, and the uncooked bones often give a good flavor, especially when the wing ends, giblets and any other offcuts are included. The quality of stock resulting from a cooked carcass depends on how meaty it is. Using a chicken quarter is the practical choice if you want a well-flavored stock, but do not want to "waste" a whole bird. Also the meat may be diced, and added to a sauce to serve with pasta.

MAKES ABOUT 1½ QUARTS

- 1 chicken quarter
- 1 onion, sliced
- 1 large carrot, sliced
- 2 celery stalks, sliced
- 1 bay leaf
- 1 sprig of sage
- 4 sprigs of parsley or a handful of parsley stalks
- 1 sprig of thyme
- 1 teaspoon black peppercorns
- generous 1½ quarts water

Put the chicken quarter in a saucepan. Add the onion, carrot, celery, bay leaf, parsley, sage, thyme and peppercorns. Pour in the water, and bring to a boil. Reduce the heat, and cover the pan; then simmer for 1½ hours.

Let the stock cool before straining it. Salt is not added to the stock, as it can be added to the recipe in which the stock is used.

Chinese-style Stock

A combination of pork and chicken makes a flavorsome stock.

MAKES ABOUT 1½ QUARTS

- 1 pound meaty pork spareribs, chopped into short lengths
- 2 chicken drumsticks
- 1 onion, thinly sliced
- 1 carrot, thinly sliced
- 1 celery stalk, thinly sliced
- generous 1½ quarts water

Put the pork spareribs, chicken drumsticks, onion, carrot and celery in a saucepan. Pour in the water, and bring slowly to a boil. Skim off any scum that rises to the surface of the water, then cover the pan, and reduce the heat. Simmer the stock for 2 hours. Strain the stock, and use as required. Salt is not added to the stock, as it can be added to the recipe in which the stock is used. Alternatively, soy sauce may be used as the seasoning in oriental dishes.

Japanese Stock

You will find packages of dried bonito fish and the dried konbu or kelp (seaweed) in oriental supermarkets and special stores. Dried bonito is often sold in small envelopes (or packages containing several envelopes), each containing about 1 tablespoon. I find that health food stores also stock the dried seaweed.

MAKES ABOUT 1½ QUARTS

- 1 piece of wakame or konbu (dried seaweed)
- 1 tablespoon dried bonito fish
- 1½ quarts water

Put the dried wakame or konbu in a saucepan. Add the bonito fish, and pour in the water. Heat gently until boiling. Cover the pan, remove it from the heat, and let sit for 30 minutes. Pour the stock through a fine strainer.

Rich Tomato Sauce

This is made with canned passata (tomato purée) and enriched with extra tomato paste as well as red wine.

MAKES ABOUT 900 ML/1½ PINTS

- 3 tablespoons olive oil
- 2 garlic cloves, crushed
- 1 onion, chopped
- 1 small carrot, diced
- 1 celery stalk, diced
- 1 bouquet garni
- 3 tablespoons tomato paste
- 2½ cups passata
- 1¼ cups robust red wine
- salt and freshly ground black pepper
- 2 teaspoons sugar

Heat the oil in a large saucepan. Add the garlic, onion, carrot, celery and bouquet garni. Stir well, then cover the pan, and cook for 15 minutes.

Stir in the tomato paste, passata and wine. Add seasoning to taste, and bring to a boil. Reduce the heat, cover the pan, and simmer gently for 1 hour.

Remove the bouquet garni; then liquidize the sauce until it is smooth. Stir in the sugar, reheat and taste for seasoning before serving.

White Sauce

MAKES ABOUT 3 CUPS

- 3 tablespoons butter
- ⅓ cup all-purpose flour
- 2½ cups milk
- salt and freshly ground white or black pepper

Melt the butter in a saucepan. Stir in the flour, then reduce the heat a little, and slowly pour in the milk, stirring all the time. Continue stirring until the sauce boils. Reduce the heat, and simmer the sauce for 3 minutes, stirring occasionally. Add salt and pepper to taste, and use as required.

COOK'S TIP

Flour, used to thicken a sauce, has to be cooked beyond simply reaching boiling point, otherwise it will taste raw in the finished sauce. The flour may be cooked for 2 minutes after it has been stirred into the butter, and before the milk is added. Alternatively, the sauce may be simmered for 2–3 minutes, or longer, after it has boiled.

FLAVORINGS FOR WHITE SAUCE

BUTTER SAUCE
Whisk in ⅓ cup butter after the sauce has simmered, then add seasoning to taste.

PARSLEY SAUCE
Stir in 6 tablespoons chopped fresh parsley at the end of the cooking time.

TARRAGON SAUCE
Stir in 2–3 tablespoons chopped fresh tarragon at the end of the cooking time.

CHEESE SAUCE
Stir in 1 cup grated sharp Cheddar cheese at the end of the cooking time. Stir over a low heat until the cheese has melted.

EGG SAUCE
Stir in 4 finely chopped hard-cooked eggs at the end of the cooking time. Add 2–3 tablespoons chopped fresh parsley or tarragon, or snipped chives, if liked.

MUSHROOM SAUCE
Cook 2 cups thickly sliced button mushrooms in the butter before adding the flour. As the mushrooms begin to cook, they yield a lot of liquid, continue cooking until this has evaporated before stirring in the flour and finishing the sauce.

Light, Fresh Tomato Sauce

This sauce has a light tomato flavor and pale red color. It is the ideal accompaniment or coating for those times when you do not want to mask delicate foods with a strong tomato flavor, or when you simply want a lighter background flavor of tomato.

MAKES ABOUT 3¾ CUPS

- 2 tablespoons olive oil
- 2 garlic cloves, crushed
- 1 onion, chopped
- 2 small carrots, chopped
- ⅓ cup diced lean rindless bacon (optional)
- 2¼ pounds tomatoes, quartered
- 1¼ cups young or light red wine
- 1 bay leaf
- salt and freshly ground black pepper
- 2–3 teaspoons sugar

Heat the olive oil in a large saucepan. Add the garlic, onion and carrots. Cook, stirring occasionally, for 5 minutes. Add the bacon and stir; then cook for a further 5 minutes.

Stir in the tomatoes, wine, bay leaf and some seasoning. Bring to a boil, reduce the heat, and cover the pan. Let the sauce bubble gently – somewhere between boiling and simmering – for 30 minutes.

Remove the bay leaf; then liquidize the sauce. Press it through a fine strainer. Reheat it, and add sugar to taste with salt and pepper as required before use.

Rich Tomato Sauce, and in the smaller bowl, Light Fresh Tomato Sauce

Béchamel Sauce

All the flavoring options given for the White Sauce recipe on page 58 may be applied to a béchamel sauce. The difference between béchamel and white sauces is that the additional flavorings of bay, mace and onion are infused with the milk before the sauce is made.

MAKES ABOUT 3 CUPS

- *1 small onion, halved*
- *1 blade of mace*
- *1 bay leaf*
- *2½ cups milk*
- *3 tablespoons butter*
- *⅓ cup all-purpose flour*
- *salt and freshly ground white or black pepper*

Put the onion, mace and bay leaf in a saucepan. Add the milk, and heat slowly until it is just reaching boiling point. Remove the pan from the heat before it boils, cover and set the milk aside until it is cold. Then heat the milk gently again until it is almost boiling, and remove the onion, mace and bay leaf.

Melt the butter in another saucepan over a high heat. Stir in the flour, reduce the heat a little; then slowly pour in the milk, stirring all the time. Continue stirring until the sauce boils. Reduce the heat, and simmer the sauce for 3 minutes, stirring occasionally. Add salt and pepper to taste, and use as required.

White Wine Sauce

MAKES ABOUT 3 CUPS

- *⅓ cup butter*
- *1 onion, finely chopped*
- *1 small carrot, finely chopped*
- *1 celery stalk, finely chopped*
- *1 bouquet garni*
- *1 blade of mace*
- *⅓ cup thinly sliced small button mushrooms*
- *⅓ cup all-purpose flour*
- *2½ cups dry white wine*
- *salt and freshly ground black pepper*
- *2 tablespoons chopped parsley (optional)*

Melt the butter in a saucepan. Add the onion, carrot, celery, bouquet garni, blade of mace and mushrooms. Stir well, then cover the pan, and cook the mixture for 15 minutes.

Stir in the flour. Then stir continuously while pouring in the wine, and bring to a boil. Reduce the heat, cover the pan, and simmer the sauce gently for 15 minutes. Taste and add salt and pepper; then stir in the parsley.

RED WINE SAUCE

Follow the above recipe, but use red wine instead of the white wine. A robust wine may be used if the sauce is to be served with rich meats, game or duck, and any cooking juices from these ingredients should be added to the sauce to enhance its flavor and suitability for the main ingredient. Also, add 2 tablespoons mushroom ketchup and 1 tablespoon tomato paste with the wine. For a lighter sauce, up to half the quantity of wine may be replaced with a suitable stock.

Bolognese Sauce

This is a favorite sauce for serving with all types of pasta, particularly spaghetti. It is also used in a variety of other dishes, including baked lasagne. The sauce freezes well for at least 3 months.

SERVES 4

- *2 tablespoons olive oil*
- *1 large onion, chopped*
- *2 garlic cloves, crushed*
- *2 celery stalks, diced*
- *1 green bell pepper, deseeded and diced*
- *1 bay leaf*
- *2 cups lean ground beef*
- *2 cups lean ground pork*
- *2 tablespoons tomato paste*
- *2 tablespoons chopped fresh oregano or marjoram*
- *1 large sprig of thyme*
- *1 tablespoon all-purpose flour*
- *salt and freshly ground black pepper*
- *scant 2 cups robust red wine*
- *2 × 14-ounce cans chopped tomatoes*
- *2 1/2 cups sliced small button or crimini mushrooms*

Heat the oil in a heavy-bottomed saucepan or flameproof casserole. Add the onion, garlic, celery, green bell pepper and bay leaf. Stir well, then cover, and cook for 15 minutes.

Stir in the ground beef and pork, and cook, stirring for 5 minutes. Add the tomato paste, oregano or marjoram, thyme and flour. Stir well, then add plenty of seasoning, and pour in the wine and tomatoes. Bring to a boil, stirring occasionally, then lightly mix in the mushrooms, and reduce the heat so that the sauce just simmers. Cover and cook for 1 hour, or until the meat is tender.

Remove the lid, and simmer for a further 30 minutes, until the liquid has reduced slightly, and the sauce is full-flavored. Taste for seasoning before serving.

Hot-and-sour Sauce

This is an idea taken from hot-and-sour soup, which is the authentic Chinese dish that marries the flavors of pepper with vinegar. I enjoy the flavor of the soup, and thought it would lend itself well to being used as a dressing for egg noodles or won tons.

SERVES 4–6

- *2½ cups Chinese-style Stock (see page 57)*
- *2 large, dried Chinese mushrooms*
- *1 tablespoon oil*
- *1 teaspoon sesame oil*
- *2 garlic cloves, finely chopped*
- *1 ounce peeled fresh ginger root, cut into fine strips*
- *1 small carrot, cut into matchstick strips*
- *1 red chili, deseeded and chopped*
- *2 ounces canned bamboo shoots, cut into matchstick strips*
- *6 scallions, shredded diagonally*
- *2 tablespoons light soy sauce*
- *1 tablespoon cornstarch*
- *2 tablespoons water*
- *1 teaspoon tomato paste*
- *¼ teaspoon ground white pepper*
- *2 tablespoons white wine vinegar*

Pour the stock into a small saucepan, and add the mushrooms. Heat gently until boiling, then reduce the heat, and simmer, uncovered, until the stock reduces to about 2 cups and the mushrooms have softened. Cool slightly; then remove the mushrooms, squeezing the liquid from them into the pan. Strain the stock through fine cheesecloth, if necessary, to remove any grit from the mushrooms. Thinly slice the mushrooms.

Heat the oil and sesame oil in a saucepan. Add the garlic, ginger, carrot, chili and bamboo shoots, and stir-fry for 2–3 minutes. Then add the scallions and mushrooms. Stir well, pour in the stock, and add the soy sauce. Bring to a boil, reduce the heat, and cover the pan. Simmer the sauce for 5 minutes.

Blend the cornstarch with the water, tomato paste, pepper and vinegar. Stir in some of the hot sauce, then pour the mixture into the saucepan, and bring to a boil, stirring all the time. Reduce the heat, and simmer the sauce, uncovered, for 5 minutes, or until thickened.

Taste the sauce for seasoning (more pepper may be added if the flavor is not sufficiently hot, and more vinegar may be added for a very tangy sauce).

Garlic Cream

Cooked garlic and potatoes puréed together with cream and butter make a delicious dressing for plain, cooked pasta. Serve with any pasta, and offer freshly grated Parmesan cheese as an accompaniment.

SERVES 4

- *6 garlic cloves, peeled*
- *½ small onion, chopped*
- *1 medium potato, peeled and diced*
- *1 bay leaf*
- *salt and freshly ground black pepper*
- *¼ cup butter*
- *1¼ cups light cream*
- *2 tablespoons finely chopped parsley*

Put the garlic cloves, onion, potato and bay leaf in a small saucepan. Add water to cover and a little salt. Bring to a boil, reduce the heat, and cover the pan. Simmer until the potatoes are tender (about 10 minutes).

Drain the potatoes, onion and garlic in a fine strainer. Discard the bay leaf; then purée the vegetables in food processor or blender, or press them through a fine strainer. Heat the butter and cream together in a saucepan until the butter has melted and the cream is hot, but do not let the cream boil. Slowly pour the cream into the vegetable purée, and process briefly until smooth.

Add salt and pepper to taste, then stir in the parsley, and serve the sauce at once.

Sweet-and-sour Sauce

Sweet-and-sour Sauce is the classic accompaniment for Crispy Won Tons (see page 52). It is also good with egg noodles, which are cooked, then drained and stir-fried for a few minutes in a little oil and sesame oil, then tossed with the sauce for a flavorsome side dish.

SERVES 4

- 2 tablespoons oil
- 1 teaspoon sesame oil
- 1 large onion, roughly chopped
- 1 large green bell pepper, deseeded and cut into large dice
- 1 large carrot, cut into matchstick strips
- 6 tablespoons tomato ketchup
- 2/3 cup dry sherry
- 2 tablespoons sugar
- 4 tablespoons cider vinegar
- 4 tablespoons soy sauce
- 8-ounce can pineapple rings in syrup
- 2 teaspoons cornstarch

Heat both oils in a saucepan. Add the onion, green bell pepper and carrot. Stir-fry the vegetables for 5 minutes, until they are lightly cooked, but still crunchy.

Stir in the tomato ketchup, sherry, sugar, vinegar and soy sauce. Drain the pineapple, and mix a little of the syrup with the cornstarch to make a smooth, thin paste. Add the remaining syrup; then pour this mixture into the sauce.

Bring to a boil, stirring all the time, then reduce the heat, and simmer for 5 minutes. Cut the pineapple rings into chunks, and add them to the sauce. Remove from the heat, and use as required.

Walnut and Watercress Paste

MAKES ABOUT 1¼ CUPS

- *1½ cups walnuts*
- *1 bunch of watercress, leaves only*
- *4 scallions, chopped*
- *1 garlic clove*
- *juice of 1 lemon*
- *4 tablespoons walnut oil*
- *⅔ cup light salad oil*
- *salt and freshly ground black pepper*
- *freshly grated Parmesan cheese, to serve (optional)*

Purée the walnuts, watercress leaves, scallions, garlic, lemon juice and walnut oil to a thick paste in a food processor or blender.

Slowly trickle in the light salad oil with the machine running. Add salt and pepper to taste; then let sit for at least 30 minutes before serving.

Stir well, and spoon the paste over pasta. Serve with freshly grated Parmesan cheese, if liked.

Mayonnaise

I like mayonnaise made with olive oil, but many people find the flavor too strong, in which case a mixture of olive and sunflower oils may be used.

MAKES ABOUT 1¼ CUPS

- *2 egg yolks*
- *salt and freshly ground white pepper (black pepper leaves little specks)*
- *½ teaspoon Dijon mustard or other mild, smooth mustard*
- *½ teaspoon superfine sugar*
- *juice of 1 lemon*
- *1 cup olive oil or half and half olive and sunflower oil*

Put the egg yolks and salt and pepper to taste in a small bowl. Add the mustard, sugar and half the lemon juice. Use an electric beater to cream the ingredients together thoroughly. Add 1 tablespoon of the oil, and continue mixing until the ingredients are pale.

Then slowly trickle in the oil, mixing all the time. Do not pour the oil in any faster than at a trickle, or the eggs may curdle. When the mayonnaise begins to thicken and becomes very pale, you can add the oil in a slightly faster steady stream. If at any time there seems to be a slight excess of oil that has not been worked in, then stop pouring, and mix in the surface oil before adding any more.

Finally, stir in the remaining lemon juice, and taste for seasoning.

FLAVORINGS FOR MAYONNAISE

GARLIC MAYONNAISE
Add 1 crushed or finely chopped garlic clove to the Mayonnaise.

LEMON MAYONNAISE
Add the grated rind of 1 lemon to the finished Mayonnaise.

HERB MAYONNAISE
Add 2 tablespoons finely chopped parsley, 1 tablespoon finely chopped fresh dill and 1 tablespoon snipped chives. The herbs may be varied according to the recipe requirements – 1 tablespoon finely chopped fresh tarragon or 2 tablespoons shredded fresh basil may be added, for example.

ANCHOVY MAYONNAISE
Stir in 1–2 tablespoons anchovy paste, 1 tablespoon snipped chives and 1 tablespoon chopped capers.

Red Bell Pepper and Herb Paste

A light, slightly tangy and mild cheese makes the ideal base for this paste of sweet red bell peppers and fresh, summery herbs. This is good with hot pasta, and also makes a tasty dressing for cold pasta – an ideal way of using up leftovers. Simply serve the pasta on a base of salad greens; and top with the paste.

MAKES ABOUT 1¼ CUPS

- *2 garlic cloves, peeled*
- *2 large red bell peppers*
- *4 ounces New York State Cheddar or similar crumbly cheese*
- *⅔ cup olive oil*
- *salt and freshly ground black pepper*
- *4 tablespoons finely chopped parsley*
- *4 tablespoons snipped chives*
- *1 tablespoon chopped fresh tarragon*

Blanch the garlic cloves in boiling water for 2 minutes; then drain. Skewer one of the bell peppers on a large metal fork, and rotate it over a gas flame until the skin is charred. Then rub off the skin under cold water. Repeat with the second bell pepper. Alternatively, char both peppers under a hot broiler, turning them until the skin is blistered on all sides.

Deseed and cut up the bell peppers; then purée them in a food processor or blender with the garlic, cheese and a little of the olive oil. Gradually pour in the remaining oil while the machine is running to make a smooth paste. Stir in salt and pepper to taste, the parsley, chives and tarragon, and serve.

Almond and Parsley Paste

A food processor or blender makes this a simple recipe, but it can be made by hand by first passing the nuts through a mouli grater, which will grind them, then pounding them to a paste with finely chopped parsley and finely grated cheese. Then the oil can be slowly pounded into the mixture. Toss this paste with pasta verde or tomato-flavored pasta to make a delicious, light meal.

Grind the almonds and parsley together in a food processor (or as above if making by hand) until quite fine. Cut the Jarlsberg cheese into chunks, add these to the nuts, and process the mixture until it begins to bind into a stiff paste. Add a little of the oil, and process to a thick paste; then gradually trickle in the remaining oil as the machine is running.

Stir in the chives and seasoning to taste; then let the paste sit for at least an hour before serving.

SERVES 4

- *8 ounces blanched almonds*
- *½ cup parsley*
- *4 ounces Jarlsberg cheese*
- *about a scant 1 cup olive oil*
- *3 tablespoons snipped chives*
- *salt and freshly ground black pepper*

Pesto

This is a classic accompaniment for plain, boiled pasta, and it is deserving of its famous reputation.

As quite a bit of oil is used, the sauce will keep well in a jar in the refrigerator for many months. If you definitely want to keep the sauce for a long time, sterilize small airtight jars in which to keep it by washing them in a sterilizing solution (available for home brewing or for cleaning babies' bottles). Once you start using the sauce in a jar, use it up within one to two weeks as it can easily become contaminated with micro-organisms from the cutlery dipped into it. It is important to remember this and not to treat pesto as you would a chutney or a true preserve.

MAKES ABOUT 2½ CUPS

- 1 cup pine nuts
- 1½ cups grated Parmesan cheese
- 4–6 garlic cloves
- 1 cup sprigs of basil (use the soft stalk ends and leaves only, trimming off any tough stalks that will not purée)
- about 2 cups good virgin olive oil
- salt and freshly ground black pepper

Process the pine nuts and Parmesan cheese in a food processor until fairly finely ground, but not binding together. Add the garlic and basil; then process the mixture until the herb is finely chopped, and the mixture begins to clump together.

Pour in a little olive oil, and process the mixture to a smooth, thick paste. Then continue trickling in the olive oil with the food processor running. Add enough to make a thin paste. Stir in seasoning to taste. Store in dry, sterilized, airtight jars in the bottom of the refrigerator. Stir well before use.

COOK'S TIP

Pesto can be made quite easily in a blender. The important point to remember is to process the mixture in batches, and combine them all at the end. Pesto is not like a mayonnaise – it does not combine irreversibly in a liaison – so there is nothing wrong with making it in this way.

Garlic Butter

Crush the garlic over the butter, then chop the crushed part of the clove to insure it mixes evenly with the butter.

SERVES 4

- ¾ cup butter
- 2 garlic cloves, crushed and chopped (see above)
- freshly ground black pepper
- 2 tablespoons finely chopped parsley
- freshly grated Parmesan cheese, to serve

Cream the butter with the garlic; then add pepper to taste and the parsley. Toss with hot, freshly cooked pasta, and serve with freshly grated Parmesan cheese.

Herb Butter

Parsley, dill, chives, tarragon, chervil, thyme, basil and oregano are all suitable for this flavorsome butter. Mint may also be used, fairly sparingly, and a little very finely chopped rosemary may be added.

SERVES 4

- ¾ cup butter
- 2 tablespoons chopped parsley
- 2 tablespoons snipped chives
- 2 tablespoons mixed herbs
- freshly ground black pepper
- a squeeze of lemon juice

Cream the butter with the herbs. Mix in pepper to taste and a little lemon juice.

Spiced Anchovy Butter

This is delicious with pasta verde or tomato-flavored pasta.

SERVES 4

- 2-ounce can anchovy fillets
- 1 garlic clove, crushed
- 2 tablespoons ground coriander
- 1 teaspoon ground mace
- ¾ cup butter
- squeeze of lemon juice
- 2 tablespoons finely chopped fresh parsley
- freshly ground black pepper

Drain the oil from the anchovies into a small saucepan. Add the garlic, coriander and mace, and cook gently for 5 minutes, stirring all the time. Remove from the heat, and let cool.

Meanwhile, pound the anchovies to a smooth paste; then beat them into the butter. Gradually beat in the spices, adding in all the oil from the saucepan, too, and add a squeeze of lemon juice. Mix in the parsley and pepper to taste.

Truffle Butter

Toss this with plain, cooked, fresh pasta and serve with a simple Good Green Salad (see page 312).

SERVES 4–6

- ¾ cup butter
- 2 preserved black truffles (from a jar or can)
- 1 tablespoon finely snipped chives
- 1 tablespoon finely chopped parsley

Cream the butter until it is soft. Add the lemon juice from the jar or can of truffles, and beat it into the butter. Slice the truffles; then cut them into fine strips.

Beat the chives and parsley into the butter; then gently mix in the truffles. The butter may be frozen for up to 2 months.

Lemon Anchovy Butter

Toss this butter with freshly cooked pasta, and serve with lemon wedges so that diners can add a little juice to their pasta if liked. The butter is especially well suited to serving with black squid ink pasta, but other fresh pasta also tastes superb served this way.

SERVES 4

- 2-ounce can anchovy fillets in olive oil
- 1–2 garlic cloves, crushed and chopped
- grated rind of 1 lemon
- ½ cup unsalted or lightly salted butter
- freshly ground black pepper
- dash of Worcestershire sauce
- 4 tablespoons chopped parsley

Pound, mash or process the anchovies with the oil from the can to make a smooth paste. Mix in the garlic and lemon rind. Soften the butter; then gradually beat in the anchovy mixture. Add freshly ground black pepper and Worcestershire sauce to taste. Finally, mix in the parsley.

69

Shrimp Butter

Toss this with freshly cooked pasta to make a delicious supper dish. Spaghetti, mafaldine, tagliatelle, small to medium pasta shells or any long or small pasta shapes are good with this butter coating them.

SERVES 4

- ¾ cup unsalted butter
- 1 small onion, very finely chopped
- ½ teaspoon ground mace
- 1¾ cups peeled, cooked, finely chopped shrimp
- 3 tablespoons chopped fresh dill
- salt and freshly ground black pepper

Melt a quarter of the butter in a small saucepan. Add the onion, and cook gently for about 20 minutes, or until it is well cooked and softened, but not browned. Stir in the mace and cook for 1 minute; then remove the pan from the heat.

Mix the cooked onion with the remaining butter. If most of the butter is quite soft, then let the onion mixture cool; if not, it will soften the bulk of the butter ready for mixing in the shrimp. Beat in the shrimp; then add the dill and seasoning to taste.

LITTLE PASTA COCKTAILS

Toss freshly cooked soup pasta with Shrimp Butter; then serve in shell dishes on a base of finely shredded lettuce and cucumber cut into matchstick strips. Garnish with whole, cooked shrimp, lemon wedges (so that guests may squeeze a little juice over their cocktails if liked) and sprigs of dill.

Greek Yogurt Topping

This is good with garlic-flavored pasta or dough that is seasoned with spices. It is important to use a mild salad onion as a regular onion is too overpowering for this topping.

SERVES 4

- *2-inch length of English cucumber, peeled and finely diced*
- *salt and freshly ground black pepper*
- *1 red or white onion, finely chopped*
- *4 tablespoons chopped parsley*
- *2 tablespoons chopped fresh tarragon or cilantro leaves*
- *4 firm, ripe tomatoes, peeled, deseeded and diced*
- *2 tablespoons chopped capers*
- *2 bottled or canned mild green chilis, chopped*
- *2 cups Greek yogurt*

Put the diced cucumber in a strainer over a bowl. Sprinkle generously with salt, and let sit for 30 minutes. Pat the cucumber thoroughly on doubled pieces of paper towel.

Mix the onion, parsley, tarragon or cilantro, cucumber, tomatoes, capers and chilis. Then stir in the yogurt and taste for seasoning, adding freshly ground black pepper as required, but the cucumber should contribute sufficient salt. Serve within about 30 minutes of mixing.

Fresh Tomato and Red Bell Pepper Dressing

SERVES 4

- 1 pound ripe tomatoes, peeled (see Cook's Tip, right), de-seeded and quartered
- ½ small onion, roughly chopped
- 1 garlic clove, crushed
- 1 red bell pepper, deseeded and roughly chopped
- 1 teaspoon superfine sugar
- leaves from 1 sprig of oregano
- leaves from 2 sprigs of mint
- salt and freshly ground black pepper
- generous ¾ cup olive oil

Purée the tomatoes, onion, garlic, red bell pepper, sugar, oregano and mint together in a blender or food processor. Mix in salt and freshly ground black pepper to taste. With the machine running, slowly trickle in the olive oil. Taste for seasoning and serve freshly prepared.

COOK'S TIP

To peel tomatoes, put them in a deep, heatproof bowl, then pour freshly boiled water over them, covering them completely. Let sit for 30–60 seconds (the more ripe the tomatoes, the quicker the skins loosen). Keep an eye on them because if you leave ripe tomatoes for too long, they begin to cook and soften.

Drain the tomatoes, and split the skins with the point of a knife; then they should peel or slide off easily. Alternatively, if you work fairly quickly, it is possible to use a slotted spoon to lift the tomatoes from the boiling water individually without causing the remaining fruit to become too soft or, if the tomatoes are very ripe, blanch a few at a time. Note, too, that once the tomatoes have been drained for any length of time, they no longer peel easily.

An alternative method of peeling one or two tomatoes is to skewer them individually on a metal fork, and rotate them over a gas flame until the skin blisters and splits. Then simply rinse the tomato under cold water, and slide off the skin.

Crab Dressing

Crab Dressing is best served with pasta shapes rather than long thin pasta, but it still tastes great with other types of pasta. For a lighter, low-calorie, dressing, use fromage frais instead of the sour cream. A cucumber salad side dish will complete the meal.

SERVES 4

- 1 tablespoon tomato paste
- ½ teaspoon superfine sugar
- ½ teaspoon Dijon mustard or other mild, smooth mustard
- 4 tablespoons snipped chives
- 3 tablespoons chopped fresh dill
- 1¼ cups sour cream
- 1½ cups crabmeat
- salt and freshly ground black pepper

Mix the tomato paste, superfine sugar, mustard, chives and dill together. Stir in the sour cream until the flavoring ingredients are evenly combined. Flake the crabmeat into the cream mixture, and add salt and pepper to taste. If possible, chill the mixture for 1 hour before serving to let the flavors develop; then leave at room temperature for 20–30 minutes before serving so that the dressing is not too cold.

Fresh Tomato and Red Bell Pepper Dressing.

Light Cheese Dressing

This makes a delicious summer supper or lunch. Offer a Good Green Salad (see page 312) as an accompaniment. Cut up some crusty Italian bread to mop every last bit of the dressing from the bowls!

SERVES 4

- *1 large garlic clove, finely chopped*
- *1 tablespoon olive oil*
- *2 scallions, finely chopped*
- *8 green olives, pitted and chopped*
- *1 cup ricotta cheese*
- *²⁄₃ cup fromage frais*
- *4 large sprigs of basil, finely shredded*
- *salt and freshly ground black pepper*
- *freshly grated nutmeg*

Put the garlic and olive oil in a small saucepan, and heat gently until the garlic is just beginning to sizzle. Cook for 2 minutes, without overheating the oil to the point when the garlic would brown (the aim is to take the raw taste off the garlic, not cook it thoroughly). Remove the pan from the heat, and let cool slightly.

Scrape the garlic and oil into a bowl. Stir in the scallions, olives, ricotta, fromage frais and basil. Add salt, pepper and nutmeg to taste.

RICOTTA AND TRUFFLE PASTE TOPPING

White truffle paste is superb with ricotta cheese. Mix about 2 tablespoons of the paste into 1 cup cheese.

Parmesan with Roasted Pine Nuts

An alternative to straight Parmesan, this delicious topping may be tossed with pastas that have first been dressed with butter or oil. It also goes well with poultry, meat, game and vegetable sauces.

SERVES 4

- 6 tablespoons pine nuts
- 2 tablespoons finely chopped parsley
- 1 tablespoon finely chopped fresh marjoram
- ¾ cup grated Parmesan cheese

Put the pine nuts in a small, heavy-bottomed saucepan. Dry-roast them by cooking them over a low to medium heat, shaking the pan often, until they are evenly and lightly browned. Remove from the heat, and let cool.

Mix the parsley and marjoram with the Parmesan; then stir in the pine nuts.

Tuna Sauce

This is one of my favorite staple standbys.

SERVES 2

- 7-ounce can tuna in oil
- 1 small onion, finely chopped
- 1 bay leaf
- ¼ cup all-purpose flour
- 1¼ cups milk
- 2 cups sliced button mushrooms
- salt and freshly ground black pepper
- 2 tablespoons dry sherry
- 2 tablespoons chopped parsley

Drain the oil from the tuna into a saucepan. Add the onion and bay leaf. Cover and cook gently for 15 minutes. Stir in the flour; then cook, stirring, for 2 minutes.

Slowly pour in the milk, and add the mushrooms. Bring to a boil, stirring all the time, and simmer, stirring, for 2 minutes. Add salt and pepper to taste; then the sherry and parsley. Simmer for a further 2 minutes. Finally, flake the tuna, and stir it into the sauce. Serve at once, poured over freshly cooked pasta.

Olive Paste

This is a homemade version of bought paste. It has more herbs and is rich with garlic, and it tastes great tossed with all sorts of pasta. For a dramatic dish, toss the paste with squid-ink colored pasta, and serve with freshly grated Parmesan cheese. Offer a dish of fresh tomatoes sprinkled with shredded basil and warmed crusty bread as accompaniments.

MAKES ABOUT 1¼ CUPS

- 12-ounce pitted black olives in brine, drained
- 2 garlic cloves
- 1 tablespoon capers
- leaves from 2 sprigs of thyme
- leaves from 2 sprigs of oregano
- 6 fresh sage leaves
- ⅔ cup olive oil
- salt and freshly ground black pepper

Put the olives, garlic, capers, thyme, oregano and sage in a food processor or blender. Add a little oil, and process until the mixture forms a thick paste; then slowly trickle in the remaining olive oil while the machine is running. Taste and add salt and pepper as required. Store in a covered jar in the refrigerator for up to 1 month.

Spicy Brazil and White Cheese Topping

This makes an unusual and delicious topping for pasta shapes. Try it on homemade spicy pasta or on ready-made chili-flavored pasta.

SERVES 4

- *4 ounces shelled Brazil nuts*
- *2 tablespoons finely crushed or coarsely ground coriander seeds*
- *1 tablespoon white cumin seeds*
- *1½ cups grated white cheese*
- *2 tablespoons chopped fresh cilantro leaves*

Using a serrated knife, slice the Brazil nuts. Do not try to cut neat slices of an even thickness, but, instead, cut some pieces as part shavings, others as thin slices. Try to avoid having too many large chunks, though.

Put the nuts in a small, heavy-bottomed saucepan with the coriander and cumin seeds. Dry-roast the nuts and spices together over a low to medium heat, shaking the pan often, until the seeds give up their aroma and the nuts are beginning to brown. Do not overcook the mixture, or it will taste bitter. Set the pan aside, and let cool.

Mix the white cheese with the cilantro, and stir in the cold nuts and seeds. Serve with hot, freshly cooked pasta.

Anchovy and Green Olive Paste

Lime and scallion add a surprisingly refreshing flavor to this paste. The paste may be kept in a covered container in the refrigerator for up to a week.

MAKES ABOUT 1¼ CUPS

- *12-ounce can pitted green olives in brine, drained*
- *2-ounce can anchovy fillets, drained*
- *1 garlic clove, crushed*
- *⅔ cup olive oil*
- *grated rind and juice of 1 lime*
- *4 scallions, very finely chopped*
- *salt and freshly ground black pepper to taste*

Put the olives, anchovies and garlic in a food processor or blender. Add a little of the oil, and process to a thick paste; then trickle in the remaining oil while the machine is running. Stir in the lime rind and juice, scallions and salt and pepper to taste.

Mixed Olive and Bell Pepper Topping

A colorful topping with a pleasing flavor to turn a simple bowl of pasta into a memorable lunch. Serve with a Good Green Salad (see page 312) and Lemon and Herb Rolls (see page 308).

SERVES 4

- *6 tablespoons olive oil*
- *2 garlic cloves, finely chopped*
- *1 mild red or white onion, quartered and thinly sliced*
- *2 large green bell peppers, deseeded and diced*
- *2 large red bell peppers, deseeded and diced*
- *10 black olives, pitted and thinly sliced*
- *10 green olives, pitted and thinly sliced*
- *4 tablespoons chopped parsley*
- *salt and freshly ground black pepper*
- *lemon wedges, to serve*

Heat the olive oil in a large skillet. Add the garlic, onion, and green and red bell peppers. Toss the mixture over a medium to high heat for 2 minutes. Remove the pan from the heat, stir in the black and green olives and parsley, and add salt and pepper to taste. Toss the hot mixture, with all the oil from the pan, with freshly cooked pasta. Serve with lemon wedges for guests to squeeze over their servings.

Herbed Cheese and Walnut Topping

This makes a satisfying, tasty supper of the simplest pasta. Try it on colorful shapes, or toss it with some quick-cook macaroni. Dressing the pasta with a little butter or olive oil and finely chopped garlic first will suit garlic lovers. This recipe gives generous portions for 4 servings of pasta.

SERVES 4

- *2 cups coarsely grated Cheddar cheese*
- *4 tablespoons finely chopped parsley*
- *1 tablespoon chopped fresh thyme*
- *4 tablespoons snipped chives*
- *1 cup very finely chopped walnuts*

Mix the cheese, parsley, thyme, chives and walnuts; then serve sprinkled over piping hot pasta, and toss well.

Pasta with Garlic and Basil

Pasta tossed with lots of garlic and warm olive oil is a classic Italian snack in which generous quantities of oil may be used according to the taste of the individual diner. This is a comparatively modest dressing.

SERVES 4

- *6 tablespoons good olive oil*
- *3 garlic cloves, finely chopped*
- *freshly ground black pepper*
- *handful of sprigs of basil, shredded*
- *freshly grated Parmesan cheese, to serve*

Heat the oil in a small saucepan. Add the garlic, and cook gently for 3 minutes. Toss the oil and garlic with freshly cooked, piping hot pasta, and add pepper to taste. Lightly mix in the basil, and serve at once, with freshly grated Parmesan cheese.

Pasta Shells with Garlic and Basil

Pasta with Fresh Tomatoes

Make this when ripe plum tomatoes are available, or use full-flavored home-grown fruit. Serve with Olive Bread (see page 308).

SERVES 4

- 2 tablespoons olive oil
- ¼ cup butter
- 1 small onion, finely chopped
- 1 garlic clove, crushed
- 1½ pounds plum tomatoes, peeled (see Cook's Tip, page 72), deseeded and cut into chunks
- 1 teaspoon superfine sugar
- salt and freshly ground black pepper
- 4 tablespoons chopped parsley
- 2 tablespoons chopped fresh tarragon or 1 tablespoon chopped fresh thyme
- 3 large sprigs of basil, shredded

Heat the olive oil and butter together in a saucepan. Add the onion and garlic. Cook, stirring, for 15 minutes, or until the onion has softened. Stir in the tomatoes and sugar, and salt and pepper to taste. Cook, stirring, until the tomatoes are hot. Then stir in the parsley and tarragon or thyme. Toss the mixture with freshly cooked pasta; then gently toss in the basil.

Red Bell Pepper Paste with Sun-dried Tomatoes

This has a full, rich flavor.

MAKES ABOUT 1¼ CUPS

- *8 sun-dried tomatoes*
- *⅔ cup red wine*
- *⅔ cup water*
- *4 garlic cloves, peeled*
- *2 bay leaves*
- *4 red bell peppers*
- *⅔ cup olive oil*
- *salt and freshly ground black pepper*

Put the sun-dried tomatoes, wine, water, garlic and bay leaves in a small saucepan. Bring to a boil, reduce the heat, and cover the pan. Simmer for 30 minutes; then let cool. When cold, drain the tomatoes, reserving the cooking liquid, and discard the bay leaves.

Meanwhile, skewer one of the bell peppers on a large metal fork, and rotate it over a gas flame until the skin is charred. Then rub off the skin under cold water. Repeat with the remaining peppers. Alternatively, the peppers may be charred by placing them under a hot broiler and turning until the skin has blistered on all sides.

Deseed and cut up the peppers; then place them in a food processor or blender with the drained tomatoes and garlic. Boil the reserved cooking liquid rapidly until it has reduced to about 4 tablespoons; then add it to the peppers, and purée them. Trickle in the oil while the machine is running. Stir in salt and pepper to taste.

Pasta Carbonara

Pasta Carbonara

The pasta must be freshly drained and piping hot when added to this creamy, lightly scrambled egg mixture. Regular cooked ham or finely shredded bacon (though it must be well cooked before the eggs are added) can be used instead of expensive prosciutto. This is a favorite sauce for long pasta, such as spaghetti or tagliatelle.

SERVES 4

- *1 pound pasta*
- *salt and freshly ground black pepper*
- *12 ounces prosciutto*
- *8 eggs*
- *⅔ cup light cream*
- *¼ cup butter*
- *3 tablespoons finely chopped parsley*

Cook the pasta in boiling salted water until just tender.

Meanwhile, trim any excess fat from the ham, and cut it into fine shreds. Beat the eggs with the cream, a little salt and plenty of pepper.

Melt the butter in a large, heavy-bottomed skillet or saucepan. Add the ham, and cook, stirring, for 3 minutes. Then pour in the egg mixture, and cook over a low heat, stirring all the time, until the eggs are very lightly scrambled, but not setting into lumps.

Drain the pasta, and add it to the pan; then turn it in the sauce for a few seconds. Stir in the parsley, and serve at once.

Macaroni Cheese

SERVES 4

FOR THE PASTA
- *12 ounces short-cut macaroni*
- *salt and freshly ground black pepper*
- *¼ cup butter*
- *1 large onion, finely chopped*
- *1 bay leaf*
- *⅓ cup all-purpose flour*

- *2½ cups milk*
- *1 cup grated sharp Cheddar cheese*

FOR THE TOPPING
- *¼ cup grated sharp Cheddar cheese*
- *½ cup fresh bread crumbs*

Cook the macaroni in boiling salted water according to the instructions on the package; then drain it well.

Meanwhile, melt the butter in a large saucepan, and add the onion and bay leaf. Cover the pan, and cook the onion gently for about 30 minutes, or until it has softened, but not browned. Stir in the flour; then reduce the heat a little, and slowly add the milk. Bring to a boil, stirring all the time. Simmer the sauce gently for 2 minutes.

Stir in the cheese until it has melted completely; then add salt and pepper to taste. Stir in the macaroni, and heat for 2 minutes. Pour into a flameproof dish.

Mix the topping ingredients, sprinkle over the macaroni cheese, and brown under a hot broiler. Serve at once.

Flavored Oils

Oils may be flavored with herbs or spices ready for dressing hot or cold pasta. The choice of base oil depends on your preference, and how you intend to use it. I use olive oil, which I find is the ideal accompaniment for pasta, whether it is hot or cold in salads. Strong nut oils (walnut or hazelnut) may be flavored with powerful herbs like thyme or rosemary, then diluted with melted butter (for hot pasta) or light oil (for cold pasta). The following are merely a few suggestions – use any strong herbs, in any combination, with garlic if liked.
Use the oil as a base for sautéing ingredients for a sauce, or simply trickle it over hot, freshly cooked pasta as a dressing, adding freshly grated Parmesan cheese and freshly ground black pepper to taste.

GARLIC OIL

Peel 3 large garlic cloves, and cut them in half lengthways. Place in a screw-topped jar or bottle, and pour in about 2½ cups oil. Let sit for 2 weeks before use. If the oil is to be kept for a long period, then remove the garlic cloves after this time.

CHILI OIL

Slit 1 green or red chili, scrape out the seeds, and rinse (take care not to splash any water into your eyes while doing this) and dry the pod. Put the chili in a screw-topped jar or bottle. Pour in about 2½ cups oil and let sit for 2 weeks before use. If the oil is to be kept for a long period, then remove the chili. For a very hot oil, use 2 dried red chilis instead of the fresh chili, and leave them in the oil permanently.

SAGE OIL

Wash and dry a large sprig of sage. Bruise the leaves slightly by crumpling them with your fingers; then put the herb in a screw-topped jar or bottle. Pour in about

2½ cups oil, and leave for 2 weeks. Crush the leaves slightly; then strain the oil. This is particularly good as a base for sauces containing pork or chicken.

TARRAGON OR ROSEMARY OIL

These are two strong herbs so the resulting oil is quite powerful. Crush a couple of large sprigs of either herb, and put them in the oil, making up as Sage Oil. These are good with lamb, chicken or pork.

BAY AND GARLIC OIL

Crush 4 bay leaves slightly; then put them in a screw-topped jar or bottle with 2 peeled and split garlic cloves. Pour in about 2½ cups oil, and leave for 2 weeks, crushing the bay leaves occasionally to encourage them to flavor the oil. Remove the bay and garlic if the oil is to be kept for longer periods.

Flavored Vinegars

Vinegars may be flavored using the same method that is used to flavor oils (see above). The ideas given for oil are just a few of the many possibilities, and, following the same principle, many different flavors can be created.
Unlike oils, the flavoring ingredients can be left in the vinegar indefinitely, giving a more intense flavor, which is desirable as vinegar is used in smaller quantities than oil. White or red wine vinegar may be used as a base or white distilled malt vinegar, but the flavor of the latter is slightly harsh. I prefer to use cider vinegar, which has a milder flavor and is more suitable for use with pasta.
Another idea is to combine the vinegars with unflavored oil to make a dressing for cold pasta. Alternatively, a little flavored cider vinegar can be an excellent sharpening ingredient for rich sauces or for achieving a sweet-and-sour result.

FROM LEFT
1   Walnut oil with thyme   2   Olive oil with bay and garlic   3   Sunflower oil with chili
4   Red wine vinegar with tarragon   5   Cider vinegar with sage

SUPERLATIVE SOUPS

◆

THIS CHAPTER AIMS TO BROADEN THE VIEW THAT SOUP AND PASTA TOGETHER SPELL JUST ONE THING – MINESTRONE. 🐚 ALL LARGE SUPERMARKETS OFFER AT LEAST ONE OR TWO TYPES OF SOUP PASTA AND YOU WILL FIND SOME CLEVER MINIATURE SHAPES IN BETTER ITALIAN DELIS. SO, ADDING PASTA TO YOUR FAVORITE SOUP IS A GOOD WAY TO MAKE IT EVEN BETTER.

APART FROM THE ITALIAN SOUPS, LIGHT ORIENTAL SOUPS ALSO USE THEIR OWN FORMS OF PASTA, FROM CHUNKY WON TON TO FINE VERMICELLI. 🐚 FOR A DRAMATIC DINNER PARTY STARTER, WHY NOT TRY BRIGHT BORTSCH SERVED AS A CLEAR SOUP, COMPLETE WITH TINY, MUSHROOM-FILLED PASTA SHAPES?

IF YOU MAKE YOUR OWN PASTA DOUGH, THE POSSIBILITIES FOR MAKING CLEVER SOUP GARNISHES ARE EXCITING. 🐚 STAMP OUT ATTRACTIVE SHAPES TO MAKE CLEAR SOUPS MORE INTERESTING, OR BOIL, THEN DRAIN AND DEEP-FRY TWISTS, SHAPES OR NOODLES TO ADD A CRUNCHY CONTRAST TO HEARTY SOUPS.

Crab and Corn Soup with Crunchy Pasta

This quick and easy soup looks like an oriental soup but is not based on an oriental recipe.

SERVES 4

- ¼ cup butter
- 1 onion, chopped
- 1 medium potato, diced
- 1 bay leaf
- salt and freshly ground black pepper
- 2½ cups fish stock
- 4 ounces fresh or dried tagliatelle
- 10-ounce can cream-style corn
- 7-ounce can crabmeat
- grated rind of 1 lemon
- 3 tablespoons chopped fresh dill
- ½ teaspoon paprika
- oil, for deep-frying
- 1¼ cups light cream

Melt the butter in a saucepan. Add the onion, potato, bay leaf, and salt and pepper to taste. Stir well; then cover the pan, and cook gently for 15 minutes. Pour in the stock, and bring to a boil. Reduce the heat so that the soup simmers; then cover the pan, and cook for 20 minutes.

Meanwhile, cook the tagliatelle in a large saucepan of boiling salted water, allowing 15 minutes for dried pasta, or 3 minutes for fresh pasta. Drain well and set aside.

Purée the soup in a blender or food processor. Stir in the cream-style corn and crabmeat, and heat gently to simmering point. Then reduce the heat to the lowest setting.

Mix the lemon rind, dill and paprika. Heat the oil for deep-frying to 350°F, or until a cube of day-old bread browns in about 30 seconds. Cut up the tagliatelle slightly; then deep-fry it for a few seconds, until crisp and golden. Drain on paper towels, and sprinkle with the dill mixture.

Stir the cream into the soup, and heat gently without boiling. Taste for seasoning; then serve at once, topping each portion with some of the crispy pasta.

Fishball Soup with Rice Vermicelli

SERVES 4

FOR THE SOUP
- 1 tablespoon oil
- 2 celery stalks, cut into fine matchstick strips
- 1 carrot, cut into fine matchstick strips
- 4 scallions, shredded lengthways
- 1 quantity Chinese-style Stock (see page 57)
- salt and freshly ground black pepper

- 1 cup rice vermicelli
- 4 leaves of Chinese cabbage, shredded

FOR THE FISHBALLS
- 1 pound cod fillet, skinned
- 2 tablespoons cornstarch
- 1 scallion, very finely chopped
- grated rind of ½ a lemon
- 1 tablespoon light soy sauce

Make the Fishballs first. Finely chop the cod or process it in a food processor, but take care not to reduce it to a soft purée. Mix the cornstarch, scallion, lemon rind and soy sauce into the fish, pounding it well until all the ingredients are thoroughly combined, and the mixture binds together. Stir well; then wet your hands, and shape teaspoonfuls of the mixture into small balls. Keep wetting your hands to prevent the mixture sticking.

Then make the soup. Heat the oil in a large saucepan. Add the celery, carrot and scallions. Cook, stirring, for 2 minutes; then add the Stock and salt and pepper to taste. Bring to a boil, reduce the heat, and cover the pan. Simmer for 5 minutes. Add the Fishballs, and simmer gently for a further 5 minutes, or until they are just cooked. Add the vermicelli and Chinese leaves, and continue to cook for 5 minutes.

Taste the soup for seasoning before ladling it into individual bowls to serve.

Seafood Chowder

SERVES 4

- 2 tablespoons oil
- 2 leeks, sliced
- 1 small onion, halved and thinly sliced
- 1 carrot, diced
- 1 celery stalk, diced
- 1 potato, diced
- 2½ cups fish stock
- 1 bouquet garni
- 1 pound cod fillet, skinned
- 2½ cups milk
- 8 scallops, shelled
- ¾ cup quick-cook macaroni
- salt and freshly ground black pepper
- 2 cups shelled, cooked mussels
- 2 cups peeled, cooked shrimp
- 4 tablespoons chopped parsley
- freshly grated Parmesan cheese, to serve

Heat the oil in a large saucepan. Add the leeks, onion, carrot, celery and potato. Cook, stirring, until the leeks have reduced, and the onion has softened slightly but not browned. Pour in the stock; then bring to a boil.

Add the bouquet garni, reduce the heat, and cover the pan. Simmer for 20 minutes.

Meanwhile, put the cod in a saucepan, and add the milk. Heat gently until the milk is just about to simmer; then poach the fish for 2–3 minutes, until it is barely cooked. Remove the fish from the milk, and set it aside on a plate. Poach the scallops in the milk for 2–3 minutes, until just cooked. Set the milk aside.

Flake the cod, discarding any bones, and slice the scallops. Add the macaroni and salt and pepper to the soup, and bring back to a boil. Then reduce the heat, cover and cook for about 7 minutes, or until the macaroni is just tender. Pour in the poaching milk, and heat, stirring all the time.

Taste the soup for seasoning; then add the cooked cod, scallops, mussels and shrimp. Gently stir in the parsley, and heat for 2–3 minutes, or until the seafood is hot. Serve at once, with freshly grated Parmesan cheese.

Shrimp and Pasta Bisque with Rouille

Uncooked shrimp are sold frozen and sometimes fresh or defrosted with their heads removed. As the shrimp are poached, their shells turn pink.

SERVES 4

FOR THE BISQUE
- ¼ cup butter
- 1 onion, finely chopped
- 1 small carrot, diced
- 1 celery stalk, diced
- 1 bay leaf
- 1 sprig of parsley
- 1½ cups diced potato, peeled
- 12 uncooked jumbo shrimp, heads removed
- 4 tablespoons brandy
- 1¼ cups dry white wine
- 2½ cups water
- salt and freshly ground black pepper
- 1 cup soup pasta shells or other soup pasta
- ⅔ cup light cream

FOR THE ROUILLE
- 2 garlic cloves, peeled
- 1–2 red chilis, deseeded and chopped (see Cook's Tip, right)
- 2 egg yolks
- 2 tablespoons fresh white bread crumbs
- 2 tablespoons lemon juice
- generous ¾ cup olive oil

TO GARNISH
- paprika
- chopped parsley

TO SERVE
- 1 short French bread stick

Make the Rouille first. Purée the garlic, chilis, egg yolks, bread crumbs and lemon juice in a food processor or blender. Alternatively, the ingredients may be gradually pounded to a paste in a mortar; then the yolks and lemon juice beaten in. Gradually trickle in the olive oil, with the machine running, to make a thick, fiery mayonnaise. Transfer to a serving bowl, cover and chill.

Next, make the Bisque. Melt the butter in a saucepan. Add the onion, carrot, celery, bay leaf, parsley and potato. Cook, stirring, for 5 minutes. Then add the shrimp. Cook, stirring gently for 5 minutes. Add the brandy, and pour in the wine. Heat until simmering; then simmer gently for 5 minutes.

Remove the pan from the heat, and use a slotted spoon to lift out the shrimp. Shell the shrimp, and return the shells to the pan. Slice the flesh, and set it aside.

Pour the water into the soup, add plenty of seasoning, and bring it back to a boil. Reduce the heat, cover the pan, and let simmer for 20 minutes.

Purée the soup in a blender or food processor; then press it through a fine strainer to remove any large bits of shell. Rinse out the saucepan; then pour the soup back into it, and bring it to a boil. Add the pasta, reduce the heat, and cover the pan. Simmer for 15 minutes, or until the pasta is cooked.

Slice the French bread fairly thinly, and toast the slices until golden on both sides. Taste the soup for seasoning; then stir in the reserved shrimp flesh, and heat for a few seconds. Stir in the cream, and heat for a few seconds without boiling; then garnish with a little sprinkling of paprika and parsley. Offer the toasted bread and Rouille with the soup.

COOK'S TIP

Chilis vary considerably in strength, and personal preferences also differ widely, so adjust the number of chilis accordingly.

To prepare chilis, cut off the stalk end and scrape out the seeds (which are especially hot) and pith from inside; then rinse the shells well before slicing or chopping them.

Take care when rinsing the chilis, wash your hands thoroughly after handling them, and avoid touching your eyes while working with them. The juices are a severe irritant to delicate skin and eyes.

Chicken Noodle Soup

SERVES 4–6

- 1 large, boneless chicken breast, skinned
- 1 tablespoon oil
- 1-inch piece fresh ginger root, peeled and cut into thin strips
- 1 carrot, cut into fine matchstick strips
- 2-ounce can bamboo shoots, cut into fine matchstick strips
- 4 scallions, shredded diagonally
- 1 quantity Chinese-style Stock (see page 57)
- salt and freshly ground black pepper
- about 6 fresh spinach leaves, washed and finely shredded (optional)
- 4 ounces fresh wheat noodles or Chinese egg noodles

Cut the chicken into thin slices; then cut these into fine strips. Heat the oil in a saucepan, and stir-fry the chicken with the ginger until lightly browned. Add the carrot, bamboo shoots and scallions. Stir for a few seconds before stirring in the stock.

Bring to a boil, reduce the heat, and cover the pan. Simmer the soup for 30 minutes. Season, add the spinach, if using, and noodles, and cook for a further 10 minutes. Taste for seasoning before serving.

Chicken and Leek Broth with Mushroom Cappelletti

This makes a hearty meal on a cold winter's day. You can substitute ready-made filled pasta for the homemade suggestion given below if you like.

SERVES 6

- 2 chicken quarters
- 1 large onion, sliced
- 2 large carrots, diced
- 2 quarts chicken stock
- 1 tablespoon oil
- 1 garlic clove, crushed
- 1 bay leaf
- 1 pound leeks, sliced
- 4 tablespoons chopped parsley
- salt and freshly ground black pepper
- 1 quantity Mushroom Cappelletti (see page 222)

Put the chicken quarters in a saucepan with the onion and half the carrot. Pour in the stock, and bring to a boil. Reduce the heat, cover the pan, and cook for 1 hour.

Lift the chicken from the stock. Discard the skin, and cut all the meat off the bones. Dice the meat.

Heat the oil in a large saucepan. Add the garlic, bay leaf and leeks. Cook, stirring, for 3 minutes; then pour in the soup and add the chicken meat. Add the parsley and a little seasoning; then bring to a boil. Reduce the heat, cover and simmer for 5 minutes.

Add the prepared Mushroom Cappelletti to the soup. Bring back to a boil; then reduce the heat, and simmer for about 5 minutes, or until the Cappelletti are tender. Taste for seasoning before serving.

Beef and Beer Soup

SERVES 4–6

- 1 tablespoon oil
- 3 cups diced, lean stewing beef
- 2 large onions, thinly sliced
- 2 carrots, sliced
- 2 celery stalks, sliced
- 3 cups sliced mushrooms
- 1 bouquet garni
- 1 blade of mace
- 2 quarts water
- salt and freshly ground black pepper
- 1¼ cups strong beer
- 1 tablespoon sugar
- 2 tablespoons tomato paste
- 1 cup soup pasta

Heat the oil in a large saucepan. Add the beef, and brown the pieces all over; then use a slotted spoon to remove them from the pan. Brown the onions next, cooking them over a medium heat for about 25 minutes, so that they slowly begin to brown without burning.

Stir in the carrots, celery and half the mushrooms. Return the beef to the pan, and add the bouquet garni and mace. Pour in the water, and add plenty of seasoning and the beer. Bring to theail, then reduce the heat, and cover the saucepan. Simmer the soup for 2 hours, or until the meat is very tender.

Stir in the remaining mushrooms, sugar and tomato paste. Taste for seasoning; then add the pasta, and simmer for 10 minutes, or until the pasta is just cooked. Serve piping hot.

Spicy Beef Soup

SERVES 4

- 8 ounces lean frying steak, cut into short, thin strips
- pinch of five-spice powder
- 1 red chili, deseeded and thinly sliced (see Cook's Tip, page 90)
- 2 tablespoons oil
- 1 teaspoon sesame oil
- 1 small carrot, cut into fine matchstick strips
- 4 scallions, shredded diagonally
- 1 piece of lemon grass or strip of pared lemon rind
- 4 tablespoons dry sherry
- 2½ pints Chinese-style Stock (see page 57) or chicken stock
- salt and freshly ground black pepper
- 1⅓ cups sliced button mushrooms
- 1 cup vermicelli

Season the steak with the five-spice powder, and mix it with the chili. If possible, cover and let marinate for several hours or overnight.

Heat the oil and sesame oil together in a saucepan. Stir-fry the steak with the chili until the meat has browned lightly. Stir in the carrot, scallions, lemon grass or rind, and cook for 1 minute. Then pour in the sherry and stock. Add seasoning to taste, and bring to a boil. Reduce the heat, cover the pan, and simmer the soup for 40 minutes.

Add the mushrooms and vermicelli, and bring back to a boil; then reduce the heat, and cook gently for 10 minutes. Taste for seasoning before serving.

Piquant Pork and Shrimp Soup with Coconut Cream

SERVES 4

FOR THE SOUP

- 4 ounces lean boneless pork, cut into very fine strips
- 1 tablespoon oil
- 1 red chili, deseeded and finely sliced (see Cook's Tip, page 90)
- 1 garlic clove, crushed and chopped
- pared rind of ½ lime, cut into fine shreds
- 2½ pints chicken stock
- 4 scallions, finely chopped
- 2-inch piece English cucumber, thinly peeled and cut into thin strips

- 1 cup peeled, cooked shrimp, defrosted and drained if frozen
- juice of ½ lime
- salt and freshly ground black pepper
- 1 cup rice vermicelli

FOR THE COCONUT CREAM

- 1 tablespoon oil
- 1 tablespoon finely chopped fresh ginger root
- 1 scallion, finely chopped
- 1 tablespoon smooth peanut butter
- 3 tablespoons instant coconut milk
- 6 tablespoons boiling water

Put the pork in a non-metallic bowl. Add the oil, chili, garlic and lime rind. Mix well, cover and leave to marinate for 2 hours.

Then put the meat and marinade into a heavy-bottomed saucepan, and stir-fry until the meat is cooked and has lightly browned. Stir in the stock, and bring to a boil. Reduce the heat so that the soup simmers. Add the scallions and cucumber. Cover and simmer for 15 minutes. Add the shrimp, lime juice, and salt and pepper to taste. Stir in the vermicelli, and let cook over a very low heat for 10 minutes.

Meanwhile, make the Coconut Cream. Heat the oil in a small saucepan. Add the ginger and scallions, and stir-fry for 5 minutes, but do not allow the mixture to become too hot as it is likely to burn. Stir in the peanut butter, coconut milk and boiling water. Remove from the heat, and transfer to a serving bowl.

Ladle the soup into serving bowls, and pass the Coconut Cream around separately, so that it may be stirred into the soup to taste just before it is eaten.

Spicy Beef Soup.

95

Pistou Soup

This is the French version of minestrone, served with the paste that gives the soup its name, a close relative of pesto.

SERVES 6–8

FOR THE SOUP
- 2 tablespoons olive oil
- 2 onions, chopped
- 4 celery stalks, sliced
- 1¼ cups diced carrots
- 1¼ cups diced turnips
- 1 pound baby potatoes, scrubbed
- 1 pound tomatoes, peeled (see Cook's Tip, page 72), deseeded and quartered
- 2 quarts vegetable stock or water
- 1 bouquet garni
- salt and freshly ground black pepper
- 1½ cups shelled fresh peas
- 8 ounces green beans, cut into short lengths
- 2 small zucchini, sliced
- 2 × 15-ounce cans navy beans, drained
- ¾ cup vermicelli

FOR THE PISTOU
- handful of fresh basil
- 2 garlic cloves
- 3 ounces Gruyère cheese
- 1-ounce piece Parmesan cheese
- ⅔ cup olive oil

First, make the soup. Heat the oil in a large saucepan. Add the onions, celery, carrots, turnips and baby potatoes. Cook, stirring, for 10 minutes; then add the tomatoes, and pour in the stock or water. Add the bouquet garni, and salt and pepper to taste. Bring to a boil; then reduce the heat, and cover the pan. Simmer the soup gently for 45 minutes.

Add the peas, and simmer for a further 10 minutes. Then add the green beans, zucchini, navy beans and vermicelli. Bring the soup back to a boil, partially cover the pan, and simmer for 10 minutes.

Make the pistou while the soup is cooking. Place the basil, garlic, Gruyère and Parmesan in a food processor or blender, and process them until finely chopped. Add some of the oil; then continue processing the mixture until it forms a paste. Trickle in the remaining olive oil while the machine is running.

Taste the soup for seasoning. Stir in the pistou, and remove the pan from the heat. Serve at once.

Minestrone

I love all sorts of hearty soups and this is one of my favorites. Minestrone makes a warming meal, served with plenty of fresh bread and Parmesan cheese. Try making the Olive Bread (see page 308) to serve as an accompaniment.

SERVES 6–8

- ⅔ cup dried navy beans
- 2 tablespoons olive oil
- 2 cups chopped, rindless bacon
- 2 garlic cloves, crushed
- 2 onions, chopped
- 6 celery stalks, sliced
- 2 large carrots, cut in large dice
- 2 large potatoes, cut in chunks
- 2 quarts chicken or bacon stock
- 1 bouquet garni
- 2 × 14-ounce cans chopped tomatoes
- 4 ounces green beans, cut into short lengths
- 2 small zucchini, halved lengthways and sliced
- 3 cups shredded cabbage
- 1 cup soup pasta
- salt and freshly ground black pepper
- 4–6 tablespoons chopped parsley
- freshly grated Parmesan cheese, to serve

Soak the navy beans overnight in cold water to cover.

Next day, drain the beans, put them in a saucepan, and add plenty of fresh cold water to cover. Bring to a boil, and boil for 10 minutes; then reduce the heat, and cover the pan. Simmer the beans for 30 minutes.

Meanwhile, heat the oil in a large saucepan. Add the bacon, garlic, onions, celery and carrots. Cook, stirring all the time, for 15 minutes, or until the bacon is cooked. Then add the potatoes, stock and bouquet garni. Stir in the drained navy beans. Bring the soup to a boil, reduce the heat, and cover the pan. Simmer for 1 hour.

Stir in the tomatoes, green beans, zucchini, cabbage and pasta, and bring back to a boil. Add salt and pepper to taste. Cook for a further 10 minutes, or until the vegetables are cooked, and the pasta is just tender. Taste for seasoning before stirring in the parsley and serving with Parmesan cheese.

Minestrone Soup.

Quick Bortsch with Uzska

There are many variations on this beet soup, but, if you want to make a soup in which to serve the tiny tortellini-type pasta, then it ought to be clear and well flavored. This quick version bypasses the process of making and clarifying your own stock by using canned consommé, and it works very well. If you cannot find fresh, uncooked beets, then use 12 ounces cooked, vacuum-packed beets, but do not use the type that has added acid or vinegar.

SERVES 4

- ¼ cup butter
- 1 onion, chopped
- 1½ cups finely shredded cabbage
- 1 carrot, diced
- 1 bay leaf
- 1 sprig of thyme
- 1¾ cups peeled, diced, fresh, uncooked beets
- 2 × 10-ounce cans concentrated beef consommé
- 1¼ cups light red wine
- 1¼ cups water
- salt and freshly ground black pepper
- 1 tablespoon superfine sugar
- 3 tablespoons cider vinegar
- 1 quantity Uszka (see page 224)

Melt the butter in a saucepan. Add the onion, cabbage, carrot, bay leaf and thyme. Cover and cook for 15 minutes.

Stir in the beets, consommé, wine and water. Add salt and pepper to taste, and bring to a boil. Reduce the heat so that the soup just simmers, then cover the pan tightly, and cook for 1¼ hours (do not boil the soup rapidly).

Meanwhile, make the Uszka as given on page 224, then set them aside ready to cook at the last minute, just before serving the soup.

Strain the soup through a cheesecloth-lined strainer. Rinse out the saucepan; then return the strained soup to it. Heat the soup, then add the sugar and vinegar, and stir until the sugar has dissolved. Set the soup aside over a low heat to keep hot until the Uszka are cooked.

Cook the Uszka as given in the recipe, and place some in warmed serving bowls. Taste the soup for seasoning and for the balance of sweet and sour, adjusting if necessary, then ladle it over the Uszka. and offer the remaining Uszka separately. Serve at once.

Zucchini Soup

SERVES 4

- ¼ cup butter
- 1 large onion, finely chopped
- 1 bay leaf
- pared rind of 1 lemon
- 1 tablespoon all-purpose flour
- 1½ quarts chicken stock
- 1 cup pasta spirals
- 2 ounces small young zucchini, thinly sliced
- 1 tablespoon chopped fresh tarragon
- salt and freshly ground black pepper

Melt the butter in a large saucepan. Add the onion, bay leaf and lemon rind. Stir well, then cover the pan, and cook gently for 15 minutes. Stir in the flour, then pour in the stock, and bring to a boil, stirring. Reduce the heat, cover the pan, and simmer for 10 minutes.

Add the pasta to the soup, and bring it back to a boil. Then reduce the heat, partially cover the pan, and continue to simmer for 15 minutes. Stir in the zucchini and tarragon, together with salt and pepper. Bring back to a boil, then cover and simmer for a further 5 minutes, or until the pasta and zucchini are tender. Taste for seasoning before serving.

Cabbage Soup with Spätzle

SERVES 6

- ¼ cup butter
- 1 large onion, halved and thinly sliced
- 2 garlic cloves, finely chopped
- 2 large carrots, halved and sliced
- 2 celery stalks, sliced
- 1 bay leaf
- 1 pound lean bacon, for boiling in one piece
- 2 quarts water
- ½ quantity Spätzle (see page 50)
- 6 cups shredded cabbage
- salt and freshly ground black pepper
- 6 tablespoons chopped parsley

Melt the butter in a large saucepan. Add the onion, garlic, carrots, celery and bay leaf. Cook, stirring, for 5 minutes. Place the piece of bacon in the pan, and pour in the water. Bring slowly to a boil, and, as the water boils, skim off and discard any scum that rises to the surface. Reduce the heat, if necessary, to keep the water just simmering; then cover the pan, and cook for 45 minutes.

Meanwhile, make the Spätzle batter, and cook as given on page 50. Drain them, and set aside.

Remove the meat from the pan, and dice it, discarding any fat. Return the meat to the soup, and add the cabbage. Taste for seasoning, stir in salt and pepper, and bring back to a boil; then reduce the heat, and cover the pan. Simmer for 15 minutes. Add the Spätzle and parsley, and cook for a further 5 minutes; then serve piping hot.

Artichoke Soup with Walnut-dressed Pasta

SERVES 4–6

- ¼ cup butter
- 1 small onion, chopped
- 1 pound Jerusalem artichokes, peeled and diced
- 1 bay leaf
- 2½ cups chicken or vegetable stock
- salt and freshly ground black pepper
- 1 cup orecchiette
- 1¼ cups milk
- 2 tablespoons walnut oil
- ½ cup finely grated Gruyère cheese
- 2 tablespoons finely chopped walnuts
- 2 tablespoons finely chopped parsley

Melt the butter in a large saucepan. Add the onion, artichokes and bay leaf. Stir well; then cover and cook for 10 minutes. Pour in the stock, and add a little salt and pepper. Bring to a boil, reduce the heat, and simmer for 20 minutes.

Cook the orecchiette in a large saucepan of boiling salted water for 15 minutes, or until tender.

Meanwhile, purée the soup in a liquidizer or food processor. Rinse out the saucepan; then return the soup to it, and stir in the milk. Reheat the soup without boiling it; then taste for seasoning.

Drain the pasta, and toss the oil, cheese, walnuts and parsley into it. Serve the soup, and spoon some of the hot pasta into the bowls. Offer the remainder separately.

Thin Tomato Soup with Spinach Tortellini

This is an ideal recipe for ready-made tortellini or other filled pasta.

SERVES 4

- 1 tablespoon oil
- ¼ cup butter
- 1 garlic clove, crushed
- 1 large onion, halved and thinly sliced
- 2 celery stalks, diced
- 1 large carrot, chopped
- 4 tablespoons tomato paste
- ½ teaspoon sugar
- 2 × 10-ounce cans concentrated beef consommé
- 2½ cups water
- salt and freshly ground black pepper
- ½ quantity tortellini with Spinach and Ricotta Stuffing (see pages 191 and 198) or 8 ounces ready-made spinach tortellini
- 3 sprigs of basil, shredded

Heat the oil and butter in a saucepan. Add the garlic, onion, celery and carrot. Cook, stirring, for 5 minutes; then stir in the tomato paste and sugar. Pour in the consommé and water. Add salt and pepper to taste, and bring to a boil. Reduce the heat, cover the pan, and simmer gently for 20 minutes.

Cook the tortellini in boiling salted water, allowing about 3 minutes for homemade pasta or following the instructions on the package for bought pasta. Drain the tortellini, then add them to the soup and taste for seasoning. Stir in the basil, and serve at once.

Carrot and Parsnip Soup with Crispy Spiced Pasta

Carrots and parsnips marry well in this simple, delicious soup. If you do not want to make your own pasta for the crunchy garnish, then deep-fry ordinary cooked pasta shapes, and toss them with good curry powder cooked in a little butter.

SERVES 4–6

FOR THE SOUP
- 1 tablespoon oil
- 1 large onion, chopped
- 1 pound parsnips, cut into chunks
- 1½ cups sliced carrots
- 1 medium potato, cut into chunks
- 3¾ cups chicken or vegetable stock
- salt and freshly ground black pepper
- ⅔ cup light cream or yogurt

TO GARNISH
- scant ¼ quantity Curry-spiced Rich Egg Pasta Dough (see page 45)
- oil, for deep-frying
- chopped fresh cilantro leaves

First, make the soup. Heat the oil in a large saucepan. Add the onion, parsnips, carrots and potato. Stir well, then cover and cook for 10 minutes. Pour in the stock, and bring to a boil. Reduce the heat, cover the pan, and simmer for 20 minutes, or until the vegetables are tender.

Purée the soup in a food processor or blender; rinse out the pan, and return the soup to it. Add salt and pepper to taste.

Now, prepare the pasta garnish. Roll out the pasta thinly, and stamp out decorative shapes, using aspic cutters, or cut it into strips, then into small triangles. Cook the pasta in boiling salted water for 3 minutes; then drain it well.

Heat the oil for deep-frying. Toss the pasta in a little flour; then fry the pieces until crisp and golden. Drain thoroughly on paper towels. Heat the soup, then stir in the cream or yogurt, and heat for a few seconds without boiling. Taste for seasoning, and serve sprinkled with cilantro and topped with the pasta.

Mushroom Soup with Watercress

SERVES 4

- 1 tablespoon olive oil
- 1 onion, chopped
- 6 cups sliced button mushrooms
- 2 tablespoons all-purpose flour
- 3¾ cups chicken stock
- salt and freshly ground black pepper
- 1 cup ditali
- 1¼ cups milk
- 1 bunch watercress

Heat the oil in a saucepan. Add the onion and half the mushrooms. Cook over medium heat, stirring often, until the mushrooms are well reduced, and the liquid that they yield has evaporated. Stir in the flour, then slowly pour in the stock, and bring to a boil, stirring all the time. Simmer for 5 minutes. Purée the soup in a liquidizer, and rinse out the saucepan; then return the soup to it, and add seasoning to taste.

Bring the soup to a boil. Add the remaining mushrooms and the ditali. Reduce the heat, cover the pan, and simmer for 15–20 minutes, or until the pasta is tender.

Stir in the milk and watercress, then heat through, stirring, and taste for seasoning before serving.

Won Ton Soup

SERVES 4

1 quantity Pork Won Tons
(see page 258)
1 tablespoon oil
4 scallions, shredded
diagonally
1 carrot, cut into fine
matchstick strips

1 quantity Chinese-style
Stock (see page 57)
4 ounces broccoli, divided
into small florets
salt and freshly ground black
pepper

First make the Pork Won Tons as given in the recipe on page 258.

Heat the oil in a large saucepan. Add the scallions and carrot, and stir-fry for 3 minutes. Then pour in the stock, and bring to a boil. Reduce the heat, cover the pan, and simmer for 10 minutes. Add the broccoli, and cook for 5 minutes.

Make sure the soup is simmering steadily; then add the Pork Won Tons. Simmer for 5 minutes, stirring them around occasionally, until they are tender, and the filling has cooked through. Taste the soup for seasoning, and serve.

Bean Curd and Rice Stick Soup

SERVES 4

¾ cup firm bean curd
2 tablespoons sake
2 tablespoons Japanese soy
sauce
3 scallions, finely chopped

1 carrot
1 quantity Japanese Stock
(see page 57)
1 cup ribbon rice sticks

Cut the bean curd into neat diamond shapes, and put them in a shallow dish. Sprinkle with the sake, soy sauce and scallions, and set aside to marinate for 1 hour.

Meanwhile, peel the carrot. Use a canelle knife or small pointed knife to cut strips down the length of the carrot (if using a knife, then cut "V" strips into the carrot along its length); then cut it into thin slices.

Pour the stock into a saucepan, and add the decorative carrot slices. Bring to simmering point; then cook for 5 minutes. Add the rice sticks, and cook for a further 10 minutes. Remove the soup from the heat.

Divide the bean curd between serving bowls. Spoon some of the rice sticks and carrots into the bowls; then ladle in the broth. Serve at once.

Won Ton Soup.

HOTPOTS AND STEWS

THE IDEA BEHIND THIS CHAPTER IS TO BRING TOGETHER A RANGE OF DISHES THAT ARE MORE OR LESS A MEAL IN THEMSELVES, WITH, PERHAPS, SOME BREAD OR A SALAD ACCOMPANIMENT.

INSTEAD OF BEING COOKED AND SERVED SEPARATELY, THE PASTA IS ADDED TO MOIST STEWS OR CASSEROLES, THEN COOKED UNTIL TENDER. ❦ THIS DOES LIMIT THE CHOICE OF PASTA AS LARGE OR LONG SHAPES DO NOT COOK SUCCESSFULLY IN THE LIMITED QUANTITY OF LIQUID. ❦ VERY THICK SHAPES TEND TO REQUIRE LONGER COOKING AND MORE WATER, SO THIN PASTA AND SMALL SHAPES ARE IDEAL.

WHEN PASTA IS ADDED TO A LIQUID ALREADY SLIGHTLY THICKENED WITH OTHER INGREDIENTS, THE COOKING TIME IS INCREASED. ❦ SO, DO NOT BE SURPRISED AT THE LENGTH OF COOKING SUGGESTED AFTER THE PASTA IS ADDED TO A STEW.

IF YOU THINK THIS IS GOING TO BE A COLLECTION OF MEAT STEWS PACKED WITH MACARONI, THEN READ ON AND I HOPE YOU WILL CHANGE YOUR MIND.

Seafarer's Hotpot

SERVES 4

- ¼ cup butter
- 1 garlic clove, crushed
- 1 onion, chopped
- 3 cups sliced mushrooms
- ¼ cup all-purpose flour
- 3¾ cups fish stock
- 1¼ cups dry cider
- 14-ounce can chopped tomatoes
- salt and freshly ground black pepper
- ¾ cup frozen peas
- 3 cups pasta shells
- 1½ pound white fish fillet, skinned and cut in chunks
- 2 cups peeled, cooked shrimp
- 4 tablespoons chopped parsley

Melt the butter in a large, flameproof casserole or heavy-bottomed saucepan. Add the garlic and onion; then cook, stirring occasionally, for 5 minutes. Add the mushrooms, and stir well; then stir in the flour, and slowly pour in the stock. Bring to a boil, stirring all the time. Add the cider, tomatoes, and salt and pepper to taste. Bring back to a boil; then add the peas and pasta. Reduce the heat so that the sauce simmers. Cover the pan, and cook gently for about 20 minutes, or until the pasta is tender. Stir occasionally during cooking to prevent the pasta sticking to the pan.

Stir in the fish, and cook gently for a further 5 minutes. Then add the shrimp and parsley, and cook for a further 5 minutes, until the fish is cooked and the shrimp are hot. Taste for seasoning; then serve piping hot.

Grecian Lamb Casserole

Orzo or minestra are the small Greek pasta shapes that resemble large rice grains when raw. They absorb the juices in this rich, herby casserole to make a splendid meal. Serve a light, crisp salad as a palate-cleansing side dish.

SERVES 4

- 2¼ pounds stewing lamb, chopped into bite-size pieces
- 1 tablespoon olive oil
- 2 large onions, chopped
- 3 garlic cloves, crushed
- 1 bay leaf
- 2 tablespoons chopped fresh oregano
- 14-ounce can chopped tomatoes
- 3¾ cups water
- salt and freshly ground black pepper
- 2 cups orzo
- 4 tablespoons chopped parsley
- French bread, to serve

Preheat the oven to 350°F.

Trim any excess fat from the lamb. Heat the oil in a large, flameproof, ovenproof casserole, and brown the lamb well all over.

When the pieces of meat have browned, add the onions, garlic, bay leaf and oregano, and mix well. Continue to cook for about 5 minutes, to take the raw taste off the onions before adding any liquid.

Pour in the tomatoes and water; then add plenty of salt and some pepper. Heat until the liquid is just simmering. Cover the casserole, and bake in the preheated oven for 1½ hours, or until the lamb is tender.

Taste the sauce for seasoning, add the orzo, and cook for a further 30 minutes, or until the pasta is tender. Serve at once, with plenty of French bread to mop up the delicious juices.

Smoked Fish Hotpot

Smoked fish tastes really good with pasta. I have used spirals here, but shells or other shapes that cook reasonably quickly may be used.

SERVES 4

- 2 tablespoons olive oil
- 1 large onion, halved and thinly sliced
- 1 red bell pepper, deseeded and sliced
- grated rind of 1 lemon
- 2 tablespoons all-purpose flour
- 3¾ cups fish stock
- salt and freshly ground black pepper
- 2 cups pasta spirals
- 1½-pound smoked fish fillet, skinned
- ¼ cup butter (optional)
- 4 eggs, hard-cooked and roughly chopped

Heat the olive oil in a flameproof casserole or heavy-bottomed saucepan. Add the onion, pepper and lemon rind. Cook, stirring occasionally, for 10 minutes. Stir in the flour; then slowly pour in the stock. Add salt and pepper, and bring to a boil, stirring all the time. Add the pasta; then reduce the heat so that the sauce simmers.

Place the fish on a suitable plate to cover the pan. Top with the butter if using, and cover with a saucepan lid or foil. Put the fish on top of the pan in place of its lid, and simmer gently for 20–30 minutes, or until the pasta is cooked. Stir occasionally to prevent the pasta sticking.

Flake the fish, discarding the skin and any bones. Lightly mix it into the pasta with all the butter from steaming (if used) and the hard-cooked eggs. Taste for seasoning, and serve at once.

Mediterranean Medley

SERVES 4

- 1 eggplant, cubed
- salt and freshly ground black pepper
- 4 tablespoons olive oil
- 8 chicken thighs, skinned
- 2 garlic cloves, finely chopped
- 2 tablespoons chopped fresh or 1 tablespoon dried oregano
- 2 onions, halved and sliced
- 1 green bell pepper, halved, deseeded and sliced
- 1 bay leaf

- 2 tablespoons golden raisins
- 1¼ cups red wine
- 2½ cups chicken stock
- 14-ounce can chopped tomatoes
- 2 cups rigatoni or penne
- 10 black olives, pitted and halved
- 4 tablespoons pine nuts
- 4 tablespoons chopped parsley
- harissa (red chili condiment), to serve

Put the eggplant in a colander, and sprinkle each layer with salt; then let sit over a bowl for 30 minutes. Rinse and drain well.

Heat half the olive oil in a large, flameproof casserole or heavy-bottomed saucepan. Fry the pieces of eggplant until lightly browned in parts, but not softened. Use a slotted spoon to remove them from the pan. Add the remaining oil, and brown the chicken pieces; then remove them also. Add the garlic, oregano, onions and green bell pepper to the fat remaining in the pan. Cook, stirring, for 5 minutes.

Stir in the bay leaf and the aubergine cubes, then return the chicken pieces to the pan, and sprinkle with the golden raisins. Pour in the wine, stock and tomatoes. Add salt and pepper, and bring to a boil. Reduce the heat, and cover the pan; then cook gently for 30 minutes.

Add the rigatoni or penne, stirring them down into the sauce, and displacing the chicken so that they are covered with sauce. Bring back to simmering point, and cover the pan tightly. Cook gently for a further 20 minutes. Add the olives, and continue to cook for about 10 minutes, or until the pasta is cooked.

Meanwhile, put the pine nuts in a small, heavy-bottomed saucepan, and cook, shaking the pan often, over a medium heat until the pine nuts are lightly browned. Remove from the heat.

Taste the casserole for seasoning. Sprinkle the pine nuts and parsley over, and serve with harissa, which may be added to taste by the diners.

Braised Turkey with Fennel

SERVES 4

- 1½ pounds boneless turkey breast, cut into chunks
- 2 tablespoons all-purpose flour
- salt and freshly ground black pepper
- ¼ cup butter
- 2 fennel bulbs, sliced

- 1 onion, finely chopped
- 2½ cups dry white wine
- 2¼ cups chicken stock
- 1 fresh bouquet garni
- 3 cups anellini or other pasta rings
- ⅔ cup sour cream

Preheat the oven to 350°F.

Toss the pieces of turkey breast with the flour and plenty of salt and pepper. Melt the butter in a large, flameproof, ovenproof casserole, and brown the turkey pieces all over; then add the fennel and onion. Turn the vegetables and turkey together over the heat for about 5 minutes. Then pour in the wine and stock. Add the bouquet garni and anellini, and bring to a boil; then remove from the heat.

Stir the pasta and turkey mixture, and cover the casserole tightly. Bake for about 40 minutes, until the pasta is cooked, and the fennel is tender. Stir in the sour cream, and taste for seasoning before serving.

Mediterranean Medley.

Pheasant Galantine with Walnut Cappelletti

This is an ideal dinner party dish. It does take a lot of preparation, but, once this is over, the attention to detail at the last minute is fairly straightforward. Side dishes of red cabbage stir-fried with onions and French beans will make a memorable meal.

SERVES 4

- *1 pheasant, boned (see Cook's Tip below)*
- *8 ounces venison sausages*
- *⅔ cup finely chopped, cooked ham*
- *2 onions, finely chopped*
- *1 eating apple, peeled, cored and finely chopped*
- *1 tablespoon chopped fresh sage*
- *2 teaspoons chopped fresh thyme*
- *2 tablespoons chopped parsley*
- *salt and freshly ground black pepper*
- *¼ cup butter*
- *⅔ cup diced, rindless smoked bacon*
- *1 small carrot, finely diced*
- *1 celery stalk, finely diced*
- *1⅓ cup sliced mushrooms*
- *1 bottle of red wine*
- *2 bay leaves*
- *1 quantity cappelletti with Walnut Stuffing (see pages 190 and 197)*

Lay the pheasant out on a board, skin-side down. Skin the venison sausages, and put the meat in a bowl. Add the ham, half the chopped onion, the apple, sage, thyme, parsley and plenty of seasoning. Pound the ingredients together with the back of a mixing spoon to combine them thoroughly. Then place the stuffing down the middle of the pheasant. Fold the bird over the stuffing, and use a trussing needle with cooking thread or string to sew it up.

Preheat the oven to 350°F.

Melt the butter in a flameproof, ovenproof casserole. Brown the outside of the Pheasant Galantine lightly; then remove it from the pan, and set aside.

Add the remaining onion, bacon, carrot, celery and mushrooms to the fat in the pan. Cook for 2–3 minutes, then pour in the wine and add the bay leaves. Stir in salt and pepper to taste, and heat the wine to just below simmering point. Lower the Pheasant Galantine into the casserole. Cover and bake in the oven for 1½ hours. Turn the Galantine halfway through cooking.

Meanwhile, make the walnut-filled cappelletti as given on pages 190 and 197. Just before taking the Pheasant Galantine from the oven, cook the cappelletti in boiling salted water for 2 minutes, so that they are three-quarters cooked, but not quite tender. Drain well.

Carefully lift the Pheasant Galantine from the casserole. Remove the bay leaves from the sauce, and taste for seasoning. Tip in the cappelletti. Stir to coat the cappelletti in sauce, then cover the casserole, and return it to the oven while you carve the Galantine. The cappelletti will finish cooking in the sauce.

> ### COOK'S TIP
> Some butchers will bone the pheasant if you ask ahead, but if you are doing it yourself, you need a sharp, pointed knife and a pair of kitchen scissors. Place the pheasant on a board, breast-side down. Cut through the skin and meat into the bone all along the back of the bird. Then slide the point of the knife under the meat, close to the bone, down one side. Work all the meat off the carcass, from the middle of the bird down the side as far as the breastbone. Scrape the meat off the leg joints, carefully turning the meat and skin inside out off the bones. Snip the meat off or around the joint ends with scissors. When the meat is free from the bones on one side, turn the board around, and work down the other side. Leave the meat attached along the top of the soft breastbone as you work. Finally, carefully cut the meat off the breastbone, taking the merest sliver of bone to avoid puncturing the skin (it is important to keep the skin whole while doing this).

Gnocchi-topped Chicken

This is a great way of turning simple semolina gnocchi into a special dinner party dish. For a formal main course, serve Sautéed Leeks with Spinach (see page 314) and some lightly sautéed zucchini as accompaniments.

SERVES 4

- *1 quantity Semolina Gnocchi (see page 49)*
- *2 tablespoons olive oil*
- *4 boneless chicken breasts, skinned*
- *1 onion, halved and thinly sliced*
- *2 garlic cloves, crushed*
- *6 sage leaves, shredded*
- *1⅓ cups sliced mushrooms*
- *4 tablespoons brandy (optional)*
- *⅔ cup red wine*
- *2½ cups passata*
- *salt and freshly ground black pepper*
- *⅔ cup shredded, lean cooked ham*
- *¼ cup melted butter*

Make the Semolina Gnocchi as given on page 49, and cut it into squares or circles.

Preheat the oven to 375°F.

Heat the olive oil in a flameproof casserole that can be placed in the oven. Brown the chicken pieces all over; then use a slotted spoon to remove them from the pan. Add the onion and garlic, and cook for 5 minutes, stirring occasionally. Add the sage and mushrooms, and stir for a few minutes. Pour in the brandy, wine and passata, and bring to a boil, stirring. Remove from the heat, and taste for seasoning.

Return the chicken pieces to the pan, spooning the sauce over them, and sprinkle the ham over the top. Arrange the Semolina Gnocchi, overlapping, on top of the chicken; then brush with the butter. Bake in the preheated oven for about 40 minutes, until the chicken is cooked through, and the Semolina Gnocchi are golden brown and well-crusted.

Marinated Pork with Sautéed Sprouts and Pasta

SERVES 4

- 3 cups cubed, lean boneless pork
- ¼ teaspoon ground allspice
- ½ teaspoon paprika
- 8 juniper berries, crushed
- 4 fresh sage leaves, finely shredded
- 1 bay leaf
- 2 cups red wine
- ¼ cup butter or 2 tablespoons butter and 1 tablespoon oil

- 1 large onion, thinly sliced
- 1 large carrot, diced
- salt and freshly ground black pepper
- 2 cups water
- 2 cups pasta bows
- 8 ounces small Brussels sprouts
- ⅔ cup sour cream, to serve (optional)

Place the pork in a dish. Add the allspice, paprika, juniper berries, sage, bay leaf and wine. Mix well, cover and marinate overnight in the refrigerator.

Melt half the butter or butter and oil in a flameproof casserole or heavy-bottomed saucepan. Drain the meat well, reserving the marinade. Brown the pork in the butter or butter and oil; then add the onion and carrot. Cook, stirring, for 5 minutes, to soften the vegetables slightly. Add the salt and pepper to taste, the reserved marinade and water. Heat until only just simmering, then cover the casserole or pan, and cook for 45 minutes, stirring once or twice during this time.

Stir in the pasta, pressing it down into the cooking liquid, and bring the liquid to a boil. Reduce the heat, and cover the casserole or pan tightly; then simmer gently for a further 25 minutes, stirring occasionally, until the pasta is tender, and much of the liquid has been absorbed.

Toward the end of cooking, melt the remaining butter or butter and oil in a small saucepan. Add the sprouts, and toss them in the butter. Cover the pan, and cook the vegetables slowly for 10 minutes.

Stir the sprouts, and their cooking juices, into the hotpot. Taste for seasoning, and serve at once, offering a bowl of sour cream to be swirled into individual portions, if liked.

Rigatoni and Vegetable Curry

The idea of curried pasta may sound rather weird, but this combination tastes extremely good.

SERVES 4

- 2 tablespoons butter
- 1 large onion, chopped
- 2 celery stalks, sliced
- 2 large carrots, halved lengthways and sliced
- 1 green bell pepper, deseeded and diced
- 1 large garlic clove, crushed
- 1 bay leaf
- 2 tablespoons peeled, finely chopped, fresh ginger root

- 6 ounces cauliflower, divided into small florets
- 2 parsnips, halved lengthways and sliced
- 1 tablespoon good-quality curry powder
- 1½ quarts chicken or vegetable stock
- salt and freshly ground black pepper
- 2 cups rigatoni

Melt the butter in a large, flameproof casserole or heavy-bottomed saucepan. Add the onion, celery, carrots, green bell pepper, garlic, bay leaf and ginger. Cook, stirring occasionally, for 5 minutes.

Stir in the cauliflower and parsnips; then mix in the curry powder. Pour in the stock, stir well, and add salt and freshly ground black pepper to taste. Bring to a boil, then cover the casserole or pan, and reduce the heat as necessary so that the liquid boils steadily, but not too furiously, for 5 minutes.

Stir in the rigatoni, and bring back to a boil. Cover the casserole or pan again, and cook as before for about 20 minutes, or until the rigatoni is tender. Stir occasionally to insure that the mixture does not stick to the casserole or pan. When cooked, much of the liquid is absorbed, leaving the curry juicy, but not wet.

Marinated Pork with Sautéed Sprouts and Pasta.

113

Hotpot of Venison Meatballs

Ground venison is available from some supermarkets and butchers. It makes a simple pot of meatballs and pasta, but is rich and delicious.

SERVES 4

FOR THE VENISON MEATBALLS	FOR THE SAUCE
• *1 onion, grated*	• *1 onion, sliced*
• *1 cup fresh bread crumbs*	• *1 carrot, halved and sliced*
• *1 garlic clove, crushed*	• *1 celery stalk, sliced*
• *1 teaspoon ground mace*	• *1 bay leaf*
• *1¹/₃ cups finely chopped or*	• *2 sprigs of sage*
ground, rindless bacon	• *1 tablespoon all-purpose*
• *4¹/₂ cups ground venison*	*flour*
• *1 teaspoon finely chopped*	• *2¹/₂ cups chicken stock*
fresh rosemary	• *2¹/₂ cups red wine*
• *salt and freshly ground black*	• *1 tablespoon tomato paste*
pepper	• *2 tablespoons mushroom*
• *1 egg*	*ketchup*
• *1 tablespoon oil*	• *2 cups pasta twists*
	• *4 tablespoons chopped*
	parsley

First, make the Venison Meatballs. Mix the onion, bread crumbs, garlic, mace, bacon, venison, rosemary, plenty of salt and pepper, and the egg in a bowl. Pound the ingredients together with the back of a mixing spoon until they are thoroughly combined. Wet your hands; then shape the mixture into 16 meatballs, kneading the meat together firmly so that they are smooth and well bound on the outside. Rinse your hands under cold water frequently to prevent the meat from sticking to them.

Heat the oil in a large, flameproof casserole or heavy-bottomed saucepan. Brown the meatballs all over, then use a slotted spoon to remove them from the pan and set aside.

Next, prepare the sauce. Add the onion, carrot, celery, bay leaf and sage to the casserole or saucepan. Cook, stirring occasionally, for 5 minutes. Then stir in the flour, and pour in the stock and wine. Add the tomato paste and mushroom ketchup with salt and pepper to taste. Bring to a boil, stirring all the time. Reduce the heat so that the sauce barely simmers, and return the meatballs to the casserole or saucepan. Cover and cook gently for 45 minutes.

Add the pasta, and continue to cook for a further 30 minutes, stirring once or twice, until the pasta is tender.

Taste for seasoning, and stir in the parsley before serving.

Gingered Lamb with Broccoli

Tangy ginger is good with rich lamb, and slightly crunchy broccoli completes the meal-in-a-pot. Use any fresh pasta shapes instead of the paglia e fieno.

SERVES 4

• *2 tablespoons olive oil*	• *1 bay leaf*
• *1 large onion, halved and*	• *2 sprigs of rosemary*
thinly sliced	• *4 tablespoons redcurrant jelly*
• *2 tablespoons peeled, finely*	• *salt and freshly ground black*
chopped, fresh ginger root	*pepper*
• *5 cups diced, lean, boneless*	• *12 ounces fresh paglia e fieno*
lamb	• *2 tablespoons butter*
• *2¹/₂ cups medium cider*	• *1 pound broccoli*
• *2¹/₂ cups chicken stock*	• *²/₃ cup sour cream*

Gingered Lamb with Broccoli

Preheat the oven to 350°F.

Heat the oil in a large, flameproof, ovenproof casserole. Add the onion and ginger, and cook, stirring, for 5 minutes. Then add the lamb, and continue to cook for about 10 minutes, to seal the meat.

Pour in the cider and stock. Add the bay leaf, rosemary and redcurrant jelly, and salt and pepper to taste. Stir until the jelly has melted. Cover the casserole, and bake in the preheated oven for 1¼–1½ hours, or until the lamb is tender.

Taste the sauce for seasoning before adding the pasta. Gently stir the pasta down into the sauce. Cover the casserole, and continue to cook for about 15 minutes, or until the pasta is tender. The pasta takes longer to cook than when added to a saucepan of boiling water, and it should be allowed time to absorb the cooking juices.

Meanwhile, cut the broccoli into small florets, and melt the butter in a large saucepan. Add the broccoli to the pan, and stir well. Cover and cook for 5 minutes, shaking the pan occasionally. The broccoli will cook in the butter and steam from cooking, and, after this time, it should be tender, but still crisp.

Lightly mix the broccoli with the lamb and pasta, then partly swirl in the cream, and serve at once.

115

Contemporary Cock-a-leekie

Pasta is the ideal ingredient for bringing this soup-cum-stew of boiled chicken with leeks and prunes right up to date. Select large pasta shapes for this recipe.

SERVES 6

- *1 cup diced rindless bacon*
- *3-pound chicken*
- *1 large carrot, sliced*
- *1 large onion, sliced*
- *strip of pared lemon rind*
- *1 fresh bouquet garni*
- *1 blade of mace*
- *salt and freshly ground black pepper*

- *5 cups sliced leeks (see Cook's Tip below)*
- *1 pound lumache*
- *6 ounces ready-to-eat prunes, pitted and quartered*
- *4 tablespoons chopped parsley*

COOK'S TIP

Gritty leeks ruin a dish, but how do you get them really clean? Trim the roots and any damaged ends off; then slit the leek lengthwise about halfway through (through the green leaves). Open the leek out, and hold it under running cold water, lifting and separating the leaves. Shake off the excess water before cutting up as required.

Alternatively, for sliced leeks, trim and rinse the leeks; then slice them, and wash the slices in a colander, separating any large ones into rings. Indeed, this is the best way of washing leeks for this recipe.

Put the bacon in a large, heavy-bottomed saucepan, and heat gently until the fat begins to run from the bacon. Then increase the heat, and cook until the bacon is lightly browned.

Meanwhile, make sure the chicken is ready for the pot, that its giblets have been removed, and it is securely trussed. Brown the bird as best you can on all sides; then turn it so that it lies breast-side down in the pot. Add the carrot, onion, lemon rind, bouquet garni, blade of mace and plenty of salt and pepper. Pour in water to cover the chicken completely. Bring the water to a boil, skimming off any scum that rises to the surface. Then top up with water if necessary. Reduce the heat so that the water simmers. Cover the pan, and cook for about 2 hours, turning the chicken over halfway through cooking until the bird is cooked through and tender.

Carefully remove the chicken from the pot, draining the stock into the pan. Add the leeks, pasta and prunes. Bring the soup liquid to a boil, then reduce the heat slightly so that the liquid bubbles at a fast simmer. Partially cover the pan, and cook for 15–20 minutes, or until the pasta is tender. Stir occasionally to make sure that the pasta does not stick to the pan.

Meanwhile, discard the skin from the chicken, and cut the meat off the carcass, carving it in neat pieces. Taste the pasta mixture for seasoning; then stir in the parsley. Ladle the pasta and leeks into large bowls, and top with the chicken.

Beef and Chestnut Stew

Dried chestnuts are available from health food stores as well as some delis. They readily absorb the flavor of the rich cooking liquor in this beef stew, and their floury texture goes well with the beef and pasta to make a satisfying meal. Serve a light vegetable accompaniment with the stew – such as some sautéed zucchini, lightly cooked carrots, cauliflower or Brussels sprouts.

SERVES 4

- *1 cup dried chestnuts*
- *1 tablespoon oil*
- *2/3 cup dried, rindless bacon*
- *2 1/4 pounds lean stewing beef*
- *2 onions, sliced*
- *1 1/3 cups sliced crimini mushrooms*
- *1 fresh bouquet garni*
- *strip of pared orange rind*

- *salt and freshly ground black pepper*
- *2 1/2 cups water*
- *2 1/2 cups stout*
- *1 tablespoon tomato paste*
- *2 cups multicolored pasta shapes*
- *2 tablespoons raisins*
- *sprigs of parsley and halved orange slices, to garnish (optional)*

Put the chestnuts in a bowl, and cover with cold water. Let soak for 4–6 hours.

Pre-heat the oven to 325°F.

Heat the oil in a large, flameproof, ovenproof casserole. Add the bacon and beef, and cook, stirring often, until the beef is sealed, and has lightly browned. Add the onions and mushrooms, and continue to cook for a further 5 minutes, or until the onions are beginning to soften slightly, and the mushrooms have reduced in volume.

Drain the chestnuts, and stir them into the meat mixture. Add the bouquet garni and orange rind with plenty of salt and pepper. Pour in the water, stout and tomato paste, and heat until the liquid is just simmering. Cover the pan, and bake in the preheated oven for 3 hours. Stir the stew occasionally during cooking.

Taste the sauce for seasoning. Add the pasta and raisins, and cook for a further 20–30 minutes, or until the pasta is tender. Remove the orange rind and bouquet garni before serving, or as you ladle out the stew. A garnish of parsley and orange slices may be added to individual portions or to one side of the stew, if you are serving it for a special meal.

117

Long-braised Beef with Tomatoes and Onions

SERVES 6

- 3-pound piece of braising steak
- 6 sage leaves
- 8 ounces rindless bacon slices
- salt and freshly ground black pepper
- paprika
- freshly grated nutmeg
- 6 cups thinly sliced onions
- 2¼ pounds tomatoes, peeled (see Cook's Tip, page 72) and sliced
- 4 tablespoons chopped parsley
- 2 tablespoons chopped fresh thyme
- 2 bay leaves
- 4 tablespoons brandy
- 8 ounces spaghetti

Preheat the oven to 400°F.

The braising steak should be cut in a large, neat piece. Lay the sage leaves on top of the meat. Stretch the bacon slices by laying them on a board, and "spreading" them with the blade of a large kitchen knife. Season the outside of the beef well with salt, pepper, paprika and a little nutmeg. Wrap the slices around the beef, and tie it neatly into shape.

Layer the onions and tomatoes in the bottom of a large ovenproof casserole dish. Sprinkle the layers with plenty of salt and pepper, the parsley and thyme. Add the bay leaves between the onions and tomatoes; place the piece of beef on top.

Warm the brandy in a small saucepan. Have a match ready, and ignite the spirit immediately it is poured over the meat. Cover the casserole tightly, using foil as well as a lid to keep in all the moisture released during cooking. Bake in the preheated oven for 30 minutes, then reduce the temperature to 325°F, and cook for 4 more hours. It is best to leave the meat tightly sealed in the casserole during this time.

Break the spaghetti into short pieces, then drop them into a large saucepan of boiling water, and boil for 5 minutes. Drain well. Remove the covering from the meat. Stir the juices around the meat, and add the spaghetti to them. Cover the casserole again and cook for a further 20 minutes, or until the spaghetti is tender.

Carve the beef, and serve it with the cooked spaghetti and vegetable accompaniments or a side salad.

Ragoût of Rabbit

Prepared boneless rabbit meat is excellent for making casseroles and sauces to go with pasta. Rabbit pieces may also be cooked in this rich ragout and served with pasta that has been boiled separately.

SERVES 4

- 1½ pounds diced, boneless rabbit
- 2 tablespoons all-purpose flour
- salt and freshly ground black pepper
- ½ teaspoon ground mace
- 2 teaspoons chopped fresh rosemary
- 1 tablespoon chopped fresh or 1 teaspoon dried oregano
- 2 tablespoons olive oil
- 1 pound pickling onions, peeled
- 2 garlic cloves, peeled
- 1 cinnamon stick
- 1 bay leaf
- 2½ cups red wine
- 2½ cups chicken stock
- 8 ounces button mushrooms
- 2 cups dried cappelletti or other small pasta shapes

Toss the rabbit with the flour, plenty of salt and pepper, mace, rosemary and oregano. Heat the oil in a flame-proof casserole or heavy-bottomed saucepan. Quickly brown the meat all over. Add the onions, garlic, cinnamon stick and bay leaf. Cook, stirring occasionally, for about 5 minutes, until the onions are beginning to cook. Pour in the wine and stock, and bring to a boil, stirring all the time.

Reduce the heat so that the sauce just simmers, and cover the casserole or pan. Cook gently for 1 hour. Taste the sauce for seasoning (it should be well seasoned to allow for the pasta and mushrooms which will counter-act the sauce). Remove the cinnamon stick. Stir in the mushrooms and cappelletti. Cover the pan. Cook gently for a further 30 minutes, stirring once or twice, until the pasta is tender.

Smoked Sausage and Pasta Hotpot

Cabbage, bacon and apple go together well with macaroni in this simple supper dish that is easy to prepare and delicious with its crusty topping.

SERVES 6-8

- *2 cooking apples, quartered, peeled, cored and sliced*
- *4 tablespoons superfine sugar*
- *1-pound smoked sausage, sliced (see Cook's Tip right)*
- *2 large onions, halved and thinly sliced*
- *5 cups shredded white cabbage*
- *3 cups quick-cook macaroni*
- *salt and freshly ground black pepper*
- *2 bay leaves*
- *1 1/2 quarts medium cider*
- *1 cup fresh white bread crumbs*
- *1/2 cup grated, sharp Cheddar cheese*

Preheat the oven to 350°F.

Mix the apples with the sugar. Layer the sausage, onions, cabbage, apples and macaroni in a large, oven-proof casserole. Sprinkle the layers generously with seasoning, and add the bay leaves between the other ingredients. Pour in the cider, cover the casserole, and bake in the preheated oven for 1 1/2 hours.

Mix the bread crumbs and cheese. Sprinkle this over the top of the casserole, and cook, uncovered, for a further 20 minutes, or until browned. Serve at once.

> ### COOK'S TIP
> Buy one of the meaty Polish sausages for this recipe. Wiejska, for example, a large boiling ring flavored with garlic, is delicious stewed until succulent and tender.

MAIN COURSE SAUCES

— ◆ —

FOR A PASTA COURSE OR MEAL TO BE A SUCCESS, THE SAUCE AND THE CHOSEN PASTA MUST WORK TOGETHER.

THINK IN TERMS OF THE TASTE OF THE SAUCE AND ITS TYPE, THEN DECIDE ON THE PASTA ACCOMPANIMENT. ❧ LIGHTLY FLAVORED DELICATE SAUCES GO WELL WITH FINE PASTA. ❧ FOR EXAMPLE, A THIN SAUCE OF SHRIMP WOULD BE RUINED BY SERVING IT WITH CHUNKY RIGATONI OR HUGE SHELLS – IT WOULD BE RATHER LIKE CUTTING DOORSTEP SLICES OF BREAD AND BUTTER TO

 SERVE WITH THE FINEST, THINNEST PIECES OF SMOKED SALMON. ❧ ON THE OTHER HAND, A RED-HOT CHILI AND GARLIC SAUCE BASED ON A THIN MIXTURE OF TOMATO AND OIL WILL WORK JUST AS WELL WITH CHUNKY PASTA AS IT WILL WITH FINE SPAGHETTI BECAUSE IT IS STRONG ENOUGH TO STAND OUT WHATEVER IT IS SERVED WITH. ❧ REMEMBER, FINE FLAVOR, FINE PASTA.

THE COLOR AND ARRANGEMENT OF PASTA WITH A SAUCE ALSO DESERVES FORETHOUGHT. ❧ SIMPLY LADLING THE SAUCE OVER THE PASTA IS NOT ALWAYS THE BEST OPTION. ❧ INSTEAD SERVE THE TWO ALONGSIDE EACH OTHER IN SHALLOW BOWLS, WHEN THE SAUCE IS A CHUNKY ONE, OR ELSE OFFER THE PASTA SEPARATELY GARNISHED.

EVEN IF THE PASTA AND THE SAUCE ARE SLIGHTLY OUT OF STEP WITH EACH OTHER IN TERMS OF FLAVOR, APPEARANCE AND TEXTURE, *ALL* THE PASTAS TASTE GOOD WITH *ALL* THE SAUCES. ❧ THE ONLY COMBINATION TO AVOID IS AN ORIENTAL PASTA WITH AN ITALIAN SAUCE OR VICE VERSA.

Simple Fish Sauce

This is an ideal way to cook frozen fish fillets or steaks. Smoked fish can be used instead of plain white fish for a little variety, and cooked seafood, such as peeled cooked shrimp, can be added to the sauce for extra texture and flavor. Serve the sauce on a bed of tagliatelle verde or on fettuccine flavored with squid ink. This is a sauce that can be served with any pasta you like.

SERVES 4

- 1½-pound cod fillet
- 1 bay leaf
- 2½ cups milk
- 3 tablespoons butter
- 1 small onion, finely chopped
- 1 small carrot, finely diced
- ⅓ cup all-purpose flour
- 3 cups sliced button mushrooms
- 1 tablespoon horseradish sauce (optional)
- 3 tablespoons chopped parsley
- 1 tablespoon chopped capers
- salt and freshly ground black pepper
- freshly grated Parmesan cheese, to serve

Place the cod in a saucepan or deep skillet. Add the bay leaf, and pour in the milk. Heat gently until the milk is just coming to simmering point. Then remove from the heat, and let cool.

When the fish has cooled, lift it from the milk, and flake the flesh off the skin in large pieces. Reserve the milk.

Melt the butter in a saucepan. Add the onion and carrot, and stir well. Cover and cook for 15 minutes, until the onion has softened.

Meanwhile, strain the reserved milk.

Stir the flour into the onion mixture, then stir in the milk, and bring the sauce to a boil. Add the mushrooms, and cook gently, stirring, for 3 minutes. The liquor from the mushrooms will thin the sauce slightly.

Add the horseradish sauce, parsley, capers, salt and pepper to the sauce, and taste it to check the seasoning. Then add the fish. Cook gently for 2–3 minutes, until the fish is hot. Serve at once, offering freshly grated Parmesan cheese with the sauce and pasta.

Fresh Tuna Sauce

A fresh green chili and some lime juice add satisfying piquancy to this sauce, which has an avocado and sour cream topping. Serve it with shells or other small pasta shapes.

SERVES 4

- 1-pound fresh tuna steak, skinned and cut into 1-inch cubes
- 4 tablespoons olive oil
- grated rind and juice of 1 lime
- 2-ounce can anchovy fillets
- 2 garlic cloves, crushed
- 1 green chili, deseeded and chopped (see Cook's Tip, page 90)
- 1 tablespoon chopped fresh oregano
- 1 onion, finely chopped
- 1 red bell pepper, deseeded and chopped
- 2 × 14-ounce cans chopped tomatoes
- 1⅓ cups sliced mushrooms
- salt and freshly ground black pepper
- 2 avocados
- ⅔ cup sour cream
- 2 tablespoons chopped fresh cilantro

Put the tuna steak in a dish. Pour the olive oil, lime rind and juice over, then cover, and let marinate for 2–4 hours.

Drain the oil from the anchovies into a saucepan, setting the anchovies aside. Add the garlic, chili, oregano, onion and bell pepper. Cook, stirring, for 10 minutes.

Then add the tuna, with the marinade, the tomatoes and mushrooms. Chop the anchovies, and stir them into the sauce with salt and pepper to taste. Heat until just simmering, cover, and cook over a low heat for 40 minutes.

When the fish is cooked, quarter the avocados, and remove the pits and peel; then slice the flesh across into pieces.

Ladle the sauce over a bed of freshly cooked pasta, then swirl with sour cream, and sprinkle with chopped cilantro. Finally, top with the avocado, and serve at once.

Clam Sauce

Clam sauce is a traditional accompaniment for spaghetti. Clams vary enormously in size, and it is not always possible to get the small ones that are about the size of large cockles or mussel shells, so if you can only get big clams, chop them up when cooked.

SERVES 4

- 2 pounds fresh clams
- 4 tablespoons olive oil
- 1 large onion, finely chopped
- 3 garlic cloves, crushed
- 2¼ pounds tomatoes, peeled (see Cook's Tip, page 72), deseeded and diced
- ½ teaspoon sugar
- salt and freshly ground black pepper
- 6 tablespoons chopped parsley
- freshly grated Parmesan cheese, to serve

Clean the clams, and cook them following the instructions in the Cook's Tip and first step of the method on page 126. Strain the cooking liquid through cheesecloth; then boil it, uncovered, until it has reduced to 1¼ cups. Remove the clams from their shells, reserving a few in their shells for garnishing if you like, and set aside.

Heat the olive oil in a saucepan. Add the onion and garlic, and cook gently for 10 minutes.

Then stir in the tomatoes, sugar, plenty of seasoning and the cooking liquor from the clams. Bring to a boil, reduce the heat, and simmer the sauce, uncovered, for 30 minutes.

Add the clams and parsley to the sauce. Taste for seasoning, then pour it over freshly cooked spaghetti, and toss together well before serving. Garnish with any reserved clams, and offer Parmesan cheese with the sauce.

Scallop and Bacon Dressing

**This is a good mixture for folding into freshly cooked
tagliatelle verde.**

SERVES 4

- *2 tablespoons olive oil*
- *2 tablespoons butter*
- *1½ cups diced, rindless bacon*
- *2 large leeks, sliced (see Cook's Tip, page 116)*
- *12 fresh scallops, shelled and sliced*
- *8 ounces tomatoes, peeled (see Cook's Tip, page 72), deseeded and roughly chopped*
- *salt and freshly ground black pepper*
- *6 tablespoons chopped parsley*

Heat the olive oil and butter in a large skillet, wok or saucepan. Add the bacon and leeks; then cook, stirring often, for 20 minutes, or until the leeks are tender.

Add the scallops, and continue to cook slowly for about 3 minutes, turning, rather than stirring, the mixture until the scallops are just firm (the cooking time will depend on the size of the pan and the heat, but it is important to avoid overcooking the scallops as they can quickly become tough).

Add the tomatoes and seasoning to taste, and stir lightly until they are hot. Stir in the parsley just before serving the mixture.

Crab and Zucchini Sauce

**When fresh crab is available, then use it instead of the
tinned crabmeat. This is a good way of making the
small yield from a fresh crab serve four.**

SERVES 4

- *1 quantity White Wine Sauce (see page 60)*
- *8 ounces zucchini, thinly sliced*
- *⅔ cup full-fat soft cheese with herbs and garlic*
- *7-ounce can crabmeat, drained*
- *salt and freshly ground black pepper*
- *a little chopped fresh dill*
- *2-ounce jar lumpfish roe, to serve*
- *sprigs of dill, to garnish (optional)*

First make the sauce as given on page 60.

Add the zucchini, and poach them gently for 5 minutes, until they are lightly cooked (tender, but not soft).

Stir in the soft cheese until melted; then add the crabmeat and salt and pepper to taste.

Ladle the sauce over the chosen pasta; then top each portion with a little chopped dill and a quarter of the lumpfish roe. Garnish with a sprig of dill, if liked, and serve at once.

Poached Salmon in Pink Sauce

SERVES 4

- 1½-pound salmon fillet
- 1¼ cups white wine
- ⅔ cup water
- 1 bay leaf
- 2 tablespoons butter
- ¼ cup flour
- 2 tablespoons tomato paste
- finely grated rind of 1 lemon
- 2 egg yolks
- 1¼ cups light cream
- 1 tablespoon chopped gherkin
- 2 tablespoons chopped parsley
- 2 tablespoons snipped chives
- salt and freshly ground black pepper
- fresh herbs, to garnish

Place the salmon fillet in a saucepan, cutting it into pieces as necessary to fit. Pour in the wine and water. Add the bay leaf, and heat, slowly, until just simmering. Remove the pan from the heat, cover and set it aside until the liquid has cooled. Remove the salmon fillet, and flake the fish off the skin in chunks. Then pour the liquor through a fine strainer and set aside.

Melt the butter in a saucepan. Stir in the flour, and cook, stirring, for 2 minutes. Pour in the salmon cooking liquor, and bring to a boil, stirring all the time. Add the tomato paste and lemon rind. Add the salmon, and allow to heat through very gently.

Beat the egg yolks with the cream; then stir in some of the sauce from the salmon. Pour the cream mixture into the sauce, and heat gently without boiling. Stir in the gherkin, parsley and chives, and season to taste; then serve promptly, pouring the sauce over some freshly cooked pasta. Garnish with fresh herbs.

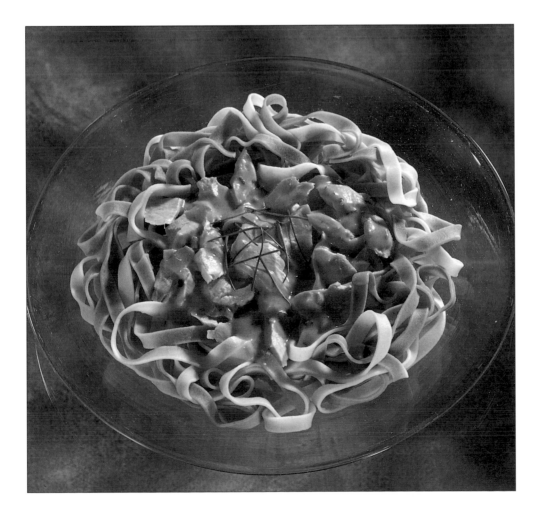

Seafood Sauce

You can vary the seafood used in this sauce according to what is available and personal taste, using the ingredients list below as a guide for your own variations.

SERVES 4

- *1 pound fresh mussels*
- *1 pound fresh cockles or small clams (optional)*
- *1¼ cups water*
- *2 tablespoons olive oil*
- *1 garlic clove, crushed*
- *1 onion, chopped*
- *2 celery stalks, thinly sliced*
- *1 carrot, diced*
- *1⅓ cups sliced mushrooms*
- *¼ cup all-purpose flour*
- *1¼ cups light red wine*
- *1 tablespoon tomato paste*
- *salt and freshly ground black pepper*
- *4 squid sacs, sliced (see Cook's Tip, page 266)*
- *1-pound white fish fillet, skinned and cut into chunks*
- *8–12 uncooked jumbo shrimp*
- *8 fresh scallops, shelled and sliced*
- *freshly grated Parmesan cheese, to serve*

COOK'S TIP

This is how to clean and cook live mussels, clams and cockles.

Thoroughly scrub the shells, and scrape off any barnacles. Discard any open or broken shells which do not close when tapped sharply.

Traditionally, shellfish require purging by leaving them to stand in cold water so that they egest any sand from their shells. Leave the shellfish to soak overnight in a large bucket of cold water with a handful of oatmeal added, leaving the bucket in a cold place.

Next day, drain and rinse the shellfish. Remove the "beards" from the mussels – the group of fine, black hairs that protrude from the shells. Pull them away sharply.

The two important points to remember are, first, to discard opened uncooked shellfish that do not shut when tapped, and, second, to discard any shells that do not open during cooking. In both cases, there is a risk of poisoning as these shellfish are dead, and may contain toxins.

Clean the mussels and cockles or clams, if using (see Cook's Tip below). Put them in a large saucepan, and pour in the water. Bring the water to a boil, then reduce the heat so that the water simmers, and cover the pan. Cook, shaking the pan occasionally, for about 10 minutes, or until all the shells have opened (discard any that do not open). Reserve a few mussels in their shells for garnishing, if you like, then remove the other mussels and cockles or clams from their shells and set aside.

Strain the cooking liquid through cheesecloth, and boil it to reduce it to about 1¼ cups, if necessary. Set this aside.

Heat the olive oil in a saucepan. Add the garlic, onion, celery and carrot. Stir well, cover the pan, and cook gently for 20 minutes, shaking the pan occasionally, until the vegetables are tender, but not browned.

Add the mushrooms and stir in the flour. Slowly pour in the strained cooking liquor and wine. Bring to a boil, stirring, and add the tomato paste. Stir in salt and freshly ground black pepper to taste. Add the squid to the sauce, cover and simmer gently for 15 minutes.

Then add the white fish, and continue to cook, covered, for 10 minutes. Next, add the shrimp, and cook for 5 minutes. Add the scallops, and poach gently for 5 minutes. Lastly, add the cooked mussels and cockles or clams. Heat for a few minutes without simmering or boiling. Taste for seasoning, and serve. Offer freshly grated Parmesan cheese with the sauce and pasta, and garnish with the reserved mussels in their shells, if liked.

Smoked Mackerel with Horseradish Cream

This is a mixture to toss with pasta rather than pour over it.

SERVES 4

- *2 tablespoons butter*
- *1 small onion, chopped*
- *1 1/3 cups sliced button mushrooms*
- *1 pound smoked mackerel fillet, skinned and flaked*
- *4 tablespoons horseradish sauce*
- *1 1/4 cups light cream*
- *2 tablespoons chopped fresh dill*
- *salt and freshly ground black pepper*

Melt the butter in a saucepan. Add the onion, and cook, stirring, for about 10 minutes, or until the onion has softened but not browned. Stir in the mushrooms, and cook for a further 5 minutes.

Then add the mackerel, and heat it slowly. Stir in the horseradish, cream and dill with salt and pepper to taste. Heat the sauce gently without boiling it. Toss the sauce with freshly cooked pasta, and serve at once.

Mussels in Lemon Cream Sauce

Ladle this flavorsome sauce over bowls of freshly cooked pasta shells. Serve with plenty of crusty bread to mop up the juices.

SERVES 4

- *2 pounds fresh mussels*
- *1 1/4 cups dry white wine*
- *2 bay leaves*
- *pared rind of 1 lemon*
- *2 tablespoons butter*
- *1 garlic clove, finely chopped*
- *1 small onion, finely chopped*
- *1 celery stalk, diced*
- *1 tablespoon all-purpose flour*
- *salt and freshly ground black pepper*
- *1 egg yolk*
- *1 1/4 cups light cream*
- *2 tablespoons chopped fresh dill*
- *2 tablespoons chopped parsley*
- *freshly grated pecorino or Parmesan cheese, to serve*

Prepare the mussels as given on page 126 (see Cook's Tip).

Slowly heat the wine, bay leaves and lemon rind in a large saucepan until boiling. Add the mussels, and bring the wine to a boil; then reduce the heat, and cover the pan. Cook for about 10 minutes, shaking the pan occasionally, until all the mussels are open (discard any that do not open). Remove from the heat, and shell the mussels, reserving a few in their shells, if liked, for garnishing.

Strain the cooking liquid from the mussels through fine cheesecloth. Remove the lemon rind, and cut it into fine shreds. Discard the bay leaf.

Heat the butter in a saucepan. Add the onion, celery and lemon rind. Stir well, and cover the pan; then cook for 15 minutes, or until the vegetables have softened.

Stir in the flour, then gradually stir in the strained cooking liquor, and bring to a boil, stirring. Simmer for 3 minutes.

Season the sauce to taste. Add the mussels, and heat gently without boiling. Beat the egg yolk with the cream. Stir in a ladleful of hot sauce, then pour the mixture back into the saucepan, and heat without allowing the sauce to simmer. Stir in the dill and parsley, and serve, offering pecorino or Parmesan cheese separately. If you have reserved some mussels in their shells, use them to garnish the plates of pasta and sauce.

Scallops in Vegetable Sauce

SERVES 4

- 1 leek, sliced (see Cook's Tip, page 116)
- 4 ounces broccoli, divided into small florets
- 2 tablespoons butter
- 1 tablespoon olive oil
- ¼ cup all-purpose flour
- 1¼ cups fish stock
- 1¼ cups dry white wine
- salt and freshly ground black pepper
- 8 ounces snow peas
- 12 fresh scallops, halved or thickly sliced if large
- ¼ cup grated Parmesan cheese
- 4 sprigs of basil, shredded

Heat the butter and oil in a saucepan. Add the leek and broccoli; then cook for 5 minutes, or until reduced in volume. Stir in the flour, then slowly pour in the stock and wine and bring to a boil, stirring. Add a little salt and pepper; then simmer, uncovered, for 3 minutes.

Add the snow peas, and simmer for a further 3 minutes. Then add the scallops, and continue to cook slowly, below simmering point, for about 5 minutes, or until the scallops are just firm (do not allow the sauce to bubble rapidly, or the scallops will quickly toughen).

Stir in the Parmesan, and taste for seasoning; then add the basil, and serve at once.

Lobster and Spinach Topping.

130

Lobster and Spinach Topping

This is a good way in which to use the small ready-cooked lobsters that are easily available from supermarkets, and also sold frozen.

SERVES 4

- 2 small, cooked lobsters (about 1 pound each)
- ¼ cup butter
- 1 small onion, finely chopped
- 2¼ pounds fresh spinach, trimmed, washed and left wet
- salt and freshly ground black pepper
- 8 ounces oyster mushrooms, halved if large
- squeeze of lemon juice
- ⅔ cup fromage frais
- 2 tablespoons freshly grated Parmesan cheese
- lemon wedges, to serve (optional)

Twist off the lobster claws and legs. Crack the claws with nut crackers, and use a meat skewer to pick out all the meat. Break the legs at the joints, and pick out all the meat. Lay one of the lobsters on a board on its back. Use a sharp, pointed knife to cut through the shell along the tail, underneath the firm bright shell which overlaps the jointed section. Do this along both sides so that you can pull off the softer area of shell covering the tail meat. Lift out the tail meat in one piece; then slice it.

Melt half the butter in a large saucepan. Add the onion, and cook, stirring often, for about 10 minutes, or until it has softened but not browned.

Add the wet spinach, cover the pan, and steam it for about 7 minutes, or until it has reduced and is tender. Stir well; then add salt and pepper to taste. Keep hot over a low heat.

Melt the remaining butter in a large skillet, and add the lobster meat with the oyster mushrooms. Sprinkle in salt and pepper. Cook, turning the mushrooms and lobster gently, until both are piping hot. Add a squeeze of lemon juice, the fromage frais and the Parmesan. Stir well; then remove the pan from the heat to prevent the fromage frais curdling.

Give the spinach a stir; then tip it on to a bed of freshly cooked pasta. Top with the lobster and mushrooms, and serve at once with lemon wedges to squeeze over the lobster, if liked.

Smoked Haddock and Egg Sauce

This is good with pasta verde, such as tagliatelle, or shells. It also makes a flavorsome filling for layered pasta dishes, such as lasagne.

SERVES 4

- 2½ cups Béchamel Sauce (see page 60)
- 1½-pound smoked haddock fillet, skinned and cut into chunks
- 4 tablespoons chopped parsley
- 4 eggs, hard-cooked and chopped
- 1⅓ cups thinly sliced button mushrooms
- a little lemon juice
- salt and freshly ground black pepper

Make the Béchamel Sauce as given on page 60, but without adding any salt and pepper.

Stir the smoked haddock into the sauce, and simmer it very gently for about 5 minutes, or until the pieces of fish are just cooked.

Stir in the parsley, eggs, mushrooms and a squeeze of lemon juice. Then add seasoning to taste. Heat gently for about 3 minutes before serving.

Creamed Monkfish with Asparagus

This delicate sauce is the perfect accompaniment for fresh pasta–tagliatelle, paglia e fieno, fettuccine, spaghetti or any slim pasta shapes. Zucchini and Basil Salad (see page 314) or Avocado and Bell Pepper Salad (see page 311) make good side dishes, and offer some crusty bread to mop up the sauce from the plates – you will not want to leave any!

SERVES 4

- *12 ounces fresh asparagus*
- *salt and freshly ground black pepper*
- *1½-pound monkfish fillet*
- *1 small onion, finely chopped*
- *1 bay leaf*
- *1 sprig of tarragon*
- *300 ml/½ pint dry white wine*
- *40 g/1½ oz butter*
- *40 g/1½ oz plain flour*
- *300 ml/½ pint single cream*
- *3 tablespoons chopped fresh dill*
- *sprigs of dill, to garnish*

Trim off any woody parts of the asparagus stalks. Then cook the stalks, covered, in the minimum of boiling salted water for about 15 minutes, or until tender.

Drain, reserving the cooking water. Pour the cooking water back into the saucepan, and boil it hard until it has reduced to about 1¼ cups. Measure 1¼ cups of the cooking water, and set it aside. Cut the asparagus into short lengths, keeping the tips of the stalks separate.

Place the monkfish fillet in a saucepan, and add the onion, bay leaf, tarragon and wine. Add seasoning to taste, and heat gently until simmering. Cover and cook for about 20 minutes, or until the fish is just cooked. Lift the fish from the cooking liquor, and cut it into slices.

Melt the butter in a saucepan. Stir in the flour, and gradually stir in the cooking liquor from the fish, with the bay leaf and onion; then pour in the reserved, reduced asparagus cooking water. Bring to a boil, stirring all the time; then simmer the sauce gently for 5 minutes. Taste for seasoning; then add the monkfish and asparagus, reserving a few tips for garnishing. Heat gently until the fish is hot, then stir in the cream, and heat briefly without allowing the sauce to boil.

Discard the bay leaf and tarragon. Stir in the dill; then serve the sauce poured over freshly cooked pasta, and topped with the reserved asparagus tips. Garnish with sprigs of dill, and serve at once.

Oysters with Julienne Vegetables in White Truffle Sauce

Serve delicate, poached oysters in nests of paglia e fieno as a light lunch or satisfying first course, with slim slices of French bread to mop up the juices. This is deserving of your best homemade pasta or good-quality ready-made pasta and, for a dramatic presentation, nest the oysters in squid-ink fettuccine. It is important to have the fettuccine cooked and ready on hot plates, so that you can serve the oysters the minute they are cooked when they are at their best.

SERVES 4

- *16 fresh oysters*
- *1 small leek*
- *1 small carrot*
- *1¼ cups dry white wine*
- *salt and freshly ground black pepper*
- *4 ounces fresh asparagus tips*
- *1¼ cups crème fraîche*
- *2 tablespoons white truffle paste*

Oysters with Julienne Vegetables in White Truffle Sauce

Thoroughly scrub the oysters. Use a short-bladed, sturdy kitchen or oyster knife to open them, protecting the hand holding the oyster with a thick oven glove as you do this. Hold the oyster with the cupped shell down. Insert the point of the knife into the hinged part of the shell; then twist it firmly, but without jerking the shell apart (which will spill the juices inside). Pour the liquor from the shell into a bowl. Then loosen the oyster from its shell, and slide it into a separate bowl. When all the oysters have been opened, strain the liquor collected from the oysters through cheesecloth to remove any particles of shell.

Put the leek and carrot in a saucepan, then pour in the wine, and add a little seasoning. Bring just to a boil, then reduce the heat, and cover the pan. Simmer gently for 5 minutes.

Add the asparagus, and cook for a further 3 minutes; then add the oysters, and cover the pan. Poach the shellfish very gently for 3–5 minutes, or until they are just firm.

Use a slotted spoon to transfer the oysters and some of the vegetables to the plates. Taste the sauce for seasoning, then stir in the crème fraîche, and heat gently for about 30 seconds without boiling. Stir in the truffle paste, and remove the pan from the heat. Spoon the sauce over the oysters and serve at once.

Swordfish and Tomato Sauce

Firm swordfish steak makes a satisfying sauce to serve with any type of pasta. Halibut, tuna or monkfish may be substituted if preferred, and, indeed, any other thick fillets of white fish will also taste good in the sauce, but cod or haddock fillets should be poached for a shorter period to avoid overcooking them. The sauce may also be layered with lasagne, and topped with Béchamel Sauce (see page 60), then baked.

SERVES 4

- 1½-pound swordfish steak, cut into chunks
- 1 tablespoon chopped fresh marjoram
- 3 tablespoons chopped parsley
- 3 tablespoons olive oil
- 1 garlic clove, crushed
- 1 onion, finely chopped
- 1 green bell pepper, deseeded and chopped
- 2½ cups passata
- ⅔ cup dry white wine
- salt and freshly ground black pepper
- 1½ cups cooked fresh or frozen peas
- grated rind of ½ lemon
- freshly grated Parmesan cheese, to serve

Put the swordfish in a bowl. Sprinkle the marjoram, parsley, olive oil and garlic over. Cover and let marinate for 2–4 hours.

Drain the oil from the fish into a saucepan. Add the onion and bell pepper; then cook, stirring often, for 15 minutes, or until the onion has softened, but not browned.

Stir in the passata and wine, and add seasoning to taste. Add the swordfish, with the herbs, and heat gently until the sauce is just about to simmer. Cover the pan, and cook gently for 20 minutes, or until the fish has cooked.

Add the peas and lemon rind, and taste the sauce for seasoning. Cook gently for a further 5 minutes, or until the peas are hot. Serve with freshly grated Parmesan.

Cucumber and Shrimp Sauce

A light sauce to make a summery meal. Shells, tagliatelle, spaghetti, spirals or cappelletti are all suitable, which indicates that almost any type of pasta will go with this sauce.

SERVES 4

- 1 tablespoon butter
- 1 small onion, finely chopped
- 1 English cucumber, peeled and diced
- ⅔ cup dry white wine
- salt and freshly ground black pepper
- 4 cups peeled, cooked shrimp, defrosted and well-drained if frozen
- 1¼ cups Greek yogurt
- 4 tablespoons freshly grated Parmesan cheese
- 3 tablespoons chopped fresh dill
- whole shrimp and cucumber slices, to garnish (optional)

Melt the butter in a saucepan. Add the onion, and stir well. Cover and cook for 5 minutes. Stir in the cucumber, cover again, and cook for a further 5 minutes. Add the wine, and heat until it is simmering; then cover the pan, and simmer for a further 15 minutes, or until the cucumber is tender.

Add salt and pepper to taste to the cucumber; then stir in the shrimp. Stir in the yogurt and cheese. Heat the mixture gently, stirring all the time (if the yogurt reaches simmering point, it will curdle, so take care to remove it from the heat as soon as the mixture is pleasantly hot enough to eat). Serve immediately, tossed with piping hot, freshly cooked pasta, and garnish with shrimp and cucumber, if liked.

Chicken Supreme

This is an old favorite, but it is a sauce that goes so well with almost any type of pasta that I never tire of it. Serve it with a bowl of tagliatelle verde and a side salad for an informal party, or toss the sauce with pasta shapes for a weekday meal.

As the sauce itself is pale, it looks particularly good if ladled over multicolored pasta shapes. The sauce can be multiplied up to serve a crowd, and it freezes well before the cream is added.

SERVES 4

- 1 tablespoon oil
- 2 tablespoons butter
- 1 small onion, chopped
- 3 boneless chicken breasts, skinned and diced
- 1/3 cup all-purpose flour
- 2/3 cup dry white wine
- 2 cups chicken stock
- 1 bouquet garni
- 12 ounces small button mushrooms
- salt and freshly ground black pepper
- 1 1/4 cups light cream
- 2 tablespoons chopped parsley

Heat the oil and butter in a flameproof casserole. Add the onion, and cook, stirring occasionally, for 10 minutes.

Add the chicken, and brown the pieces lightly all over. Stir in the flour; then cook for 2 minutes before slowly pouring in the wine and stock. Add the bouquet garni, bring the sauce to a boil, and reduce the heat so that it is just simmering.

Stir the mushrooms into the sauce (which is very thick at this stage), and add salt and pepper to taste. Cover the casserole tightly, and cook the sauce gently for 20 minutes. The liquid that the mushrooms yield during cooking will thin the sauce slightly.

Stir the cream into the sauce, and heat it through gently; then add the parsley, and discard the bouquet garni before serving the sauce.

Chicken, Garlic Sausage and Leek Sauté

A good recipe for using leftovers of a roast chicken. The sauce should be used as soon as it is made since it does not freeze or reheat successfully.
Serve it with any pasta shapes – small or large, short or long, thick or thin. Try one of the varieties of tomato-flavored pasta if you like, or pep up the mixture by serving it on a base of chili and tomato spaghetti (if available).

SERVES 4

- *¼ cup butter*
- *1 pound leeks, finely sliced (see Cook's Tip, page 116)*
- *1¾ cups diced, skinless, cooked chicken*
- *1 cup diced garlic sausage*
- *salt and freshly ground black pepper*
- *4 tablespoons good-quality ready-made mayonnaise (not home-made)*

Melt the butter in a large, flameproof casserole or heavy-bottomed saucepan. Add the leeks, and stir well; then cover the pan tightly, and cook for 7–10 minutes, or until the leeks are tender.

Stir in the chicken, garlic sausage, and salt and pepper. Cover again, and simmer for a further 5 minutes, or until the meats are thoroughly hot. If using a cast iron-based pan, which will retain enough heat to keep the sauce bubbling for a while, remove the pan from the heat, and let cool. Otherwise, set over the lowest heat.

Then stir the mayonnaise into the sauce, and taste for seasoning. Serve at once.

Brandied Chicken Livers

SERVES 4

- ¼ cup butter
- 1 onion, finely chopped
- 2 garlic cloves, chopped
- 3 cups roughly chopped chicken livers

- 4 tablespoons brandy
- 1¼ cups sour cream
- 4 tablespoons chopped parsley

Melt the butter in a skillet. Add the onion and garlic, and cook, stirring, for about 15 minutes, or until the onion has softened, but not browned.

Add the chicken livers, and cook, stirring gently and occasionally, for about 15 minutes, or until the livers have cooked.

Pour in the brandy, and immediately ignite it. When the flames have died, stir in the sour cream, and salt and pepper to taste. Heat through without boiling, and taste for seasoning. Stir in the parsley before serving the sauce on freshly cooked pasta.

137

Turkey with Navy Beans and Pesto

A simple, sautéed mixture to toss with tagliatelle, spaghetti or any other of the long pasta shapes. Spoon the Pesto over individual portions of the pasta mixture.

SERVES 4

- *1 pound skinned, boneless turkey breast, cut into thin strips*
- *3 tablespoons all-purpose flour*
- *salt and freshly ground black pepper*
- *grated rind of 1 lemon*

- *1 tablespoon olive oil*
- *2 tablespoons butter*
- *4 scallions, chopped*
- *3 cups sliced mushrooms*
- *15-ounce can navy beans, drained*
- *½ quantity Pesto (see page 67), to serve*

Dust the turkey with the flour, salt, pepper and the lemon rind. Heat the oil and butter in a large skillet. Add the turkey, and cook, turning the strips occasionally, until they are golden brown.

Add the scallions, mushrooms and beans, and continue to cook for 2–3 minutes, or until all the ingredients are hot.

Toss the cooked turkey mixture with your chosen cooked pasta, and serve topped with Pesto to taste.

Duck with Sweet Ginger Sauce

This is good with linguine, spaghetti or bucatini. Serve with the crisp Good Green Salad (see page 312) with some fresh orange segments mixed in.

SERVES 4

- *4 boneless duck breasts, skinned*
- *1 tablespoon cornstarch*
- *salt and freshly ground black pepper*
- *2 tablespoons oil*
- *1 onion, halved and thinly sliced*

- *1 bay leaf*
- *1 sprig of thyme*
- *2 cups dry cider*
- *3 pieces candied ginger, chopped*
- *1 tablespoon syrup from candied ginger jar*

Slice the duck breasts, and toss them with the cornstarch, and salt and pepper.

Heat the oil in a large skillet. Add the onion, bay leaf and thyme. Stir for about 5 minutes to start cooking the onion, then add the duck, and cook, turning and stirring the pieces, until lightly browned in parts.

Stir in the cider, ginger and ginger syrup. Bring to a boil, then reduce the heat, and simmer the sauce, uncovered, for 30 minutes. Taste for seasoning before serving.

Turkey with Navy Beans and Pesto

Cumberland Pheasant

This is a good recipe for a cock pheasant, the tougher bird of a brace. If you have the remains of a couple of roast pheasants, then remove and reserve all the meat from the bones, and stew the carcass with wine to make a stock for making the sauce; then add the reserved meat.

SERVES 4

- 1 tablespoon oil
- 1 onion, sliced
- 1 carrot, sliced
- 1 celery stalk, sliced
- 1 pheasant, cleaned
- 1 fresh bouquet garni
- 2½ cups red wine
- 2½ cups water
- salt and freshly ground black pepper

- 3 oranges
- ⅔ cup diced, rindless bacon
- 8 ounces button mushrooms
- 6 tablespoons redcurrant jelly
- ⅔ cup port
- 2 tablespoons arrowroot or cornstarch
- 3 tablespoons water

Preheat the oven to 350°F.

Heat the oil in a flameproof, ovenproof casserole, add the onion, carrot and celery, and cook for 5 minutes. Then add the pheasant, and brown it lightly all over. Add the bouquet garni. Pour in the wine and water. Stir in salt and pepper to taste; then heat gently to simmering point.

Meanwhile, pare the rind from 1 orange, in 1 or 2 wide strips, and put them in the casserole with the pheasant. Squeeze the juice from the orange, and add it to the casserole. Cover and bake in the preheated oven for 1–1¼ hours, or until the pheasant is tender.

Meanwhile, remove the segments from the remaining oranges in the following way. Slice the top and bottom off each fruit, and peel, removing all the pith. Use a sharp, serrated knife to cut the fruit segments from between the membranes that divide them. Cover and set aside.

Dry-fry the bacon in a large, heavy-bottomed saucepan over a low to medium heat until the fat runs from it. Continue to cook, stirring often, until it has browned. Remove the pheasant from the casserole; then strain the cooking liquor into the pan with the bacon. Bring to a boil, and boil hard until the liquid has reduced by half (to about 2½ cups).

While the liquid is reducing, shred the orange rind strained from the cooking liquid into fine pieces. Cut all the meat off the pheasant in neat pieces, discarding the skin.

Stir the pheasant meat, mushrooms, redcurrant jelly, orange rind and port into the reduced sauce, and continue to simmer gently for 15 minutes.

Blend the arrowroot or cornstarch to a smooth paste with the water. Stir in some of the hot sauce over a low heat; then stir the mixture into the sauce. Bring to a boil, stirring (if using arrowroot, remove the pan from the heat as soon as the sauce boils; if using cornstarch, it should be simmered for 3 minutes). Stir the pheasant meat into the sauce, and taste for seasoning before serving.

CUMBERLAND TURKEY

This recipe is also good for cooking large turkey drumsticks, which can otherwise be rather tough and dry. Simply substitute 2 large turkey drumsticks for the pheasant, and stew them in the wine for the same length of time. Remove all the meat from the drumsticks, taking care to discard all the very fine – and sometimes quite short – bones.

Pheasant with Celery, Grapes and Walnuts

The basic method and sauce ingredients used for this recipe are extremely useful for duck, chicken or turkey, as well as pheasant. I specifically used the pheasant breasts as it is more difficult to find recipes for them. Serve fresh linguine or tagliatelle as a base for the sauce.

SERVES 4

- 4 boneless pheasant breasts, skinned
- 3 tablespoons all-purpose flour
- salt and freshly ground black pepper
- 2 tablespoons butter
- 1 small carrot, finely diced
- 1 onion, chopped
- 1 sprig of rosemary
- 1 bay leaf
- 1 head of celery, sliced
- ½ cup roughly chopped walnuts
- 2 cups pint water
- ⅔ cup Malmsey Madeira
- 1 cup seedless green grapes

Slice the pheasant breasts; then toss the slices with the flour and plenty of salt and pepper. Melt the butter in a flameproof casserole or heavy-bottomed saucepan. Quickly brown the pieces of pheasant, then use a slotted spoon to remove them from the casserole or pan, and set aside.

Add the carrot, onion, rosemary, bay leaf and celery to the fat remaining in the casserole or pan. Stir well, then cover, and cook for 15 minutes, shaking often. Stir in the walnuts, and return the pheasant to the casserole or pan. Add the water, and heat until just simmering. Cover and cook for 45 minutes, or until the celery is tender.

Stir the sauce occasionally during cooking, and taste it for seasoning about halfway through, adding more salt if required. Stir in the Madeira, and bring the sauce to a boil. Remove from the heat, and check the seasoning again. Stir in the grapes, and serve at once.

Casserole of Hare

Pasta is by far the best accompaniment for this casserole. Tagliatelle, linguine, mafaldine, bucatini or any long, slightly thicker pasta shapes are ideal. The quantities can easily be doubled if you want to cook a whole hare. The cooked casserole freezes well.

SERVES 4–6

- ½ hare, chopped into small portions
- ⅓ cup all-purpose flour
- salt and freshly ground black pepper
- ½ teaspoon ground mace
- 1 teaspoon paprika
- 2 tablespoons butter
- 225 g/8 oz boneless belly of pork, skinned and diced
- 1 large onion, chopped
- 1 large carrot, diced
- 2 celery stalks, diced
- 3 cups roughly chopped open mushrooms
- 2 bay leaves
- 2 sprigs of thyme
- 2½ cups robust red wine
- 2 cups water
- ⅔ cup port

Preheat the oven to 325°F.

Dust the hare with the flour, plenty of salt and some pepper, mace and paprika.

Melt the butter in a flameproof, ovenproof casserole, and brown the pieces of hare all over. Then remove them, using a slotted spoon, and set aside. Add the pork, and brown the pieces of meat; then add the onion, carrot and celery. Cook, stirring, for 5 minutes.

Stir in any leftover flour mixture from dusting the hare, the mushrooms, bay leaves, thyme, wine and water. Bring just to a boil, stirring. Return the hare to the casserole, cover and bake in the preheated oven for 3 hours, or until the hare is completely tender.

Transfer the pieces of hare to a serving dish. Boil the cooking liquid, uncovered, for 10 minutes, to reduce it a little, then reduce the heat, and stir in the port. Taste for seasoning, and discard the herbs before serving.

Venison with Dried Peaches

A rich, dark meat sauce to serve with Spätzle (see page 50) or Potato Gnocchi (see page 46), as well as any of the chunkier pasta shapes. Tagliatelle, fettuccine, ziti or mafaldine are also good choices if you want to offer pasta and a meat sauce separately, with a vegetable accompaniment.

SERVES 4

- *1½ pounds stewing venison, trimmed of any fat and cubed*
- *8 juniper berries, crushed*
- *2 garlic cloves, crushed*
- *1 bay leaf*
- *1 sprig of thyme*
- *salt and freshly ground black pepper*
- *a little grated nutmeg*
- *1 bottle of red wine*
- *2 tablespoons dried porcini or boletus mushrooms, sliced*
- *1 tablespoon olive oil*
- *2 cups diced, rindless bacon*
- *1 pound shallots or pickling onions, peeled*
- *3 tablespoons all-purpose flour*
- *¾ cup roughly chopped dried peaches*
- *4 tablespoons redcurrant jelly*
- *3 tablespoons chopped parsley*

Place the venison in a bowl. Add the juniper berries, garlic, bay leaf, thyme, salt and pepper, nutmeg and wine. Mix well, then cover, and leave the meat to marinate for 24 hours.

Put the dried porcini or boletus in a mug or small bowl, and pour in enough hot water to cover them. Set aside to soak for 30 minutes, and preheat the oven to 325°F.

Drain the porcini or boletus, reserving the soaking liquid. Cut the porcini slices into small pieces. Strain the liquid through fine cheesecloth to remove any grit.

Drain the meat well, reserving the marinade.

Heat the oil in a large, heavy-bottomed skillet, add the bacon, and cook until the fat runs from it, stirring occasionally. Add the shallots or pickling onions, and cook until lightly browned all over; then use a slotted spoon to transfer them to an ovenproof casserole. Brown the venison in the fat remaining in the pan, then stir in the flour, and slowly pour in the marinade. Stir until the sauce just boils; then transfer the meat and sauce to the casserole.

Stir the porcini or boletus, their soaking liquid and the dried peaches into the venison mixture. Cover tightly, and bake in the preheated oven for about 3 hours, or until the meat is very tender. Stir twice during cooking.

Stir in the redcurrant jelly until it has melted, add the chopped parsley, then taste for seasoning before serving.

Venison with Dried Peaches

Venison Stroganoff

A variation on the traditional recipe using beef, this is rich and delicious with tagliatelle or paglia e fieno.

SERVES 4

- *1½ pounds venison steak*
- *2 tablespoons all-purpose flour*
- *salt and freshly ground black pepper*
- *2 tablespoons butter*
- *1 large onion, halved and thinly sliced*
- *3 cups thinly sliced mushrooms*
- *4 tablespoons brandy*
- *1¼ cups red wine*
- *6 tablespoons chopped parsley*
- *⅔ cup sour cream*

Cut the venison across the grain into fine strips. Toss these with the flour and plenty of seasoning.

Melt the butter in a large skillet. Brown the venison in the butter, then add the onion and mushrooms, and continue cooking, stirring often, for about 15 minutes, or until the onion has softened slightly.

Warm the brandy in a small saucepan. Ignite it, and pour it over the venison mixture. When the flames have died, add the wine, and bring to a boil, stirring. Simmer the sauce gently for 5 minutes. Remove the pan from the heat, stir in the parsley, and swirl in the sour cream; then serve at once.

Meatballs

Meatballs in tomato sauce are a classic topping for pasta. Serve them with spaghetti, tagliatelle, perciatelli or other long pasta. For slightly easier eating, ladle the mixture over short pasta shapes.

SERVES 4

- *4 cups ground beef*
- *1 onion, finely chopped*
- *4 tablespoons grated Parmesan cheese*
- *grated rind of 1 lemon*
- *⅓ cup very finely chopped or ground rindless bacon*
- *½ cup fresh bread crumbs*
- *1 teaspoon grated nutmeg*
- *salt and freshly ground black pepper*
- *1 large egg*
- *1 tablespoon olive oil*
- *1 quantity Light Fresh Tomato Sauce (see page 59) or Rich Tomato Sauce (see page 58)*
- *4 tablespoons chopped parsley*
- *1 large garlic clove, finely chopped (optional)*

Mix the ground beef, onion, Parmesan, half the lemon rind, the bacon, bread crumbs, nutmeg, salt and pepper to taste, and the egg. Pound the mixture with the back of a mixing spoon until the ingredients are thoroughly combined. Alternatively, the ingredients may be kneaded together by hand.

To shape the meatballs, use a teaspoon to pick up lumps of mixture. Wet your hands; then press and mold the mixture into a small, smooth ball. Repeat with the remaining mixture, which makes 20 meatballs about the size of walnuts.

Heat the oil in a large, deep, lidded skillet or flameproof casserole, and fry the meatballs for 15–20 minutes, turning and rolling them carefully with one or two spoons to make them a neat, round shape.

When the meatballs have browned all over, add the tomato sauce, and bring to a boil. Reduce the heat, cover and simmer with the meatballs for 30 minutes, stirring and turning them once during this time.

Mix the remaining lemon rind with the parsley and garlic, if using. Ladle the meatballs over the pasta base, and sprinkle with the parsley mixture. Serve at once.

Classic Meatballs with Penne

Goulash

Spätzle or potato gnocchi are ideal accompaniments for a hearty goulash, but tagliatelle or mafaldine are often the favored side dishes for a casual party menu.

SERVES 4

- *5 cups cubed stewing beef*
- *2 tablespoons mild paprika*
- *2 tablespoons all-purpose flour*
- *salt and freshly ground black pepper*
- *2 tablespoons oil*
- *2 garlic cloves, crushed*
- *2 large onions, halved and thinly sliced*
- *1 red bell pepper, deseeded and diced*
- *2¼ pounds tomatoes, peeled (see Cook's Tip, page 72), deseeded and chopped*
- *1 teaspoon sugar*
- *1¼ cups beef stock*
- *⅔ cup sour cream, to serve (optional)*

Toss the beef with the paprika, flour and plenty of salt and pepper. Heat the oil in a flameproof casserole, and brown the meat all over; then use a slotted spoon to remove it to a plate.

Add the garlic, onions and red pepper, and cook, stirring, for 10 minutes. Return the meat, and add the tomatoes. Stir in the sugar and stock. Bring to a boil; then reduce the heat so that the mixture simmers. Cover tightly, and cook slowly for 2½–3 hours, or until the meat is tender.

Stir the goulash occasionally during cooking. Taste for seasoning at the end of cooking. Sour cream may be served with the goulash if liked.

Hot Beef Sauce

SERVES 4

- 1½ pounds rump steak
- 4 garlic cloves, crushed
- 2 green chilis, deseeded and diced (see Cook's Tip, page 90)
- 2 tablespoons ground coriander
- grated rind and juice of 1 lime
- salt and freshly ground black pepper
- 2 tablespoons oil
- 2 large onions, halved and thinly sliced
- 1 red bell pepper, halved, deseeded and thinly sliced
- 14-ounce can chopped tomatoes
- 2 avocados
- 1 papaya
- 4 tablespoons chopped fresh cilantro
- ⅔ cup sour cream

Cut the steak across the grain into fine strips. Mix these with the garlic, chilis, ground coriander, grated lime rind and juice. Add plenty of seasoning, and set aside to marinate for several hours or overnight.

Heat the oil in a large skillet. Fry the steak, reserving the lime juice from marinating, until it is lightly browned. Add the onions and bell pepper; then continue to cook for about 20 minutes, or until the onion has softened.

Add the reserved lime juice and tomatoes, and bring to a boil, stirring. Taste for seasoning.

Cut the avocados into quarters, remove their pits, and peel them; then slice each section across into small pieces. Halve the papaya, scoop out the seeds, and peel the fruit. Cut the pieces of papaya in half lengthways, then across into pieces of a similar size to the avocado.

Mix the avocado, papaya and cilantro with the beef. Taste the mixture for seasoning; then serve it on a bed of cooked pasta. Top with sour cream, or offer this separately, and serve at once.

Rich Ragoût

A rich sauce of the Bolognese type, this may be served with spaghetti or long pasta. It is also especially good with shells, lumache or other shapes that will scoop up some of the sauce.

SERVES 4

- ¼ cup dried mushrooms (ceps or porcini are good)
- ⅔ cup hot water
- 2 tablespoons olive oil
- 3⅓ cups finely diced stewing beef
- 1¾ cups finely diced, lean boneless pork
- 1¾ cups chopped chicken livers
- 2 garlic cloves, crushed
- 2 onions, chopped
- 1 green bell pepper, deseeded and diced
- 1 bay leaf
- 1 tablespoon chopped fresh oregano
- 1 tablespoon chopped fresh thyme
- 4 tablespoons brandy
- 2½ cups robust red wine
- 1¼ cups passata
- salt and freshly ground black pepper
- 3 cups chopped mushrooms
- freshly grated Parmesan cheese, to serve

Soak the mushrooms in the water for 30 minutes. Then drain them well, and chop them. Strain the soaking liquor through cheesecloth to remove grit from the mushrooms, and set aside.

Heat the oil in a large, flameproof casserole or heavy-bottomed saucepan. Add the beef, pork and chicken livers, and cook, stirring, until the meats are sealed. Stir in the garlic, onions and bell pepper; then cook for a further 10 minutes.

Add the bay leaf, oregano and thyme. Pour in the brandy, wine, passata and strained soaking water. Add the prepared dried mushrooms and plenty of seasoning. Bring just to boiling point, stirring, then reduce the heat, and cover the casserole or pan. Simmer very gently for 2½ hours, or until the meat is extremely tender. Stir occasionally to insure that the meat does not stick to the bottom of the casserole or pan.

Add the mushrooms, and cook, uncovered, for 30 minutes. Taste and adjust the seasoning before serving with Parmesan cheese.

Piquant Diced Lamb

Fresh chilis bring this lamb mixture to life. It is delicious with substantial pasta shapes, such as long mafaldine or pappardelle, or chunky rigatoni, cicatelli di San Severo or lumache.

SERVES 4

- *5 cups diced, lean, boneless lamb*
- *1–2 fresh green chilis, deseeded and chopped (see Cook's Tip, page 90)*
- *2 garlic cloves, crushed*
- *salt and freshly ground black pepper*
- *grated rind and juice of 1 orange*
- *1 tablespoon chopped fresh oregano*
- *1 tablespoon ground coriander*
- *2 tablespoons olive oil*
- *1 large onion, chopped*
- *1 red bell pepper, deseeded and diced*
- *2 tablespoons all-purpose flour*
- *2½ cups lamb or chicken stock*

Mix the lamb with the chilis, garlic, plenty of salt and pepper, the orange rind, oregano and coriander. Cover and let marinate for at least 2–3 hours or overnight.

Heat the oil in a flameproof casserole, and brown the meat. Then add the onion and bell pepper, and cook, stirring, for 5 minutes.

Stir in the flour; then pour in the stock and orange juice. Bring just to a boil, then reduce the heat, and cover the pan. Simmer the sauce very gently for 1 hour. Taste for seasoning before serving.

Scotch Lamb Sauce

Serve this rich meat sauce with Potato Gnocchi (see page 46) or large pasta shapes.

SERVES 4

- 1 cup cored, diced lambs' kidneys
- 5 cups diced, lean, boneless lamb
- 3 tablespoons all-purpose flour
- salt and freshly ground black pepper
- 2 tablespoons oil
- 1 large onion, halved and thinly sliced
- 2 carrots, halved and sliced
- 1 bouquet garni
- 1 blade of mace

- 2½ cups water
- 3 tablespoons mushroom ketchup
- 1 tablespoon butter
- 1 large leek, thinly sliced (see Cook's Tip, page 116)
- 1⅓ cups sliced crimini mushrooms
- ⅔ cup whiskey
- ⅔ cup single cream (optional)
- 2 tablespoons chopped parsley

Preheat the oven to 325°F.

Mix the kidneys with the lamb; then toss both with the flour and plenty of seasoning (the mixture requires more salt than usual as the sauce makes its own stock). Heat the oil in a large, flameproof, ovenproof casserole. Brown the meat and kidney mixture; then add the onion, carrots, bouquet garni and blade of mace. Cook, stirring for 5 minutes.

Pour in the water, and stir in the mushroom ketchup. Bring just to a boil, stirring, then cover tightly, and bake in the preheated oven for 2 hours, or until the lamb is extremely tender.

Meanwhile, melt the butter in a skillet, and sauté the leek and mushrooms for 2–3 minutes, or until reduced in volume and lightly cooked. Stir the leek mixture and whiskey into the casserole. Taste for seasoning; then bake for a further 30 minutes.

Finally, remove the bouquet garni and blade of mace. Check the seasoning again; then stir in the cream (if used) and parsley before serving.

Beef with Bell Peppers

This goes well with the long types of pasta or with Potato Gnocchi or Spätzle (see pages 46 and 50).

SERVES 4

- 1 pound frying steak
- 3 tablespoons all-purpose flour
- salt and freshly ground black pepper
- 1 tablespoon chopped fresh thyme
- 2 tablespoons olive oil

- 1 large onion, halved and thinly sliced
- 2 red bell peppers, halved, deseeded and thinly sliced
- 1 green bell pepper, halved, deseeded and thinly sliced
- 2 cups beef stock

Toss the steak with the flour, plenty of seasoning and thyme. Heat the oil in a large skillet, and brown the meat strips; then add the onion, and red and green bell peppers (see Cook's Tip, page 65). Cook, stirring, for about 15 minutes, or until the onion has softened slightly.

Stir in the beef stock, and bring to a boil. Reduce the heat as soon as the sauce begins to boil, so that it simmers gently. Cover the pan, and simmer for 20 minutes. Taste for seasoning before serving.

Scotch Lamb Sauce with Potato Gnocchi

Ham and Olive Dressing

This delicious mixture is chunky, so it goes well with short, fairly large pasta shapes. Wide, long shapes, such as tagliatelle verde or mafaldine, are also suitable accompaniments.

SERVES 4

- *2 tablespoons olive oil*
- *1 large onion, thinly sliced*
- *1 garlic clove, crushed*
- *2 large sprigs of thyme*
- *1 bay leaf*
- *2 large sprigs oregano or marjoram*
- *2 large sage leaves, shredded*
- *2½ cups diced, lean, uncooked ham steak*
- *1⅓ cups sliced mushrooms*

- *1 pound tomatoes, peeled (see Cook's Tip, page 72) and roughly chopped*
- *9 black olives, pitted*
- *4 tablespoons pale cream or dry sherry*
- *salt and freshly ground black pepper*
- *freshly grated Parmesan cheese, to serve*

Heat the olive oil in a large, flameproof casserole. Add the onion, garlic, thyme, bay leaf, oregano or marjoram and sage. Stir well, cover and cook, stirring occasionally, for 15 minutes.

Add the ham, and cook until the pieces have lightly browned in parts, turning and stirring occasionally to prevent them sticking.

Stir in the mushrooms, tomatoes, olives and sherry. Add a little pepper to taste, and heat until the mixture is steadily bubbling. Cover tightly, and simmer for 5 minutes, not boiling the mixture too rapidly (when the dressing is cooked, the tomatoes should be more or less broken down, but not completely reduced to a pulp).

Taste the sauce for seasoning before serving (it is best not to add salt at the earlier stage as the ham may be quite salty). Ladle the sauce over the pasta, and serve with Parmesan and extra black pepper, if liked.

Ham and Beet Sauce

Flavorsome ham tastes terrific with slightly sweet beet and tangy orange. If you want to serve the sauce with long, thin pasta, such as spaghetti, then dice the ham and vegetables quite small so that they are easy to eat.

SERVES 4

- *2 tablespoons olive oil*
- *2½ cups diced, lean, uncooked ham steak*
- *1 large or 2 medium onions, chopped*
- *2 garlic cloves, crushed*
- *2-inch strip of pared orange rind*
- *1 carrot, diced*
- *1 bay leaf*

- *12 sage leaves, shredded*
- *1 tablespoon all-purpose flour*
- *1¼ cups red wine*
- *⅔ cup water*
- *juice of 1 orange*
- *salt and freshly ground black pepper*
- *2½ cups diced, cooked beets (see Cook's Tip below)*

COOK'S TIP

Vacuum-packed cooked beets are a good alternative to freshly boiled beets in this recipe. Avoid beets preserved with any acid or vinegar, though.

150

Ham and Beet Sauce

Heat the oil in a flameproof casserole or heavy-bottomed saucepan. Add the ham, onion, garlic, orange rind, carrot, bay leaf and sage. Stir well, then cover, and cook for 15 minutes.

Stir in the flour, and cook for about 1 minute; then pour in the wine, water and orange juice. Bring to a boil, stirring, then reduce the heat, cover and simmer for 15 minutes. Add salt and pepper to taste, and stir in the beetroot. Stir for 1–2 minutes, or until the beets are hot, before serving.

151

Smoked Pork with Sauerkraut

Spätzle (see page 50), Potato Gnocchi (see page 46) or Kopytka (see page 48) are ideal accompaniments to make a hearty meal of this full-flavored mixture. However, any other short pasta shapes may be served with this fairly chunky sauce.

SERVES 4

- 2 tablespoons olive oil
- 1 large onion, chopped
- 1 large carrot, diced
- 1 celery stalk, thinly sliced
- 1 garlic clove, crushed
- 1 bay leaf
- 1 pound sauerkraut
- 2½ cups diced smoked pork loin
- salt and freshly ground black pepper
- 1¼ cups chicken stock
- 1¼ cups dry white wine
- ⅓ cup raisins
- ¼ cup butter
- 4 teaspoons all-purpose flour
- about 8 large sprigs of dill, chopped
- a little paprika

Heat the olive oil in a large, flameproof casserole. Add the onion, carrot, celery, garlic and bay leaf. Stir well, cover the casserole, and cook for 10 minutes.

Meanwhile, drain the sauerkraut. Squeeze a handful lightly to remove excess liquid; then slice the clump with a sharp knife to shred it. Add the shredded sauerkraut, pork loin, and salt and pepper to taste to the vegetables, and stir well. Cover the casserole, and cook for a further 5 minutes.

Pour in the stock and wine, stir in the raisins, and bring just to a boil. Reduce the heat, cover the casserole tightly, and simmer the mixture for 10 minutes. While the mixture is cooking, cream the butter to a smooth paste with the flour. Bring the mixture to a boil, then stir in lumps of the paste, and continue to stir until the cooking juices have boiled and thickened slightly.

Taste the mixture for seasoning before stirring in the dill. Then serve at once, sprinkled with a little paprika.

Creamed Pork in Cider

SERVES 4

- 2 tablespoons olive oil
- 5½ cups diced, lean boneless pork
- 1 onion, chopped
- 2 eating apples, peeled, cored and diced
- 2 tablespoons raisins
- 2 tablespoons all-purpose flour
- 2½ cups dry cider
- 6 sage leaves, shredded
- salt and freshly ground black pepper
- ⅔ cup light cream
- freshly grated pecorino or Parmesan cheese, to serve

Heat the oil in a flameproof casserole or heavy-bottomed saucepan. Add the pork, and brown the pieces all over. Stir in the onion, apples and raisins. Cook for 2 minutes, then add the flour, and stir for a further 2 minutes. Pour in the cider, and add the sage with salt and pepper to taste. Heat until simmering, then cover the casserole or pan, and simmer gently for 1¼ hours, or until the pork is tender.

Taste for seasoning, and stir in the cream before serving. Offer pecorino or Parmesan with the sauce and pasta.

Smoked Pork with Sauerkraut and Potato Gnocchi

Amatriciana Sauce

Serve this thin sauce, pepped up with chili, with spaghetti, bucatini or any slim pasta.

SERVES 4

- 4 tablespoons olive oil
- 2 red chilis, deseeded and chopped (see Cook's Tip, page 90)
- 1 red bell pepper, deseeded and chopped
- 1 bay leaf
- 1 onion, chopped
- 2 garlic cloves, chopped
- 1⅓ cups diced, rindless bacon
- 2¼ pounds tomatoes, peeled, deseeded and chopped
- 1 teaspoon sugar
- salt and freshly ground black pepper
- freshly grated pecorino or Parmesan cheese, to serve

Heat the oil in a saucepan. Add the chilis, bell pepper, bay leaf, onion, garlic and bacon. Fry the mixture for 15 minutes; then add the tomatoes, sugar and plenty of seasoning. Heat until the tomatoes are bubbling merrily, then cover the pan tightly, and cook for about 45 minutes, stirring occasionally, until the sauce is thick and rich.

Taste the sauce for seasoning, then serve with pasta, and offer pecorino or Parmesan cheese separately.

Chorizo with Garbanzo Beans

A rich passata-based sauce, this brings spicy Spanish sausage and nutty garbanzo beans together. This is another sauce that will work well with almost any type of pasta, from elbow macaroni to ziti.

SERVES 4

- 2 tablespoons olive oil
- 1 onion, chopped
- 2 garlic cloves, crushed
- 1 celery stalk, diced
- 1 green bell pepper, deseeded and diced
- 1½ cups diced chorizo
- 3 cups sliced mushrooms
- 2 × 15-ounce can garbanzo beans
- 2 cups passata
- salt and freshly ground black pepper
- lots of chopped parsley
- ⅔ cup sour cream and/or freshly grated Parmesan cheese, to serve (optional)

Heat the olive oil in a saucepan. Add the onion, garlic, celery and green bell pepper. Cook, stirring often, for 10 minutes.

Stir in the chorizo, mushrooms, garbanzo beans with the liquid from the cans, passata, and salt and pepper. Bring to a boil, reduce the heat and cover the pan. Then simmer the mixture for 15 minutes.

Taste for seasoning, and stir in lots of chopped parsley just before serving. Offer sour cream and/or Parmesan cheese with the sauce, if liked.

Boscaiola Sauce

This "woodcutter's sauce" goes well with any short pasta shapes, such as penne, rigatoni, spirals or bows. If available, porcini-flavored pasta in novelty mushroom shapes may be served as a base for this sauce.

SERVES 4

- 4 tablespoons olive oil
- 4 1/2 cups sliced crimini mushrooms
- 2 garlic cloves, crushed
- 1 bay leaf
- 1 1/2 cups passata
- 2/3 cup diced prosciutto or cooked ham
- salt and freshly ground black pepper

Heat the olive oil in a large saucepan. Add the mushrooms, garlic and bay leaf; then cook, stirring occasionally, for 10 minutes.

Stir in the passata, ham, and salt and pepper to taste. Bring to simmering point, stirring, then cover the pan tightly, and simmer the sauce for a further 10 minutes. Taste for seasoning before serving.

Cotechino with Borlotti Beans

This rich, meaty sauce is delicious and satisfying. It is an ideal candidate for cooking ahead as its flavor improves when it is reheated; it also freezes well. Large pasta shapes and types that are traditionally served with meat sauces are the best accompaniments as the sauce is a chunky one. Dried gnocchi shapes, Potato Gnocchi (see page 46), Spätzle (see page 50), Kopytka (see page 48), large spirals, shells, penne, rigatoni, cicatelli di San Severo, orecchiette or gli strozzapreti are all very good with this sauce. The mixture also makes a rich filling for lasagne, topped with a Béchamel Sauce (see page 60) before baking.

SERVES 4

- 2/3 cup dried borlotti beans, soaked overnight (see Cook's Tip below)
- 1 pound cotechino or fresh Italian sausage
- 3 tablespoons olive oil
- 1 large onion, chopped
- 1 bay leaf
- 2 garlic cloves, crushed
- 1 tablespoon chopped fresh oregano
- 1 1/4 cups red wine
- 2 tablespoons tomato paste
- salt and freshly ground black pepper

Drain the beans, and boil them in plenty of fresh water for 10 minutes. Then reduce the heat slightly, partially cover the pan, and continue boiling the beans for a further 30 minutes, or until they are just tender.

Meanwhile, skin the sausage, and break or cut the meat into chunks. Cook the chunks of sausage in a heavy-bottomed flameproof casserole, stirring often, until they are browned all over. If necessary, trickle a little of the olive oil into the pan first, but there is usually plenty of fat in the sausagemeat to brown it. Use a slotted spoon to remove the sausage from the pan.

Drain off any excess fat, if necessary; then add the olive oil to the casserole. Add the onion, bay leaf, garlic and oregano, and cook, stirring occasionally, for 10 minutes. Stir in the wine, tomato paste, just a little salt and pepper, then bring to a boil, cover and simmer for 5 minutes.

Drain the beans, and stir them into the sauce with the sausage. Cover tightly, and simmer the mixture gently for 1 1/4–1 1/2 hours, or until the sausage is completely tender. Stir occasionally during cooking to prevent the mixture sticking to the pan. Taste for seasoning, and add more salt if necessary before serving.

COOK'S TIP

Never add salt to the cooking water for dried beans as it prevents them softening. Season beans, or the sauces to which they are added, only after they have been cooked, and are completely tender.

Liver with Bell Peppers and Pine Nuts

Serve this cream-dressed liver and bell pepper mixture on a bed of tagliatelle, or toss it with slim pasta shapes, such as spirals or bows.

SERVES 4

- *4 tablespoons pine nuts*
- *1 pound lambs' or calves' liver, cut into thin strips*
- *2 tablespoons all-purpose flour*
- *salt and freshly ground black pepper*
- *2 tablespoons butter*
- *2 tablespoons olive oil*
- *8 ounces rindless bacon, cut into thin strips*
- *1 large onion, halved and thinly sliced*
- *1 green bell pepper, deseeded and sliced*
- *1 red bell pepper, deseeded and sliced*
- *6 sage leaves, shredded*
- *4 tablespoons brandy*
- *²/₃ cup sour cream*
- *4 large sprigs of basil, shredded*

Dry roast the pine nuts in a small, heavy-bottomed saucepan over a low to medium heat until they are lightly browned. Shake the pan often to prevent the pine nuts overbrowning on one side. Set aside.

Dust the liver with the flour and plenty of seasoning. Heat the butter and olive oil; then fry the liver, turning often, until just lightly browned in parts, firm and cooked. Use a slotted spoon to remove the liver from the pan, and set it aside.

Add the bacon, onion, green and red bell peppers, and sage to the fat remaining in the pan. Cook, stirring, for about 15 minutes, or until the bacon and vegetables are just cooked.

Return the liver to the pan, stirring it gently with the vegetables, and pour in the brandy. Add a little salt and pepper, if necessary; then heat the liver through for about 2 minutes.

Swirl the sour cream into the liver; then turn it out onto a bed of cooked pasta. Sprinkle with the basil and pine nuts, and serve at once.

158

Creamed Eggs with Smoked Salmon

Good old scrambled eggs turn up trumps again, but this time with the help of some smoked salmon. The important point to remember when scrambling eggs for serving with pasta is that they should be cooked until just creamy; then the pasta should be tossed with them.
If they are cooked until set, then, by the time the pasta is mixed in, the eggs will be overcooked.

SERVES 4

- 4 ounces smoked salmon offcuts
- 4 tablespoons snipped chives
- 8 eggs
- ⅔ cup light cream
- salt and freshly ground black pepper
- ¼ cup butter

Cut the smoked salmon pieces into slim strips, and mix them with the chives. Beat the eggs with the cream, adding salt and pepper to taste.

Melt the butter in a saucepan over a gentle heat (do not heat it too fiercely, or the eggs will begin to set as soon as they are added to the pan). Pour in the egg mixture, and whisk it constantly over a low to medium heat until they begin to thicken.

Stir in the smoked salmon, chives and freshly cooked pasta. Serve at once.

Poached Eggs with Creamed Watercress

SERVES 4

- ¼ cup butter
- 2 bunches watercress, leaves only, chopped
- 2 scallions, finely chopped
- 1¼ cups light cream
- salt and freshly ground black pepper
- freshly grated nutmeg
- a little vinegar
- 8 fresh eggs
- sprigs of watercress, to garnish
- freshly grated Parmesan cheese, to serve

Melt the butter in a saucepan. Add the watercress and scallions. Stir over a low heat for 5 minutes; then add the cream with salt, pepper and nutmeg to taste. Set aside over a low heat.

Prepare a skillet or saucepan of water for poaching the eggs. Add salt and a splash of vinegar; then bring the water to a steady simmer. Crack the eggs into a saucer one at a time, swirl the water gently, and slide in the egg. Continue adding the eggs, swirling the water in different areas of the pan, until all are added. Poach the eggs until cooked to taste (about 3 minutes for a set white and soft yolk). Use a slotted spoon to remove the eggs from the pan, and trim their edges with a knife or kitchen scissors.

Toss freshly cooked pasta with the hot watercress cream, then transfer to heated serving plates or a suitable dish and top with the eggs. Garnish with sprigs of watercress and serve with Parmesan.

Puffed Eggs on Pasta

This is definitely not a recipe for healthy eating, but, if you have sampled – and enjoyed – deep-fried eggs, then it makes a simple family treat. Have tagliatelle, vermicelli, mafaldine or spaghetti piping hot ready to toss with the sauce, and top with the eggs. Poached or soft-boiled eggs may be served instead of deep-fried eggs.

SERVES 4

- 2 tablespoons olive oil
- 1 small onion, finely chopped
- 1 garlic clove, crushed
- 1 red bell pepper, deseeded and diced
- 1 green bell pepper, deseeded and diced
- 8 ounces tomatoes, peeled (see Cook's Tip, page 72), deseeded and diced
- salt and freshly ground black pepper
- 4 tablespoons chopped parsley
- 4 eggs
- oil, for deep-frying

Heat the olive oil in a saucepan. Add the onion, garlic, and red and green bell peppers. Stir well, then cover the pan and cook for 20 minutes, or until the vegetables have softened. Stir in the tomatoes with plenty of seasoning, and cook for a further 5 minutes. Add the parsley, and toss the mixture with freshly cooked pasta. Turn into a serving dish, and keep hot.

Heat sufficient oil to deep-fry the eggs to 350°F, or until a cube of day-old bread browns in 30 seconds. Crack an egg on to a saucer; then slide it into the hot oil. Stand well back as you do this, and work from the side of the pan, rather than above it, as the oil does spit. Use a slotted spoon to ease the egg gently off the bottom of the pan, if necessary, after a few seconds. It will float to the surface when cooked. Lift the egg with a slotted spoon at this point, and let all the oil drain off before transferring the egg to the pasta.

Cook all the eggs in the same way – they only take a few seconds to cook, and it is possible to cook two at a time. Serve the pasta topped with the eggs, immediately.

Poached Eggs with Creamed Watercress

Spaghetti with Cidered Eggs and Gruyère

Break the spaghetti up slightly before cooking it rather than leaving it in long pieces.

SERVES 4

- *3 tablespoons butter*
- *6 shallots or 1 mild white salad onion, chopped*
- *1 bay leaf*
- *⅓ cup all-purpose flour*
- *2 cups milk*
- *1¼ cups dry cider*

- *salt and freshly ground black pepper*
- *1½ cups grated Gruyère cheese*
- *6 eggs, hard-cooked and chopped*

Melt the butter in a saucepan. Add the shallots or mild onion and bay leaf. Cook, stirring, for 10 minutes, then stir in the flour, and cook for a further 2 minutes.

Gradually stir in the milk, and bring to a boil, stirring all the time. The sauce will be very thick, but it must thicken before the cider is added to prevent curdling. Gradually stir in the cider, and add salt and pepper to taste. Add the Gruyère, and continue stirring over a low heat until it has melted.

Remove the pan from the heat, stir in the eggs and spaghetti, and serve at once.

162

Chopped Herb Omelet with Mushrooms

This is a simple and tasty way to make a nutritious pasta meal. Serve a side salad as an accompaniment, such as Zucchini and Basil Salad (see page 314) or a Good Green Salad (see page 312). The pasta must be freshly cooked so that the omelet can be tossed with it immediately it has set.

SERVES 2

- 2 tablespoons butter
- 1 tablespoon olive oil
- 3 cups sliced, small button mushrooms
- 2 eggs
- salt and freshly ground black pepper
- 1 tablespoon chopped parsley
- 1 tablespoon snipped chives
- 1 teaspoon chopped fresh
- tarragon
- 2 tablespoons water
- freshly grated Parmesan
- cheese, to serve

Melt half the butter and the oil in a large saucepan. Add the mushrooms, and cook, stirring occasionally, while you cook the omelet.

Beat the eggs with salt and pepper to taste, the parsley, chives, tarragon and the water. Heat the remaining butter in a large skillet. Pour in the egg mixture, and cook over high heat until it begins to set underneath. Lift the edge of the omelet to let any runny egg flow under it onto the hot pan to cook. Continue until the egg is just set. Remove the pan from the heat.

Cut the omelet into strips, then across into small squares or pieces. Add salt and pepper to the mushrooms. Pour the mushrooms and their cooking liquor over the pasta, and mix in well. Then lightly mix in the omelet, and serve at once, offering Parmesan cheese with the pasta mixture.

Creamed Tagliatelle with Truffles

This is extremely simple to make and a real treat for truffle fans.

SERVES 4

- 2 black truffles from a jar or can
- 1¼ cups light cream
- 1 pound fresh tagliatelle
- salt and freshly ground black pepper
- ¼ cup melted butter
- freshly grated pecorino, to serve

Reserve any juices from the jar or can of truffles. Thinly slice the truffles; then cut them into fine strips. Warm the cream in a small saucepan without letting it boil.

Cook the tagliatelle in plenty of boiling salted water for about 3 minutes, until tender but not soft. Drain well, then toss the butter into the tagliatelle, and add the cream with any juices from the truffles. Mix well, and add freshly ground black pepper to taste. Divide between four hot plates, and top with the truffles; then serve the pecorino separately.

Eggs with Stilton and Beans

SERVES 4

- *8 ounces green beans, cut into short lengths*
- *salt and freshly ground black pepper*
- *2 tablespoons butter*
- *2 scallions, chopped*
- *2 tablespoons chopped fresh tarragon or chervil*
- *2 tablespoons chopped parsley*
- *4 tablespoons dry white wine or cider*
- *6 eggs, hard-cooked and roughly chopped*
- *1½ cups crumbled or chopped blue Stilton cheese*

Add the beans to boiling salted water, and bring back to a boil. Cook for 1 minute; then drain them.

Melt the butter in a saucepan. Add the scallions and beans, and cook for 2–3 minutes, stirring. Stir in the tarragon or chervil, parsley and wine or cider. Bring to a boil; then remove the pan from the heat. Add the eggs and Stilton with salt and freshly ground black pepper to taste. Stir the mixture lightly; then immediately mix it into freshly cooked pasta before the cheese melts. Serve at once.

Fondue with Pasta

This may not be conventional, but it is a good idea for serving rich cheese fondue because starchy pasta tastes excellent with it. In the past, I had often served a pasta salad as an accompaniment for a cheese fondue, so moving on one step further, to offering pasta for dipping, made good sense.

SERVES 4

FOR THE FONDUE
- *2 cups grated or finely chopped white cheese*
- *2 cups grated Gruyère or Emmental cheese*
- *3 tablespoons all-purpose flour*
- *salt and freshly ground black pepper*
- *¼ teaspoon ground mace*
- *⅔ cup dry white wine*
- *4 tablespoons brandy*
- *1 garlic clove, crushed*
- *2 tablespoons snipped chives*

FOODS TO DIP

(See Cook's Tip right)
- *celery, cut into thick slices*
- *eating apples, cored and cut into chunks*
- *one or more of the following types of pasta:*
  Potato Gnocchi (see page 46)
  cappelletti filled with Walnut Stuffing (see pages 190 and 197)
  tortellini filled with Mushroom Stuffing (see pages 191 and 224)
  Uszka (see page 194)
- *about ¼ cup melted butter*

Mix the white cheese with the Gruyère or Emmenthal, flour, salt and pepper to taste and mace.

Heat the wine, brandy and garlic in a fondue pot until it is just about to simmer. Then gradually add the cheese mixture, stirring all the time, and letting each addition melt before adding any more. Do not allow the wine base to simmer as the cheese is being added, or the fondue will curdle. Continue stirring over a low to medium heat until the fondue is smooth and thick; then stir in the chives.

Cook the chosen pasta just before serving the fondue, and toss it in the melted butter; then place it on heated serving dishes. Arrange the celery and apples on serving dishes.

Stand the pot of fondue over a spirit burner. Provide long-handled forks for diners to spear and dip the pasta, celery and apple into the fondue.

COOK'S TIP

Deep-fried filled pasta, such as ravioli or cappelletti, are excellent for dipping. Cook the pasta as normal in boiling water, then drain well, and toss in flour. Deep-fry for a few seconds until crisp and golden; then drain well on paper towels.

Smoked Mozzarella with Arugula and Watercress

The piquant combination of arugula and watercress combines well with lightly smoked mozzarella in this hot-cold dressing. Toss it with freshly cooked pasta shapes, such as spirals, elbows, rigatoni, penne or lumache.

SERVES 2

- 2 tablespoons olive oil
- 1 garlic clove, chopped
- ½ red bell pepper, deseeded and diced
- 4 black olives, thinly sliced
- 1 bunch of watercress, leaves only, roughly chopped
- 6 arugula leaves, shredded
- 1¼ cups diced, smoked mozzarella cheese
- salt and freshly ground black pepper

Heat the oil in a small saucepan. Add the garlic, red bell pepper and olives. Cook for 2 minutes, then add the watercress and arugula, and stir until the leaves are just limp.

Remove the pan from the heat, and stir in the mozzarella with salt and pepper to taste. Toss into freshly cooked pasta, and serve at once.

Feta Cheese with Coriander and Olives

SERVES 4

- 4 tablespoons coriander seeds, finely crushed or ground in a peppermill
- 4 tablespoons pine nuts
- 4 tablespoons olive oil
- 2 garlic cloves, chopped
- 4 tablespoons Greek yogurt
- 2 cups diced cheese
- 12 black olives, pitted and thickly sliced
- 4 scallions, chopped
- 2 tablespoons chopped fresh cilantro leaves

Place the coriander seeds and pine nuts in a small, heavy-bottomed saucepan, and dry-roast over low to medium heat, shaking the pan often, until the seeds begin to pop, and the pine nuts are beginning to brown lightly.

Add the olive oil and garlic to the pan, and cook gently for 2–3 minutes. Stir the hot oil mixture into freshly cooked pasta; then mix in the Greek yogurt. Add the cheese, olives, scallions and cilantro leaves. Mix lightly, and serve at once.

Blue Cheese and Cucumber Sauce

SERVES 4

- 1 tablespoon olive oil
- 1 bay leaf
- 2 garlic cloves, crushed
- 1 cucumber, peeled and diced
- ⅔ cup dry cider
- 3 cups diced Danish blue cheese
- 2 tablespoons all-purpose flour
- 4 scallions, finely chopped
- 4 tablespoons light cream
- freshly ground black pepper

Heat the olive oil in a saucepan. Add the bay leaf, garlic and cucumber. Stir well, then cover the pan, and cook for 20 minutes, shaking the pan occasionally. Pour in the cider, and heat until just about to simmer.

Reduce the heat to the lowest setting. Gradually add the cheese, stirring until each addition has melted before adding the next. Cook until the sauce has thickened, and is just at simmering point.

Stir in the scallions and cream, and add pepper to taste. Serve at once.

Goat Cheese with Grapes and Bows

This will serve six as a first course. Otherwise, hungry diners may find the portions slightly small for a hearty main meal, but it is ideal for an average appetite and lunch. The flat shape of bows is ideal for this sauce, but you can use any other pasta shapes, if you like.

SERVES 4

- 3 tablespoons olive oil
- 2 garlic cloves, crushed
- 1 onion, halved and thinly sliced
- 16 black olives, pitted and thickly sliced
- 2 cups halved, seedless green grapes
- ¾ cup soft goat cheese

Heat the oil in a saucepan. Add the garlic and onion, and cook, stirring, for 10 minutes, or until the onion has softened but not browned (at this stage, leave the pan over a very low heat if the pasta is not well on the way to being cooked).

Stir the olives and grapes into the onion, and cook for 2–3 minutes, until really hot. Quickly stir in the goat cheese, then remove the pan from the heat, and toss the sauce with hot, freshly drained pasta. Serve at once.

Goat Cheese with Grapes and Bows

169

Garlic Cheese with Sun-dried Tomatoes

SERVES 4

- 8 sun-dried tomatoes
- generous ¾ cup full-bodied red wine
- 1 small onion, finely chopped
- 3 garlic cloves, chopped
- 2 tablespoons chopped fresh oregano
- 2 bay leaves
- salt and freshly ground black pepper
- 4 tablespoons olive oil
- 8 ounces Gouda cheese, cut into cubes
- 2 pickled walnuts, chopped
- 4 tablespoons chopped fresh parsley

Use a pair of kitchen scissors to snip the sun-dried tomatoes into small pieces. Put them in a small saucepan with the wine, onion, garlic, oregano, bay leaves, and salt and pepper to taste. Heat gently until simmering. Then cover the pan, and cook for 5 minutes. Remove from the heat, and let sit for 2 hours.

Add the olive oil, cheese and walnuts to the tomato mixture, stir well, and let marinate overnight. To serve, strain the liquid from the cheese mixture into a large saucepan. Bring to a boil, and boil hard for 3 minutes, whisking occasionally. Pour this hot dressing over freshly cooked pasta. Add the strained cheese and tomato mixture, and the parsley. Toss well and serve at once.

COOK'S TIP

Teifi cheese is a firm, moist cheese rather like Gouda in texture. It is readily available from delicatessens, both plain and with a variety of flavouring ingredients added, including garlic. Gouda may be substituted, in which case 3 chopped garlic cloves should be added to the tomato and wine mixture. Alternatively, try Gapron or Gaperon, the strong French, dome-shaped peppered cheese that is heavily laced with garlic.

Dolcelatte Dressing with Fennel and Olives

SERVES 4

- 1 fennel bulb, diced
- juice of 1 lemon
- 2 tablespoons olive oil
- 1 garlic clove, crushed
- 12 green olives, pitted and sliced
- 1 tablespoon chopped capers
- salt and freshly ground black pepper
- cayenne pepper
- 3 tablespoons chopped parsley
- 3 cups diced Dolcelatte cheese

Toss the fennel with the lemon juice. Heat the oil in a saucepan. Add the fennel and garlic, and cook for about 5 minutes, until the fennel is lightly cooked, but still crunchy.

Stir in the olives, capers, salt and pepper to taste, a little cayenne and the parsley. Remove the pan from the heat, and mix in the Dolcelatte. Then pour the mixture over a bowl of freshly cooked pasta, and mix well. Serve at once.

Garlic Cheese with Sun-dried Tomatoes

171

Arrabiatta Sauce

A hot tomato sauce, spiced with chilis, this is, literally translated, an "angry" sauce. Authentically, it is served with penne (all' Arrabiatta), but it goes well with any pasta.

SERVES 4

- *3 tablespoons olive oil*
- *1 large onion, chopped*
- *2 red or green chilis, deseeded and chopped (or more if you like; see Cook's Tip, page 90)*
- *2 garlic cloves, crushed*
- *2 celery stalks, chopped*
- *1 carrot, chopped*
- *1 bay leaf*
- *2½ cups passata*
- *⅔ cup stock (chicken or vegetable)*
- *salt and freshly ground black pepper*
- *1 teaspoon sugar*

Heat the oil in a saucepan. Add the onion, chilis, garlic, celery, carrot and bay leaf. Stir well; then cover the pan, and cook for 15 minutes, shaking the pan occasionally.

Stir in the passata and stock with plenty of salt and pepper. Add the sugar, and bring to a boil. Reduce the heat, and cover the pan; then simmer the sauce gently for 30 minutes. Taste for seasoning before serving.

Ratatouille

Ratatouille and pasta are natural partners, but they are not often served together.

SERVES 4

- *1 large eggplant, cut into chunks*
- *salt and freshly ground black pepper*
- *⅔ cup olive oil*
- *2 garlic cloves, crushed*
- *1 bay leaf*
- *1 large onion, halved and thinly sliced*
- *1 large green bell pepper, deseeded and diced*
- *1 large red bell pepper, deseeded and diced*
- *8 ounces zucchini, sliced*
- *2¼ pounds tomatoes, peeled (see Cook's Tip, page 72), deseeded and quartered*
- *2 tablespoons chopped fresh marjoram*
- *6 tablespoons chopped parsley*
- *freshly grated pecorino or Parmesan cheese, to serve*

Put the eggplant in a colander, sprinkling each layer of chunks with salt. Place the colander over a bowl, and let the eggplant drain for 30 minutes. Then rinse, and dry it well.

Heat the olive oil in a large, flameproof casserole. Add the eggplant and cook, stirring for 3–5 minutes, until the pieces are lightly cooked, but not softened. Add the garlic, bay leaf, onion, bell peppers and zucchini. Stir well, add salt and pepper to taste, and then mix in the tomatoes and marjoram. Mix well, and heat until the mixture is just bubbling. Cover and cook for about 50 minutes, until the vegetables have softened to a thickened, flavorsome sauce.

Taste the ratatouille for seasoning, and stir in the parsley just before serving. Offer plenty of freshly grated pecorino or Parmesan with the Ratatouille and pasta.

Puttanesca Sauce

A thin, perky sauce, flavored with a hint of chili, this is traditionally served with spaghetti. It is thin and smooth, so ideal for any long, slim pasta, but it is just as delicious with any shapes you happen to have, especially as it is a great standby for using staple ingredients.

SERVES 4

- *2-ounce can anchovy fillets*
- *2 tablespoons olive oil*
- *1 onion, chopped*
- *1 green chili, deseeded and chopped (see Cook's Tip, page 90)*
- *1 large garlic clove, crushed*
- *2 tablespoons capers, chopped*
- *2 × 14-ounce cans chopped tomatoes*
- *16 black olives, pitted and sliced*
- *salt and freshly ground black pepper*

Drain the oil from the anchovies into a saucepan. Add the olive oil. Heat the oils; then add the onion, chili and garlic. Cook, stirring, for 10 minutes.

Meanwhile, chop the anchovy fillets. Add them to the pan with the capers, tomatoes and olives. Sprinkle in a little salt and pepper to taste, and bring just to a boil; then cover the pan, and reduce the heat. Simmer the sauce for 15 minutes.

Cauliflower and Zucchini Sauce

This is a tomato-based sauce to serve with spaghetti, fettuccine, tagliatelle, long macaroni, pappardelle or mafaldine – in other words, long types of pasta. It is also an excellent sauce for layering with lasagne.

SERVES 4

- 2 tablespoons olive oil
- 1 large onion, chopped
- 1 bay leaf
- 1 garlic clove, crushed
- 6 ounces cauliflower, divided into small florets
- 2 tablespoons chopped fresh oregano or marjoram
- 2 cups passata
- ⅔ cup water
- salt and freshly ground black pepper
- 1 pound zucchini, sliced
- 10 black olives, pitted and thickly sliced (optional)
- freshly grated Parmesan cheese, to serve

Heat the oil in a large saucepan. Add the onion, bay leaf and garlic, then stir well, and cover the pan. Cook for 5 minutes.

Add the cauliflower and oregano or marjoram, stir well, and cover the pan again. Let cook for 5 minutes. Stir in the passata, water and salt and pepper to taste. Bring to a boil, reduce the heat, and cover the pan. Simmer for 15 minutes.

Finally, add the zucchini and olives, if using. Cover and continue to simmer gently for 10 minutes. Taste for seasoning before serving the sauce. The sauce and pasta can take generous quantities of Parmesan cheese as a topping, but it is best to leave individual diner's options open.

174

Navy Bean and Ham Sauce

Canned navy beans are delicious in a creamy white sauce flavored with ham, celery and sage. Serve on a bed of tagliatelle verde or on tomato-flavored pasta shapes.

SERVES 4

- 2 tablespoons butter
- 1 small onion, finely chopped
- ¼ cup all-purpose flour
- 2 cups milk
- ⅔ cup diced, lean, cooked ham
- 8 fresh sage leaves, shredded
- 2 × 11-ounce cans navy beans, drained
- 4 tablespoons dry sherry
- 4 tablespoons light cream
- a little grated nutmeg
- salt and pepper

Melt the butter in a saucepan. Add the onion, and cook, stirring occasionally, for 8–10 minutes, until the onion has softened.

Stir in the flour; then gradually pour in the milk, stirring all the time. Bring the sauce to a boil, and simmer for 3 minutes.

Stir in the ham, sage, navy beans and sherry, and simmer for 2 minutes. Then add the cream, and season the sauce with a little nutmeg, salt and pepper to taste. Remove from the heat without allowing the sauce to boil. Pour over the pasta, and serve at once.

Fennel and Almond Sauce

This is ideal for coating pasta that is served as a side dish, for example, as an accompaniment for roast lamb or broiled meat or poultry.

SERVES 4

- *2 fennel bulbs, halved*
- *1 cup blanched almonds*
- *1 ¼ cups chicken or vegetable stock*
- *⅔ cup dry white wine*
- *salt and freshly ground black pepper*
- *1 bay leaf*
- *2 tablespoons butter*
- *1 small onion, chopped*
- *¼ cup all-purpose flour*
- *¼ cup light cream*
- *¼ cup slivered almonds, toasted, to serve*

Cut the fennel bulbs in half lengthwise. Put them in a saucepan with the blanched almonds. Add the stock, wine, salt and pepper to taste, and the bay leaf. Heat until simmering, then cover, and cook for about 45 minutes, or until the fennel is tender right through. Let it cool slightly.

Lift the fennel from the liquid with a slotted spoon. Slice and reserve two halves; then roughly chop the remaining pair, and purée them with the almonds and cooking liquid. Press the purée through a fine strainer.

Rinse out the saucepan; then melt the butter in it. Add the onion, and cook, stirring, until it is well softened, but has not browned. Stir in the flour, then gradually stir in the fennel purée, and bring to a boil. Simmer for 3 minutes. Add the sliced fennel, and stir in the cream. Taste for seasoning, and heat gently without boiling. Pour the sauce over the chosen cooked pasta, and sprinkle with the toasted almonds before serving.

Carbonara-style Leeks with Horseradish

This was one of those "the larder is bare"-type dishes that started as a good idea, that I despaired of as I mixed it together, then bounced back to give the tastebuds a real treat when we sat down to eat! The pasta should be freshly cooked, ready for stirring into the sauce, which will not like to be kept waiting.

SERVES 4

- *¼ cup butter*
- *5 cups sliced leeks*
- *8 eggs*
- *3 tablespoons creamed horseradish*
- *4 tablespoons light cream*
- *salt and freshly ground black pepper*
- *6 tablespoons freshly grated Parmesan cheese*

Melt the butter in a large saucepan. Add the leeks, stir well, then cover the pan, and cook for 15 minutes, or until the leeks are tender, and have reduced.

Meanwhile, beat the eggs with the horseradish and cream, adding plenty of salt and pepper. Stir the egg mixture into the leeks, and continue to stir over a low to medium heat until the eggs begin to set, and the mixture becomes creamy.

Stir in the pasta immediately, and cook for a few seconds. Do not continue cooking until the eggs set, or the sauce will curdle. Taste for seasoning, and serve at once.

Spicy Okra and Mango

I felt inclined to serve this with fairly substantial fresh pasta shapes – fresh Potato Gnocchi (see page 46), for example – or the dried types, which tend to be a bit thicker when cooked, such as gli strozzapreti, cicatelli di San Severo, rigatoni or lumache.

SERVES 4

- 8 ounces small, young okra
- 4 teaspoons ground coriander
- 1 large firm mango
- 3 tablespoons olive oil
- 1 large onion, chopped
- 1 large red bell pepper, deseeded, halved lengthways and sliced
- 2 garlic cloves, crushed
- 2 green chilis, deseeded and chopped (see Cook's Tip, page 90)
- 4 teaspoons chopped fresh oregano
- salt and freshly ground black pepper
- 1 lime, cut into wedges, to serve

The okra must be small, firm, bright in color and unblemished. Old fibrous or large okra will not cook successfully. Trim the stalk ends and points off the pods, then slice them thinly, and put in a bowl. Add the coriander, and toss well.

The mango should be just ripe, but still firm (fruit that is soft or too sweet will not complement the okra). Peel the mango; then slice the flesh off the large, flat central pit. Cut the slices into small pieces.

Heat the oil in a saucepan. Add the onion, bell pepper, garlic, chilis and oregano; then cook, stirring occasionally, for 10 minutes. Stir in the okra, and cook over a fairly high heat for about 3–5 minutes, until the okra slices are slightly browned in part, and just tender. Stir in the mango, taste for seasoning, and serve. Toss the okra mixture with the pasta; then arrange lime wedges around the edge of the dish so that their juice may be squeezed over to taste.

Creamy Eggplant Sauce

Serve with shells, twists, bows, rigatoni or other short shapes. Pasta flavored with vegetables makes a colorful tempting base. I cooked a novelty three-colored pasta with beet-, spinach-, and mushroom-flavored shapes, and it looked wonderful.

SERVES 4

- *1 pound eggplants*
- *salt and freshly ground black pepper*
- *5 tablespoons olive oil*
- *4 garlic cloves, crushed*
- *1 large onion, finely chopped*
- *½ cup finely ground walnuts*
- *4 tablespoons dry white vermouth or white wine*
- *1½ cups light cream*
- *4 tablespoons freshly grated Parmesan cheese*
- *4 large sprigs of basil, shredded*
- *sprigs of basil, to garnish*

Trim the ends off the eggplants, then dice them quite small, and layer them in a colander, sprinkling each layer with salt. Place over a bowl, and set aside for 30 minutes. Rinse and pat dry on paper towels.

Heat the oil in a large saucepan, and cook the garlic and onion for 10 minutes. Then add the eggplant, and stir so that the pieces are evenly coated in oil. Cook, stirring often, until the eggplant is tender (about 15 minutes, depending on the size of the pan and heat).

Stir in the walnuts, then add the vermouth or wine, and heat, stirring for a few minutes. Stir in the cream and Parmesan cheese, and heat gently, stirring all the time. Do not boil the sauce.

Remove the pan from the heat, and taste the sauce for seasoning. Stir in the basil, then ladle the sauce over freshly cooked pasta, and serve garnished with sprigs of basil.

Fresh Spinach and Scallion Cream

Take advantage of washed, ready-to-cook baby spinach leaves to make this tempting pasta topping. If you want to make a less calorie-rich meal, then use low-fat soft cheese or fromage frais instead of mascarpone. This sauce really does go with any shape or form of pasta.

SERVES 4

- *1 large red bell pepper and 6 ripe tomatoes, peeled (see Cook's Tips, pages 65 and 72), deseeded and diced, to serve (optional)*
- *salt and freshly ground black pepper*
- *2 tablespoons butter*
- *1 bunch of scallions, trimmed and chopped*
- *12 ounces young spinach leaves, washed and left very wet, stalks discarded and torn into pieces if large*
- *a little grated nutmeg*
- *1 cup mascarpone*

If you intend serving the pepper and tomato topping, then start by skinning the bell pepper and tomatoes. Then dice the flesh of the pepper and tomatoes, and mix them together, adding a little salt. Set aside.

Melt the butter in a large saucepan. Add the scallions, and cook, stirring for 2 minutes. Then add the spinach, packing it into the pan. Cover the pan tightly, and cook for 5 minutes. Shake the pan often to prevent the spinach sticking.

When the spinach has greatly reduced in volume, has wilted, and is just tender, add salt, pepper and nutmeg to taste. Then stir in the mascarpone over a low heat. When the mascarpone has melted and warmed, spoon the mixture over the chosen, freshly cooked pasta. Add the topping, if using, and serve at once.

Turnip and Bell Pepper Sauce

Turnips are a very underrated vegetable. Their slightly peppery flavor is extremely good with sweet red and yellow bell peppers, and the rather "dry" flavor of Emmental marries the two well. Insure that the vegetables are finely cut, and the sauce will be a perfectly suitable topping for long pasta, such as spaghetti, bucatini or the finest capellini.

SERVES 4

- *8 ounces small turnips*
- *juice of ½ a lemon*
- *2 large red bell peppers*
- *2 large yellow bell peppers*
- *1¼ cups dry cider*
- *¼ cup butter*
- *2 tablespoons all-purpose flour*
- *1½ cups finely grated Emmental cheese*
- *salt and freshly ground black pepper*

Peel and thinly slice the turnips. Then cut the slices into fine matchsticks. Put in a bowl, sprinkle with the lemon juice, and cover with cold water.

Char and skin the bell peppers (see page 65). Halve and deseed them; cut them in half crosswise before slicing them into fine strips.

Drain the turnips, and put them in a saucepan. Pour in the cider, and bring to a boil. Reduce the heat, cover the pan, and simmer until the turnip matchsticks are just tender (about 5 minutes). Add the bell pepper strips, and simmer for a further 2 minutes. Remove from the heat.

Melt half the butter in a small saucepan. Stir in the flour; then strain the cooking liquid from the turnip and bell peppers into the pan. Whisk the sauce until smooth and boiling. Drain the vegetables in a fine strainer over the pan to insure all the cider is added to the sauce; then return the vegetables to their empty cooking pan, and add the remaining butter. Put the pan over the lowest heat to melt the butter, and cover to keep the vegetables hot.

Stir the Emmental and salt and pepper to taste into the sauce; then heat gently until the cheese has completely melted. Pour the sauce over the chosen pasta; then toss the peppers and turnips in. Serve immediately.

Dark Mushroom Sauce

This thin, well-flavored sauce is good with thin, long pasta shapes, such as spaghetti, bucatini, perciatelli, tagliatelle or fettuccine.

SERVES 4

- *3 tablespoons olive oil*
- *2 tablespoons butter*
- *1 onion, finely chopped*
- *1 garlic clove, crushed*
- *1 pound flat mushrooms, sliced*
- *3 pickled walnuts, chopped*
- *3 tablespoons mushroom ketchup*
- *8 tablespoons dry sherry*
- *12 black olives, pitted and thinly sliced*
- *salt and freshly ground black pepper*
- *lots of chopped parsley*
- *freshly grated Parmesan cheese, to serve*

Heat the oil and butter. Add the onion and garlic, and cook for 5 minutes. Add the mushrooms, and stir well. Continue to cook, stirring until the mushrooms have reduced in volume. Then simmer the mushrooms in their own liquor until it begins to reduce. Increase the heat to evaporate the liquid, stirring to prevent the mushrooms sticking. The mushrooms are ready when they are moist, but not sitting in liquid.

Add the pickled walnuts, mushroom ketchup, sherry, olives, and salt and pepper to taste. Simmer gently for 5 minutes, stirring often. Taste for seasoning, and stir in plenty of parsley. Toss the mushrooms with the chosen pasta, and serve with plenty of freshly grated Parmesan.

Turnip and Bell Pepper Sauce

Creamed Celeriac with Baby Spinach and Dill

Celeriac is a versatile vegetable, with a mild celery-like flavor. Baby spinach leaves are a real boon: they are sold ready for cooking in many large supermarkets, and they have a delicious flavor. This simple mixture is perfect for tossing into linguine, spaghetti or tagliatelle. It also goes well with other slim shapes, such as short twists or spirals, but I would not serve it with really chunky shapes.

SERVES 4

- 2¼ pounds celeriac
- salt and freshly ground black pepper
- ¼ cup butter
- 1 leek, thinly sliced (see Cook's Tip, page 116)
- 8 ounces baby spinach leaves, washed
- ½ cup cream cheese
- 4 tablespoons chopped fresh dill
- 6 tablespoons freshly grated pecorino or Parmesan cheese

Peel the celeriac; then cut it into fairly thin slices. Cut the slices into slim sticks; then cut these into 1–2-inch lengths. Blanch the celeriac strips in boiling salted water for 2 minutes; then drain well.

Melt the butter in a large saucepan. Add the leek, stir well, and cover the pan. Cook for 10 minutes, until the leek is reduced and tender. Stir in the celeriac with salt and pepper to taste. Add the spinach, and mix well. Cover the pan, and cook for 5 minutes, or until the spinach has wilted, and the vegetables are just cooked.

Stir in the cream cheese until it has melted to make a sauce; then remove the pan from the heat. Mix in the dill and pecorino or Parmesan cheese. Taste for seasoning, and serve at once on a bed of freshly cooked pasta.

Artichoke Hearts with Prosciutto and Peas

This is made using canned artichoke hearts, but, for a very special treat, you could boil fresh artichokes, then trim them down to the tender hearts, and use those (you will need 6 fresh artichokes if you intend using fresh vegetables).

SERVES 4

- 2 × 15-ounce cans artichoke hearts, drained
- 1 tablespoon olive oil
- ¼ cup butter
- 4 ounces prosciutto, cut into short, thin strips
- 1 small onion, halved and thinly sliced
- 1 small sprig of rosemary
- 1 tablespoon all-purpose flour
- 1¼ cups chicken stock
- 1 pound fresh peas, shelled
- salt and freshly ground black pepper

Slice the artichoke hearts, and set them aside. Heat the olive oil and butter in a saucepan. Add the ham, and cook, stirring, for 5 minutes. Then add the onion and rosemary, and cook until the onion has softened, but not browned.

Stir in the flour, then gradually pour in the stock, and bring to a boil. Add the peas with a little salt and pepper to taste. Reduce the heat so that the sauce simmers, then cover the pan, and simmer for about 15 minutes, or until the peas are tender.

Stir the artichoke hearts into the sauce, and heat them through for 3 minutes. Taste for seasoning, and remove the rosemary before serving.

Fava Beans with Bacon

Fresh, young fava beans are delicious with pasta. Simply toss them with freshly cooked pasta shapes, adding hot melted butter and freshly ground black pepper to make a delicious dish. This version, with bacon and basil, works well with small or short pasta shapes.

SERVES 4

- *3 cups diced, rindless bacon*
- *2 garlic cloves, crushed*
- *1 pound young fava beans*
- *salt and freshly ground black pepper*
- *¼ cup butter*
- *3 tablespoons chopped parsley*
- *4 sprigs of basil, shredded*
- *freshly grated Parmesan or pecorino, to serve*

Heat the bacon in a heavy-bottomed skillet over a low to medium heat until the fat runs from it. Then add the garlic, and continue cooking, stirring occasionally, until the pieces are well cooked and slightly crisp.

Meanwhile, cook the fava beans in boiling salted water for 5–10 minutes, depending on how large and old they are (small, young beans will be ready very quickly; older ones will take about 10 minutes). Drain the beans, and toss them with the bacon. Add seasoning to taste, remove the pan from the heat, and add the butter.

Toss the bacon and beans with the chosen pasta, scraping all the butter from the pan. Toss in the parsley and basil, and serve at once. Offer freshly grated Parmesan or pecorino cheese with the pasta.

183

Vegetable Medley

I scribbled a large "yum" at the end of my testing notes for this sauce. Serve the mixed vegetables with shells, spirals or pasta shapes rather than with long, thin pasta.

SERVES 4

- 6 ounces cauliflower, divided into small florets
- salt and freshly ground black pepper
- 2 tablespoons olive oil
- 2 tablespoons butter
- 1 onion, chopped
- 6 ounces baby carrots, quartered lengthways and thinly sliced
- 8 ounces young zucchini, very lightly peeled (see Cook's Tip right) and thinly sliced
- 1⅓ cups sliced button mushrooms
- 1 large, leafy sprig of tarragon, chopped
- grated rind of ½ a lemon
- squeeze of lemon juice

Cook the cauliflower in boiling salted water for about 3 minutes, until lightly cooked. Drain well.

Heat the olive oil and butter in a large saucepan. Add the onion, carrots and cauliflower, and stir well; then cover the pan, and cook for 10 minutes. Shake the pan occasionally to prevent the vegetables sticking.

Add the zucchini, mushrooms, tarragon, lemon rind and juice. Stir well, cover the pan again, and cook for a further 2–3 minutes, or until the zucchini are bright green and tender, but with a bit of bite and full of flavor. Taste for seasoning before serving.

COOK'S TIP

If you use a sharp potato peeler to remove very fine slices of peel down the length of the zucchini, the outside of the vegetables becomes bright green and the flavor when cooked is excellent.

Patty Pan and Avocado Topping

Small, yellow patty pan squash are complemented by the avocado in this sautéed mixture, which makes a colorful first course, or light lunch dish. Halve the quantities if the mixture is served as a topping for a first-course portion of pasta. Fresh pasta shapes are the best base for this topping.

SERVES 4–6

- ¼ cup butter
- 2 onions, sliced
- 1 carrot, halved and thinly sliced
- 1 sprig of tarragon
- 1 pound patty pan squash, halved horizontally
- salt and freshly ground black pepper
- 4 avocados
- juice of ½ lemon
- 8 large sprigs of dill, chopped

Melt the butter in a large saucepan. Add the onions, carrot and tarragon. Stir well, cover, and cook for about 15 minutes, or until the onions have softened.

Stir in the patty pan, salt and pepper to taste, and cover the pan; then continue to cook for a further 15 minutes, stirring once or twice, until the squash are tender but not too soft.

Halve the avocados, remove their pits, and cut them into quarters lengthwise. Peel each segment of avocado and slice it crosswise. Sprinkle with the lemon juice. Stir the avocado into the patty pan mixture, add the dill, and mix well. Then taste for seasoning before serving. Toss the vegetables into a large bowl of pasta, or spoon them on top of individual dishes of pasta.

Zucchini and Cheese Sauce

This creamy sauce of wine and milk is delicious, and inexpensive. It is ideal for a light lunch dish, or make half the quantity, and toss in some small pasta shells for an interesting first course. Tagliatelle or mafaldine are suitable long pastas; elbow macaroni, shells, cartwheels or other medium-to-small shapes are also suitable.

SERVES 4

- 2 tablespoons butter
- 1 onion, chopped
- 1 green bell pepper, deseeded and diced
- 1 celery stalk, diced
- ¼ cup all-purpose flour
- salt and freshly ground black pepper
- 1¼ cups dry white wine
- 1¼ cups milk
- 1¼ cups very finely diced mozzarella
- 4 tablespoons freshly grated Parmesan cheese
- 1 pound zucchini, halved lengthwise and thinly sliced

Melt the butter in a large saucepan. Add the onion, pepper and celery, and stir well. Cover, and cook gently for 10–15 minutes.

Stir in the flour with a little salt and pepper to taste, then add the wine, and gradually bring the sauce to a boil, stirring vigorously all the time. The sauce will be very thick at this stage, but do not add any of the milk yet, or it will curdle. When the sauce has boiled, slowly stir in the milk, and gently bring it back to a boil. Reduce the heat, and simmer the sauce, stirring occasionally, for 5 minutes.

Gradually stir in the mozzarella, and continue cooking just at simmering point, stirring all the time, until the cheese has completely melted. Stir in the Parmesan, and taste for seasoning; then add the zucchini. Simmer for a further 3 minutes, to cook the zucchini lightly, or for longer if you prefer slightly softer vegetables. Toss with pasta, and serve at once.

Carrot and Celery Sauce

This may sound terribly boring, but, really, it is far from it! The creamy, lightly herbed sauce really will go with any pasta, but, to accentuate the rather delicate flavors, I would opt for smaller or longer shapes, such as orecchiette, cappelletti, small shells, twists, bows and so on.

SERVES 4

- 8 ounces carrots
- 2 tablespoons butter
- 1 small head of celery, finely sliced
- 1 large onion, halved and thinly sliced
- 2 tablespoons all-purpose flour
- 2½ cups chicken or vegetable stock
- 1 bay leaf
- salt and freshly ground black pepper
- ½ cup mascarpone cheese
- 4 large sprigs of dill, chopped
- freshly grated pecorino or Parmesan cheese, to serve

Cut the carrots into 1-inch lengths. Slice each piece lengthwise; then cut the slices into fine matchstick strips.

Melt the butter in a saucepan. Add the carrots, celery and onion, and stir well; cover and cook for 5 minutes. Stir in the flour, then gradually pour in the stock, and bring to a boil, stirring. Add the bay leaf, and salt and pepper to taste, reduce the heat, and cover the pan. Simmer the sauce for 15 minutes.

Remove the pan from the heat, and cool the sauce slightly before stirring in the mascarpone cheese and dill. Taste for seasoning, and serve with pecorino or Parmesan cheese.

Golden Rutabaga Sauce

This is simple and delicious! Toss shells, elbow macaroni or other small shapes with the pasta to make a delicious lunch dish.

SERVES 4

- *1 pound rutabaga (½ a large rutabaga)*
- *salt and freshly ground black pepper*
- *1 quantity Cheese Sauce (see under White Sauce, page 58)*
- *2 tablespoons butter*
- *1 small onion, finely chopped*

Peel the rutabaga, and cut it into thick slices; then cut these into cubes. Cook in boiling salted water for 10–15 minutes or until tender.

Meanwhile, make the Cheese Sauce as given on page 58. Also, melt the butter in a saucepan, add the onion, and cook, stirring occasionally, for about 10 minutes, or until softened.

Drain and mash the cooked rutabaga; then press it through a fine strainer into the cooked onion. Mix well, and gradually stir in the Cheese Sauce. Reheat the sauce if necessary, then pour over the cooked pasta, and serve.

COOK'S TIP

A gratin topping finishes pasta in Golden Rutabaga Sauce perfectly. Mix ¼ cup fresh bread crumbs, ¼ cup grated Cheddar cheese and some chopped parsley. Sprinkle this over the top of the pasta and sauce; then brown the topping under a hot broiler. Garnish with diced or sliced tomatoes and sprigs of parsley, if liked.

STUFFED AND FILLED PASTA

◆

*T*HIS SECTION INCLUDES A COMBINATION OF STUFFED PASTA SHAPES THAT ARE FILLED BEFORE COOKING AND OTHER DISHES THAT COMBINE COOKED PASTA WITH A FILLING BEFORE BAKING OR BROILING.

FOR SUCCESS, ALLOW PLENTY OF TIME FOR MAKING SMALL, FAIRLY FIDDLY PASTA SHAPES. ❦ ONCE YOU ARE INTO THE SWING OF MAKING AND SHAPING THEM, THOUGH, IT IS SURPRISING HOW MANY YOU CAN TURN OUT IN A RELATIVELY SHORT PERIOD OF TIME (FOR THIS REASON IT IS OFTEN WORTH MAKING A LARGE BATCH OF FILLING AND DOUGH, THEN FREEZING THE SHAPES FOR FUTURE USE).

TO FREEZE FILLED PASTA, SPREAD THEM OUT ON A TRAY LINED WITH PLASTIC WRAP AND OPEN-FREEZE THEM. ❦ PACK THEM INTO BAGS WHEN THEY ARE FIRM, THEN YOU CAN REMOVE AS MANY SHAPES AS REQUIRED AND ADD THEM STRAIGHT TO A PAN OF BOILING WATER.

A TIP FOR SPEEDING UP THE PROCESS, IF YOU DO NOT WANT TO MAKE THE DOUGH BUT FANCY TRYING INDIVIDUAL FILLINGS, IS TO BUY FRESH LASAGNE AND USE SMALL CUTTERS TO STAMP OUT CIRCLES OR MAKE MINIATURE SHEETS OF RAVIOLI. ❦ MAKING EXTRA-LARGE RAVIOLI IS ALSO A GOOD WAY OF SPEEDING UP THE PROCESS OF STUFFING PASTA.

I have used this term to describe pasta that is filled with a stuffing before cooking – shapes such as ravioli and tortellini. There is a wide variety of fillings that can be used to make different shapes. The following section includes the techniques and tips for filling and cooking pasta shapes so that you can select your own stuffing. In some of the recipes that follow, there are instructions for using a particular filling and a complementary sauce or dressing, but otherwise the general information given applies.

As well as making small shapes, there is no reason for not making larger squares, but serving fewer of them. They may not look quite so attractive, but they will taste as good. The only point to remember is not to make very large shapes with a solid, raw filling that requires lengthy boiling. If you are making large, filled shapes, the stuffing should be cooked so that it heats through quickly; otherwise the pasta will be overboiled before the stuffing is cooked.

The stuffing recipes are sufficient for filling a half quantity of the Rich Egg Pasta Dough (see page 44) or two-thirds of the Pasta Dough (also see page 44), making 72 tortellini or 36 normal-sized ravioli.

Remember that the stuffing should be full-flavored and well-seasoned, so that it stands out in the cooked pasta. The flavor of very delicate or underseasoned stuffings can be completely lost after they are encased in pasta and served with a sauce.

MAKING STUFFED CIRCLES, ROUND RAVIOLI OR CAPPELLETTI

- Make ½ quantity Rich Egg Pasta Dough (see page 44) or ⅔ quantity Pasta Dough (also see page 44).
- Roll out half the pasta dough to form a 12-inch square. Stamp out 40 1½-inch circles, dipping the cutter in flour occasionally to prevent it sticking to the dough.
- Use half the stuffing on 20 of the circles. Brush the remaining circles with a little beaten egg. Then sandwich the stuffing between the pasta circles, pinching their edges together neatly. Repeat with the remaining dough and stuffing.

MAKING SQUARE RAVIOLI

- Make ½ quantity Rich Egg Pasta Dough (see page 44) or ⅔ quantity Pasta Dough (also see page 44).
- Roll out half the pasta dough until it is slightly larger than a 12-inch square; then trim the edges neatly.
- Dot six small mounds of stuffing, spacing them evenly along the top of the dough. Then dot another five mounds evenly spaced at right angles to this row down one end of the dough. Using these as a guide to keep the mounds of stuffing evenly spaced in neat lines, place six lines of stuffing mounds on the dough, working from the top down toward the bottom edge.
- Cover the stuffing and dough loosely with plastic wrap to prevent it drying out as you roll out the covering. Roll out the remaining pasta dough until it is slightly larger than a 12-inch square.
- Brush the pasta between the mounds of stuffing with beaten egg. Then carefully lay the second sheet of dough over the top.
- Working from one edge of the dough, press the dough together along the edge; then seal it neatly between the mounds of dough. Continue pressing the dough together until all the spaces between the stuffing are sealed. It is important to work methodically in one direction; otherwise you can trap air pockets.
- Use a pastry wheel or knife to cut between the stuffing, right along the middle of the sealed paths of dough.

FILLING AND SHAPING TORTELLINI

- Make ½ quantity Rich Egg Pasta Dough (see page 44) or ⅔ quantity Pasta Dough (also see page 44).
- Cut the pasta dough in half. Roll out one portion into a 12-inch square. Cut the dough into 2-inch wide strips. Then cut these across in the opposite direction to make 2-inch squares.
- Work on about a quarter of the squares at a time, keeping the others covered loosely with plastic wrap to prevent the pasta drying out. Brush the squares with egg, and place a little of the filling in the middle. Just less than ½ teaspoon (not a measuring spoon, but a cutlery teaspoon) of filling is sufficient for each square.
- Fold the pasta diagonally over the filling, and pinch the edges together to make a triangle; then curl the long side around a finger tip, and pinch the points together to shape each tortellini.
- Repeat, using the remaining pasta to make a total of 72 tortellini.

Pinching the points together to shape the Tortellini

COOKING STUFFED PASTA

Add the pasta to salted water that is just boiling. It must not be bubbling too rapidly, as this may cause some delicate shapes to open before the pasta seals firmly around the edge, but do not let the water go off a boil.

Small shapes with a cooked filling will cook in about 3 minutes, while some shapes filled with raw meat require longer boiling, up to 15 minutes.

Large stuffed pasta shapes can be cooked by first boiling them, then coating them with a sauce and baking. This insures that the filling is cooked through without over-boiling the pasta case.

NOTE ABOUT THE RECIPES

The following recipes for a delicious array of stuffings make enough to fill about 72 tortellini, 36 ravioli or 8 cannelloni, unless otherwise stated.

Folding the pasta dough over the filling

Creamed Chicken Stuffing

This is easier to handle than a stuffing made from uncooked chicken, and it also has the advantage of cooking quickly. Mascarpone gives a particularly rich result, but cream may be substituted for it.

- 1½ cups very finely chopped or ground, skinned, boneless chicken breast
- 1 very finely chopped scallion
- ¼ cup fresh white bread crumbs
- 2 tablespoons chopped parsley
- 1 tablespoon chopped fresh sage or tarragon
- freshly grated nutmeg
- salt and freshly ground black pepper
- 1 tablespoon dry sherry
- 4 tablespoons mascarpone cheese

Mix the chicken with the onion, bread crumbs, parsley, sage or tarragon, a little nutmeg, and plenty of salt and pepper (it is easier to mix all the ingredients in this way, and to insure they are thoroughly combined, before the moist ingredients are added).

Stir in the sherry, and pound the mascarpone with the mixture until thoroughly combined. The mixture will be quite dry, but this makes it easy to handle, and the mascarpone melts during cooking to moisten the filling.

Pumpkin and Leek Stuffing

If fresh pumpkin is not available, use canned pumpkin, drained, or make the mixture using cooked and mashed rutabaga instead – the flavor is different but just as good.

- 2 tablespoons butter
- 1¼ cups finely chopped leek
- 1 cup mashed, cooked pumpkin
- 1 cup fresh white bread crumbs
- salt and freshly ground black pepper
- ½ cup finely grated Emmental or Gruyère cheese

Melt the butter in a saucepan. Add the leek, and cook, stirring occasionally, until the leek has reduced, and is tender. Remove the pan from the heat. Stir in the pumpkin, bread crumbs, and salt and pepper; then set the mixture aside until cool, if necessary. Finally, mix in the cheese.

Smoked Mackerel and Lemon Stuffing

- ½ cup fresh white bread crumbs
- 2 tablespoons milk
- 3 ounces skinned and boned smoked mackerel fillet
- grated rind of ½ a lemon
- 2 cocktail gherkins, finely chopped
- 1 teaspoon chopped fresh oregano
- 2 canned anchovy fillets, finely chopped or mashed
- salt and freshly ground black pepper

Put the bread crumbs into a small bowl. Sprinkle the milk over, and set aside for 10 minutes. Flake the fish into the bread crumbs, and mash both together until thoroughly mixed. Mix in the lemon rind, gherkins, oregano, anchovy fillets, and salt and pepper to taste.

Beef Stuffing

- 2 tablespoons butter
- 1 small onion, very finely chopped or grated
- 1 garlic clove, crushed
- 1 teaspoon chopped fresh oregano
- ½ teaspoon chopped fresh thyme
- ¼ teaspoon ground mace
- 1½ cups lean ground steak
- salt and freshly ground black pepper
- ½ cup fresh bread crumbs
- 1 teaspoon tomato paste
- 1 egg, beaten

Melt the butter in a saucepan. Add the onion and garlic, and cook, stirring, for 2–3 minutes. Remove from the heat. Stir in the oregano, thyme and mace. Then add the steak, plenty of salt and pepper, and the bread crumbs. Pound the ingredients together well; then add the tomato paste and about half the egg (reserve the remainder for brushing the pasta dough). Mix the ingredients thoroughly, so that the seasonings and flavorings are evenly distributed, and the mixture is well bound together.

193

Mushroom Stuffing

- *2 tablespoons butter*
- *⅓ cup finely chopped onion*
- *1⅓ cups finely chopped, small button mushrooms*

- *1 cup wholewheat bread crumbs*
- *salt and freshly ground black pepper*
- *1 tablespoon mushroom ketchup*

Melt the butter in a saucepan. Add the onion, and cook, stirring, for 2 minutes. Add the mushrooms, and continue to cook for a further 5 minutes, stirring occasionally.

Remove the pan from the heat, and add the bread crumbs, and plenty of salt and pepper; then stir in the ketchup. Remember to season the mixture well, so that the flavor stands out when the pasta dough is filled.

Pheasant and Bacon Stuffing

This is a good way in which to use up any leftovers from the carcass of a roast pheasant.

- 2 tablespoons butter
- ½ small onion, grated
- ⅓ cup very finely chopped or ground, lean bacon
- 4 juniper berries, crushed
- ⅓ cup finely chopped mushrooms
- 1½ cups very finely chopped or ground, cooked pheasant meat
- ½ cup fresh white bread crumbs
- 1 tablespoon chopped parsley
- 1 tablespoon chopped fresh sage
- salt and freshly ground black pepper
- 2 tablespoons light cream

Melt the butter in a small saucepan. Add the onion, bacon, juniper berries and mushrooms. Cook, stirring, until the bacon is cooked, and the mushrooms yield their juice. Then continue to cook, stirring often, until all the liquid has evaporated, leaving the mixture just moist. Stir to make sure the bacon does not stick to the pan.

Remove the pan from the heat, and mix in the pheasant, bread crumbs, parsley, sage, and plenty of salt and pepper. Then add the cream, and stir well; cover and set aside to sit for 5 minutes before using.

Veal Stuffing

- 2 tablespoons butter
- 1 small onion, very finely chopped or grated
- 1 garlic clove, crushed (optional)
- 1 teaspoon chopped fresh sage
- ½ teaspoon chopped fresh thyme
- ½ teaspoon chopped fresh marjoram
- ¼ teaspoon ground mace
- 1½ cups ground veal
- ⅓ cup very finely chopped or ground, lean rindless bacon
- ½ cup fresh white bread crumbs
- salt and freshly ground black pepper
- 2 tablespoons brandy or dry sherry

Melt the butter in a saucepan. Add the onion and garlic, if using, and cook, stirring, for 2–3 minutes. Remove from the heat. Stir in the sage, thyme, marjoram and mace. Then add the ground veal, bacon, bread crumbs, and plenty of salt and pepper.

Pound the ingredients together; then mix in the brandy or sherry to moisten the mixture.

Cheese and Date Stuffing

- 1 tablespoon olive oil
- 4 tablespoons finely chopped celery
- 1 small onion, finely chopped
- 1 garlic clove, crushed
- 1 tablespoon chopped parsley
- 1 cup fresh white bread crumbs
- ⅓ cup finely chopped, cooking dates
- ½ cup crumbled feta cheese
- ½ cup finely grated white cheese
- salt and freshly ground black pepper

Heat the oil in a small saucepan. Add the celery, onion and garlic, and cook, stirring, for 5 minutes. Remove from the heat; then add the parsley, bread crumbs and dates. Let cool slightly, if necessary, before adding both types of cheese. Pound the cheese with the other ingredients until thoroughly combined. Finally, add salt and pepper to taste.

Herbed Pork Stuffing

- 1½ cups lean ground pork
- 1 scallion, finely chopped
- 2 tablespoons chopped parsley
- 1 tablespoon chopped fresh sage
- 1 teaspoon chopped fresh tarragon or thyme or rosemary or a mixture of all three
- 1 teaspoon chopped fresh oregano
- 1 garlic clove, crushed
- ½ cup fresh white bread crumbs
- grated rind of ½ a lemon
- freshly grated nutmeg
- salt and freshly ground black pepper
- 2 tablespoons port

Put the meat into a bowl. Add the scallion, parsley, sage, tarragon, thyme or rosemary, oregano, garlic, bread crumbs, and lemon rind. Sprinkle in a little nutmeg and plenty of seasoning.

Pound the ingredients together with the back of a mixing spoon, or by kneading them into the meat with your hand. Add the port to moisten the stuffing when the ingredients are evenly combined.

Walnut Stuffing

Walnut Stuffing

- ¾ cup walnuts
- ¾ cup fresh wholewheat bread crumbs
- 2 tablespoons finely chopped onion
- 2 teaspoons chopped fresh tarragon
- salt and freshly ground black pepper
- 5 teaspoons light cream

Grind the walnuts in a food processor or blender, or by putting them through a small mouli grater. Mix the nuts with the bread crumbs, onion, tarragon, and plenty of salt and pepper. Stir in the cream to bind the mixture together.

Ham and Cheese Stuffing

- ⅓ cup finely chopped or ground, cooked ham
- ½ cup finely grated, sharp Cheddar cheese
- ½ cup fresh bread crumbs
- 4 sage leaves, chopped
- salt and freshly ground black pepper
- a little grated nutmeg
- 1 tablespoon dry sherry
- 1 tablespoon cream or milk

A food processor is ideal for preparing the ham and cheese. Mix both together, add the bread crumbs, sage, salt and pepper and a little nutmeg. Stir in the sherry and cream or milk; then pound the mixture with the back of a spoon until the ingredients are thoroughly combined.

197

Salmon-stuffed Shells

Look out for very large pasta shells in good delis or Italian grocery store. If you cannot find them, then substitute large lumache.

SERVES 4

- 9-ounce salmon fillet, skinned
- ⅔ cup water
- ⅔ cup dry white wine
- 2 tablespoons butter
- 1 small onion, finely chopped
- ¼ cup all-purpose flour
- 3 cups sliced small button mushrooms
- ⅔ cup light cream
- 6 tablespoons freshly grated Parmesan cheese
- salt and freshly ground black pepper
- ¾ cup ricotta cheese
- 1 cup fresh bread crumbs
- 2 tablespoons chopped parsley
- 2 tablespoons snipped chives
- 12–16 large pasta shells
- sprigs of herbs, to garnish

Lay the salmon in a saucepan. Add the water and wine. Heat until just simmering, then remove the pan from the heat, and let sit for 15 minutes. Drain and flake the fish, reserving the liquid, but discarding any bones.

Preheat the oven to 375°F.

Melt the butter in a small saucepan. Add the onion, and cook for 10 minutes, stirring, until it has softened. Stir in the flour; then add the cooking liquor from the salmon and the mushrooms. Bring to a boil, stirring, and simmer gently for 3 minutes. Mix in the cream, 2 tablespoons of the Parmesan, and salt and pepper to taste. Pour the mushrooms and the sauce into an ovenproof gratin dish.

Mix the salmon with the ricotta, bread crumbs, parsley, chives, and salt and pepper to taste.

Cook the pasta shells in boiling salted water for about 12 minutes, or until tender. Drain well, and rinse under cold water; then drain again.

Fill the shells with the salmon mixture. Arrange them on top of the sauce, and sprinkle the remaining Parmesan over them. Bake in the preheated oven for about 20 minutes, or until they are hot, and have browned. Serve at once, garnished with sprigs of herbs.

Salmon-stuffed Shells with Fresh Chives

Spinach and Ricotta Stuffing

- 6 ounces fresh spinach
- ½ cup ricotta cheese
- 4 tablespoons freshly grated Parmesan or pecorino cheese
- 1 scallion, very finely chopped
- 1 tablespoon chopped parsley
- 1 tablespoon chopped fresh oregano
- freshly grated nutmeg
- salt and freshly ground black pepper
- ½ cup fresh white bread crumbs

Trim the stalks from the spinach, then wash the leaves well, and put into a saucepan, leaving the leaves quite wet. Cover the pan tightly, and cook for 5 minutes over a fairly high heat, shaking the pan often. The spinach is cooked when it is wilted and just tender.

Drain the spinach in a fine strainer, pressing out all the liquid with the back of a spoon. Chop the spinach finely – preferably in a food processor. Mix the ricotta, Parmesan or pecorino (for a milder flavor), scallion, parsley and oregano into the spinach. Add a little nutmeg, and salt and pepper; then mix in the bread crumbs. Cover and let sit for 5 minutes before using.

Stuffed Lumache

Lumache ("snails") comes in a variety of sizes, and the very large ones are intended for filling with a stuffing. Here, they are nestled together on a bed of vegetables before being browned in the oven.

SERVES 4

FOR THE LUMACHE
- 2 tablespoons butter
- 1 onion, finely chopped
- 1⅓ cups finely chopped mushrooms
- 1 cup bread crumbs
- salt and freshly ground black pepper
- 1 tablespoon chopped fresh oregano
- 1 cup ricotta cheese
- 1 bunch of watercress, leaves only, finely chopped
- freshly grated nutmeg
- 16 large lumache
- 1¼ cups Béchamel Sauce (see page 60)

- 4 tablespoons freshly grated Parmesan cheese

FOR THE VEGETABLE BASE
- 2 tablespoons olive oil
- 1 large onion, halved and thinly sliced
- 1 garlic clove, crushed
- 1 green bell pepper, deseeded, halved and thinly sliced
- 1 red bell pepper, deseeded, halved and thinly sliced
- 2 medium zucchini, thinly sliced
- 6 tomatoes, peeled, deseeded and quartered

First, prepare the stuffing for the lumache. Melt the butter in a saucepan. Add the onion, and cook, stirring, for 5 minutes. Then add the mushrooms, and continue to cook, stirring occasionally, for a further 10 minutes. Mix in the bread crumbs, salt and pepper to taste and oregano. Then add the ricotta cheese and watercress. Season with a little grated nutmeg to taste, and set aside.

Preheat the oven to 400°F.

Cook the lumache in plenty of boiling salted water for about 12 minutes, or until tender. Drain well, rinse under cold water, and drain again so they do not close up.

Meanwhile, prepare the Béchamel Sauce (see page 60).

Next, prepare the vegetable base. Heat the oil in a skillet. Add the onion, garlic and bell peppers. Cook, stirring, for 15 minutes, or until the onion has softened. Stir in the zucchini, and cook for 2 minutes; then add the tomatoes with salt and pepper to taste. Cook for 2–3 minutes, to soften the tomatoes; then spoon the mixture into an ovenproof dish or four individual dishes.

Fill the lumache with the mushroom mixture, and arrange them on the vegetable base. Spoon a little Béchamel Sauce over the top of each stuffed lumache, and sprinkle with a little Parmesan. Bake for about 15 minutes, or until the tops have browned.

Rich Pork and Beef Stuffing

This is a popular filling for pasta as the combination of pork and beef, enriched with chicken livers, gives pasta an excellent flavor.

- 1 tablespoon olive oil
- 1 small onion, finely chopped
- 2 garlic cloves, crushed
- scant ¼ cup finely chopped chicken livers
- 1 teaspoon ground coriander
- 1 teaspoon chopped fresh marjoram

- 2 tablespoons chopped parsley
- ¾ cup lean ground pork
- ¾ cup lean ground steak
- ½ cup fresh white bread crumbs
- 2 tablespoons brandy
- salt and ground black pepper

Heat the olive oil in a small saucepan. Add the onion and garlic. Cook, stirring, for 2–3 minutes. Stir in the chicken livers, and cook for about a minute, or until just set. Remove the pan from the heat.

Stir in the coriander, marjoram and parsley. Mix the pork and steak in a bowl, and stir in the onion and chicken liver mixture. Pound the ingredients until thoroughly combined. Then pound in the bread crumbs, brandy, and plenty of salt and pepper.

Stuffed Lumache

Seafood Envelopes

Seafood Envelopes

Serve glazed carrots, cut into fine matchsticks, and sautéed coarsely shredded celeriac with these seafood envelopes to make a tempting and attractive main course. Two envelopes are sufficient per portion for a first course.

SERVES 4

FOR THE SEAFOOD ENVELOPES
- *¼ quantity Rich Egg Pasta Dough (see page 44)*
- *¾ cup frozen peeled, cooked shrimp, defrosted*
- *3 ounces skinned white fish, filleted, such as plaice or cod*
- *⅔ cup finely chopped small button mushrooms*
- *½ cup fresh white bread crumbs*
- *grated rind of 1 lemon*
- *2 tablespoons chopped parsley*
- *salt and freshly ground black pepper*
- *2 tablespoons light cream*

FOR THE SAUCE
- *3 tablespoons butter*
- *1 small onion, very finely chopped*
- *1 bay leaf*
- *⅓ cup all-purpose flour*
- *1¼ cups fish stock*
- *⅔ cup milk*
- *⅔ cup light cream*
- *2 tablespoons tomato paste*
- *3 tablespoons chopped fresh dill*
- *dash of Worcestershire sauce*

TO GARNISH
- *lemon wedges*
- *sprigs of fresh dill*

COOK'S TIP

I found that this recipe was more successful when I did not brush the pasta dough with egg, when pinching and sealing the edges together; but the dough will not pinch together and seal successfully if it has started to dry out on the surface at all, so, if the surface of the dough is slightly dry, brush the edge with a little beaten egg.

First, make the pasta dough as given on page 44.

Drain the shrimp; then chop them very finely (a food processor is ideal for making this filling). Chop the fish finely, until it is rather like a very thick purée. Mix the shrimp, fish, mushrooms, bread crumbs, lemon rind, parsley, salt and pepper to taste and cream. Pound the ingredients together until thoroughly combined.

Roll out the pasta dough until it is slightly larger than a 12-inch square. Trim the edges neatly; then cut the pasta into four 3-inch wide strips. Cut the strips across into 3-inch squares. Divide the filling between the 16 pasta squares. Bring the corners of the pasta up over the filling to meet in the middle, like an envelope. Pinch the edges of the pasta dough together to seal in the filling. Set aside while you make the sauce.

Melt the butter in a saucepan. Add the onion and bay leaf, and stir well; then cover the pan, and let cook for 15 minutes. Stir in the flour, and cook for 2 minutes; then stir in the stock and milk, and bring to a boil, stirring or whisking all the time. The sauce will be very thick at this stage. Simmer, stirring, for 2 minutes. Cover the surface of the sauce with dampened baking parchment, put a lid on the pan and leave over the lowest heat to keep warm.

Cook the seafood envelopes in boiling salted water for 7 minutes, keeping it just bubbling steadily, neither too fiercely nor too gently. Meanwhile, whisk the cream, tomato paste, dill, Worcestershire sauce and salt and pepper to taste into the sauce. Heat the sauce gently, if necessary, without boiling.

Drain the pasta, and arrange them on warmed serving plates. Pour a little of the sauce over; then offer the remainder separately. Garnish with lemon wedges and sprigs of dill, and serve at once.

Shrimp and Mushroom Cannelloni

- 2 tablespoons butter, plus extra for greasing
- 1 ⅓ cups chopped, small button mushrooms
- 2 scallions, chopped
- 3 cups cooked, peeled shrimp, defrosted and drained if frozen
- 1 ½ cups fresh white bread crumbs
- 2 tablespoons chopped parsley
- salt and freshly ground black pepper
- 12 cannelloni tubes
- 1 quantity Mushroom Sauce (see page 58)
- ½ cup grated Cheddar cheese
- whole cooked shrimp, to garnish (optional)

Melt the butter in a saucepan. Add the mushrooms, and cook, stirring, for about 5 minutes, or until well reduced.

Stir in the scallions, and cook for 1 minute; then add 2 cups of the shrimp, the bread crumbs, parsley, and salt and pepper to taste. Mix well; then set aside.

Preheat the oven to 350°F.

Cook the cannelloni tubes in boiling salted water for about 6 minutes, or until just tender. Drain and rinse under cold water to keep the tubes open. Drain again.

Grease an ovenproof dish with a little butter. Spoon the shrimp mixture into the cannelloni tubes; then place them in the dish.

Make the Mushroom Sauce as given on page 58, and add the remaining shrimp; then pour it over the cannelloni. Sprinkle with the cheese, and bake in the preheated oven for 25–30 minutes, or until golden-brown on top. Serve at once.

Beef Ravioli with Spicy Mushroom and Tomato Sauce

FOR THE BEEF RAVIOLI
- ½ quantity Rich Egg Pasta Dough (see page 44) or ⅔ quantity Pasta Dough (also see page 44)
- 1 quantity Beef Stuffing (see page 193)
- 1 egg, beaten

FOR THE SPICY MUSHROOM AND TOMATO SAUCE
- 4 tablespoons olive oil
- 1 large onion, finely chopped
- 2 celery stalks, finely chopped
- 2 garlic cloves, crushed
- 1–2 green chilis, deseeded and chopped (see Cook's Tip, page 90)
- 1 bay leaf
- 1 tablespoon ground coriander
- 4 cups small button mushrooms
- 2 × 14-ounce cans chopped tomatoes
- salt and freshly ground black pepper
- 2 tablespoons chopped fresh cilantro

TO GARNISH AND SERVE
- cilantro leaves, to garnish
- freshly grated Parmesan cheese, to serve

First, make the pasta dough and stuffing as given on pages 44, 190 and 193.

Roll out half the pasta dough until it is slightly larger than a 12-inch square; then trim the edges neatly. Dot six small mounds of stuffing, spacing them evenly, along the top edge of the dough. Then dot another five mounds, evenly spacing them, in a line at right angles to the first, down one end of the dough. Using these as a guide to keep the mounds of stuffing evenly spaced in neat lines, place six lines of stuffing mounds on the dough, working from the top down toward the bottom edge. Cover the stuffing and dough loosely with plastic wrap to prevent it drying out as you roll out the covering.

Roll out the remaining pasta dough so it is slightly larger than 12 inches square. Brush the pasta between the mounds of stuffing with beaten egg. Then carefully lay the second sheet of dough over the top. Working from one edge of the dough, press the dough together along the edge; then seal it neatly between the mounds of dough. Continue pressing the dough together until all

Beef Ravioli with Spicy Mushroom and Tomato Sauce

the spaces between the stuffing have been sealed. It is important to work methodically in one direction; otherwise you can trap air pockets.

Use a pastry wheel or knife to cut between the mounds of stuffing, right down the middle of the sealed paths of dough. Set the ravioli aside on floured baking sheets, dusted with flour and covered loosely with plastic wrap, while you prepare the sauce.

Heat the oil in a saucepan. Add the onion, celery, garlic, chilis, to taste, and bay leaf. Stir well, cover the pan, and cook for 15 minutes.

Stir in the ground coriander, mushrooms, tomatoes, and salt and pepper to taste. Bring to a boil; then reduce the heat, cover the pan, and simmer the sauce gently for 45 minutes.

Cook the ravioli in plenty of boiling salted water for 15 minutes. The water should just bubble, not boil too rapidly. Drain the pasta well, and transfer it to a warmed serving dish or individual dishes. Stir the chopped cilantro into the sauce; then ladle it over the pasta, discarding the bay leaf. Garnish with cilantro leaves, and serve with freshly grated Parmesan.

Chicken and Spinach Roulade

SERVES 4

FOR THE ROULADE

- ¼ *quantity Rich Egg Pasta Dough (see page 44)*
- 1⅓ *cups frozen spinach, defrosted and drained*
- *1 onion, very finely chopped*
- *1 garlic clove, crushed*
- *1 cup finely chopped or ground, skinned, boneless, cooked chicken breast*
- *1 cup ricotta cheese*
- *1 egg, beaten*
- ¼ *cup fresh bread crumbs*
- *salt and freshly ground black pepper*

FOR THE TOPPING

- *1 tablespoon light cream or milk*
- *2 fresh basil sprigs, finely shredded*
- *3 tablespoons fresh white bread crumbs*
- *2 tablespoons freshly grated Parmesan cheese*

TO GARNISH AND SERVE

- *2–3 tomatoes, sliced, to garnish*
- *sprigs of basil, to garnish*
- *Rich Tomato Sauce (see page 58) or Mushroom Sauce (also see page 58), to serve*

First, make the pasta dough as given on page 44.

Mix the spinach, onion, garlic, chicken and half the ricotta cheese. Stir in most of the egg (reserving a little to use to seal the pasta dough later); then mix in the bread crumbs, and add salt and pepper to taste.

Cut a large sheet of cooking foil measuring about 34 × 16 inches. Fold the foil in half widthways so it measures roughly 17 × 16 inches, and grease it lightly. Roll out the pasta to form a rectangle 13 × 10 inches. Spread the spinach and chicken filling over it, leaving an uncovered border of about 1½ inches around the edge. Fold the two narrow pasta edges and the long edge nearest to you over the filling. Brush the top of the folded pasta edges with beaten egg; then roll up the pasta and filling, like a jelly roll, toward the unfolded pasta edge. Roll the pasta gently, to avoid squeezing out the filling.

Brush the unfolded edge with egg, and make sure the join is well sealed, pressing the edge neatly with the end of a round-bladed knife. Then dust the roulade with flour, and gently roll it onto the prepared foil, placing the join underneath. Make sure the ends are neat; then lift the roulade on the foil into a deep roasting pan. If you have a fish kettle, this is ideal for cooking the roulade.

Pour just enough boiling water around the roulade to cover it. Add salt to the water; then cover the roasting pan tightly with foil, or put a lid on the fish kettle. Simmer the roulade for 1 hour, turning it over halfway through cooking, if necessary, should the water not be deep enough to cover it.

Meanwhile, prepare the topping. Mix the remaining ricotta cheese with the light cream or milk and basil. Stir in salt and pepper to taste. Have a large, shallow gratin dish ready for the roulade (for example, a lasagne dish or oval fish dish). Lift the roulade from the water (see Cook's Tip below), and place it in the dish. Spread the ricotta mixture over the top. Mix the bread crumbs and Parmesan together; then sprinkle this over. Brown the topping under a hot broiler. Garnish with sliced tomatoes and basil. Serve at once, cutting the roulade into thick slices, and offering either the Rich Tomato Sauce or Mushroom Sauce as an accompaniment.

COOK'S TIP

If you have cooked the roulade in a roasting pan, the best way to drain it is to pour off some of the water from the pan first, then lift the roulade on the foil; otherwise it tends to float aside slightly.

Cauliflower and Salami Cannelloni

SERVES 4–6

- 10 ounces cauliflower, divided into small florets
- salt and freshly ground black pepper
- 1 cup cream cheese
- 6 tablespoons freshly grated Parmesan cheese
- 1 cup fresh white bread crumbs
- 1 egg, beaten
- a little butter, for greasing
- 12 cannelloni tubes
- 1 cup shredded salami
- 2½ cups passata

Cook the cauliflower in boiling salted water for 6 minutes; then drain well. Leave the cauliflower for 10 minutes to cool a little; then mix it with the cream cheese, 2 tablespoons of the Parmesan, the bread crumbs, egg, and salt, and pepper to taste.

Preheat the oven to 350°F, and grease an ovenproof dish with a little butter.

Cook the cannelloni in plenty of boiling salted water for 5 minutes, or until just tender. Drain and rinse under cold water, opening the tubes as you do so. Put the cauliflower mixture into a large piping bag fitted with a plain tip, and fill the cannelloni tubes. Place them in the prepared dish.

Sprinkle the salami over the cannelloni; then spoon the passata over. Sprinkle with the remaining Parmesan, and bake in the preheated oven for 25–30 minutes, or until the cheese has browned, and the sauce is bubbling. Serve at once.

Deep-fried Cheese Puffs

These are quite scrumptious. The recipe makes quite a large number of them, and I would advise serving about six per portion for a first course or ten for a light meal. If you are well-organized enough to be able to deep-fry the pasta for a cocktail party, they are ideal for handing around with other dips and canapés. Have the pasta cooked, floured and ready to deep-fry at the last minute when entertaining.

MAKES 40

FOR THE PASTA
- *1 quantity Feta Circles (see page 220)*
- *oil, for frying*
- *flour, for coating*

TO SERVE
- *¼ iceberg lettuce, shredded*
- *1 bunch of watercress, leaves only*
- *a little olive oil (optional)*
- *lemon or lime wedges*

Make the Feta Circles, and cook them as given on page 220.

Drain the pasta thoroughly; then heat sufficient oil to deep-fry the pasta to about 375°F, or until a cube of day-old bread browns in about 30 seconds.

Place a small mound of flour in a dish, and coat the Feta Circles thoroughly, a few at a time. This is important because even if it is well-drained, freshly cooked pasta will still be a little damp, and so will spit furiously if it is not well coated in flour to absorb the surface moisture.

Fry the pasta for a few seconds, or until it has puffed up, and is crisp and golden. Drain well on paper towels. Serve, freshly cooked, on a bed of lettuce and watercress, with a little olive oil trickled over the leaves if liked. Arrange the puffs; then add lemon or lime wedges so that their juice may be squeezed over the pasta to taste.

MOZZARELLA PUFFS
Use cubes of mozzarella cheese instead of feta, dust the hot, drained puffs with grated Parmesan cheese, and serve on a tomato salad.

Pheasant Cappelletti with Dried Morels and Oyster Mushrooms

This dish elevates pasta to the dinner party menu. Serve a salad of Frisée with Dates, Olives and Onions (see page 316) or Braised Fennel (see page 314) as a classy side dish to accompany the ravioli. Use the carcass from the pheasant to make the stock for the mushroom sauce in this recipe.

SERVES 4–6

- *½ quantity Rich Egg Pasta Dough (see page 44)*
- *1 quantity Pheasant and Bacon Stuffing (see page 195)*
- *¼–⅓ cup dried morels*
- *1¼ cups pheasant or chicken stock*
- *¼ cup butter*
- *1 small onion, finely chopped*
- *1 bay leaf*
- *¼ cup all-purpose flour*
- *1¼ cups dry white wine*
- *salt and freshly ground black pepper*
- *⅔ cup light cream*
- *4 sprigs of fresh basil, finely shredded*
- *1 pound oyster mushrooms*
- *sprigs of basil, to garnish*

First, make the pasta and the pheasant stuffing, as given on pages 44, 190 and 195.

Roll out half the pasta dough to form a 12-inch square. Stamp out 40 1½-inch circles, dipping the cutter in flour occasionally to prevent it sticking to the dough.

Place a little pheasant stuffing on 20 of the circles. Brush the remaining circles with a little beaten egg. Then sandwich the stuffing between the pasta circles, pinching their edges together neatly. Repeat with the remaining dough and stuffing.

Make the sauce before cooking the pasta. Rinse the morels once or twice; then place them in a bowl. Heat the stock until it is just hot, and pour it over the morels; then cover the bowl, and set the morels aside to soak for 20 minutes or until softened.

Meanwhile, melt half the butter in a saucepan, add the onion and bay leaf, and stir well. Cover the pan, and let cook for 15 minutes.

Drain the morels, and strain the stock through fine cheesecloth to remove any grit. Set the morels aside. Stir the flour into the onion; then add the strained stock and wine, stirring all the time. Add a little salt and pepper, and bring the sauce to a boil. Reduce the heat, and cover the pan; then simmer for 15 minutes. Add the morels, cover the pan, and cook for a further 5 minutes.

Cook the Pheasant Cappelletti in plenty of boiling salted water for 3–4 minutes. Stir the cream and basil into the sauce, taste for seasoning, and warm the sauce for a few seconds without boiling it; then remove the pan from the heat, and leave, covered, on one side. Drain the cappelletti, and turn them into a serving dish. Pour the sauce over, and mix lightly.

Melt the remaining butter in a large skillet. Add the oyster mushrooms, and season them well. Toss them over a high heat for 2 minutes; then arrange the mushrooms and their cooking juices around the Pheasant Cappelletti. Garnish with sprigs of basil, and serve at once.

PHEASANT CAPPELLETTI VARIATIONS

If the budget does not stretch to buying dried morels, the pasta and its oyster mushroom accompaniment may be served with Red or White Wine Sauce (see page 60) or Light Tomato Sauce (see page 59). Alternatively, toss the freshly cooked pasta with truffle butter, serve with the sautéed oyster mushrooms, and sprinkle with shredded basil instead of making a sauce.

Ham and Cheese Ravioli with Broccoli and Leeks

SERVES 4

- *½ quantity Rich Egg Pasta dough (see page 44)*
- *1 quantity Ham and Cheese Stuffing (see page 197)*
- *1 egg, beaten*
- *8 ounces broccoli, divided into small florets*
- *salt and freshly ground black pepper*
- *2 tablespoons olive oil*
- *¼ cup butter (optional)*
- *4 cups sliced leeks (see Cook's Tip, page 116)*

First, make the pasta dough as given on page 44, and set it aside to rest while you make the filling (see page 197).

Roll out half the pasta dough until it is slightly larger than a 12-inch square; then trim the edges neatly. Dot six small mounds of stuffing, spacing them evenly, along the top edge of the dough. Then dot another five mounds, spacing them evenly too, at right angles to the first row, down one side of the dough. Using these as a guide to keep the mounds of stuffing evenly spaced in neat lines, place six lines of stuffing mounds on the dough, working from the top edge down toward the bottom edge.

Cover the stuffing and dough loosely with plastic wrap to prevent it drying out as you roll out the covering. Roll out the remaining pasta dough until it is slightly larger than a 12-inch square. Brush the pasta between the mounds of stuffing with beaten egg. Then carefully lay the second sheet of dough over the top. Working from one edge of the dough, press the dough together along the edge; then seal it neatly between the mounds of dough. Continue pressing the dough together until all the spaces between the stuffing are sealed. It is important to work methodically in one direction; otherwise you can trap air pockets.

Use a pastry wheel or knife to cut between the mounds of stuffing, right along the middles of the sealed paths of dough, to form the ravioli. Prepare the broccoli and leek mixture before cooking the pasta, but have a large saucepan of boiling salted water ready for cooking it.

Cook the broccoli in boiling salted water for 3 minutes; then drain well. Heat the oil and butter, if using, in a large saucepan. Add the leeks, and stir well. Cover the pan, and cook, shaking the pan occasionally, for about 15 minutes, or until the leeks have reduced, and are tender. Stir in salt and pepper to taste, and add the broccoli. Let cook gently while boiling the pasta.

Cook the ravioli in the boiling water for about 3 minutes, then drain it well, and turn it into a large serving dish. Pour the leek and broccoli mixture over, together with all the liquid from the pan, and mix together lightly. Serve at once.

Ham Packages

These are satisfying and flavorsome, so a Good Green Salad (see page 312) or some simply cooked vegetables are suitable accompaniments.

SERVES 4

- *¼ quantity Rich Egg Pasta Dough (see page 44)*
- *8-ounce lean, rindless ham steak, cut into four equal pieces*
- *1 tablespoon olive oil*
- *1 cup roughly chopped mushrooms*
- *4 cocktail gherkins, chopped*
- *¾ cup grated zucchini*
- *salt and freshly ground black pepper*
- *1 egg, beaten*
- *a little butter*
- *4 ripe tomatoes (preferably plum tomatoes), sliced*
- *5 ounces mozzarella cheese, thinly sliced*

First, make the pasta as given on page 44, then set it aside to rest while you prepare the filling.

The ham pieces should be fairly even in size; if not, beat the smaller piece(s) out slightly with a steak mallet or rolling pin. Heat the oil in a skillet and cook the ham pieces until browned on both sides and just cooked. Then drain them well, and set aside.

Brown the mushrooms in the remaining juices, then remove from the heat, and stir in the gherkins, zucchini, and salt and pepper. Let cool.

Roll out the pasta until it is slightly larger than a 12-inch square. Trim the edges neatly; then cut it into four 6-inch squares. Place a quarter of the vegetable mixture on each square, and top with a piece of ham. Brush the edges of the pasta dough with beaten egg; then fold the corners of the pasta over the ham, like an envelope, sealing it in. Carefully pinch and smooth the joins in the pasta.

Cook the pasta packages in boiling salted water for 5 minutes. Use a slotted spoon to remove them from the pan, and place in a buttered gratin dish or individual serving dishes that can go under the broiler. Top the pasta packages with sliced tomatoes and mozzarella cheese, and broil until golden; then serve at once.

Ham Package Variations

The filling in the ham packages makes them quite moist, but, if you like, instead of the tomato and mozzarella topping, a coating sauce can be poured over the parcels. Rich Tomato Sauce, Mushroom Sauce, or Cheese Sauce (see page 58) would all work well. Mozzarella cheese may be placed on the sauced packages, and browned under the broiler, if liked.

213

Artichoke and Cheese Cannelloni

SERVES 4

- 16 cannelloni tubes
- salt and freshly ground black pepper
- ¼ cup butter
- 1½ pounds Jerusalem artichokes, peeled and thickly sliced
- 1 small onion, finely chopped
- 1 cup ricotta cheese
- 3 tablespoons chopped parsley
- ½ cup fresh white bread crumbs
- 1 quantity Cheese Sauce (see page 58)
- 4 tablespoons fine dry bread crumbs
- 4 tablespoons freshly grated Parmesan cheese

Cook the cannelloni in boiling salted water for 6 minutes, then drain well, and rinse under cold running water to open the tubes. Lay the tubes on a clean dish cloth to dry.

Preheat the oven to 350°F, and use a little of the butter to grease an ovenproof dish.

Cook the artichokes in simmering salted water until just tender, 8–10 minutes. Drain and reserve about a third of the vegetables; then mash the remainder until smooth.

Meanwhile, melt the remaining butter in a small saucepan, and add the onion. Cook, stirring occasionally, for 15 minutes, or until it has softened but not browned.

Stir in the mashed artichokes, ricotta cheese, parsley, fresh bread crumbs, and salt and pepper to taste. Put the mixture into a piping bag fitted with a plain tip, and fill the cannelloni tubes, placing them in the prepared oven-proof dish as you do so.

Make the Cheese Sauce as given on page 58, and pour it over the cannelloni. Dice the reserved artichokes, and mix them gently with the bread crumbs and Parmesan, taking care not to mash the vegetables as you do so. Spoon the mixture over the top of the cannelloni, and bake in the preheated oven for about 40 minutes, or until the topping is crisp and golden. Serve at once.

Bacon and Pine Nut Triangles

SERVES 4–6

FOR THE BACON AND PINE NUT TRIANGLES
- ½ quantity Rich Egg Pasta Dough (see page 44) or ⅔ quantity Pasta Dough (also see page 44)
- 1 tablespoon olive oil
- ½ cup finely chopped, lean rindless bacon
- 1 small onion, finely chopped
- ⅓ cup ground or very finely chopped, pine nuts
- 6 black olives, pitted and chopped
- 1 tablespoon chopped fresh oregano
- salt and freshly ground black pepper
- 1 egg, beaten

TO SERVE
- 8 ounces ripe tomatoes, peeled (see Cook's Tip, page 72), deseeded and roughly chopped
- 4 sprigs of basil, shredded
- 1 quantity White Wine Sauce (see page 60)
- sprigs of basil, to garnish
- freshly grated Parmesan cheese

First, make the pasta dough as given on page 44, and set it aside to rest.

Heat the olive oil in a small saucepan. Add the bacon and onion; then cook, stirring, for 8–10 minutes. Remove the pan from the heat, and stir in the pine nuts, olives, oregano, and salt and pepper to taste. Set aside to cool.

Roll out half the pasta dough to form a 12-inch square. Cut the dough into 2-inch wide strips; then cut these across into 2-inch squares. Work with a third of the squares at a time, keeping the remainder loosely covered with plastic wrap to prevent the pasta drying out.

Brush the squares with beaten egg. Place a tiny mound of stuffing in the middle of a square (you need less than half a teaspoon – cutlery spoon, that is, not a measure – for each square). Then fold one corner of the pasta diagonally over the filling, and pinch the edges together

214

to seal the mixture in a triangular-shaped pasta. Repeat with the remaining rolled squares, using about half the filling. Then roll the remaining dough out, and repeat the process with the remaining filling.

Prepare the serving ingredients before cooking the pasta. Mix the tomatoes with the basil, and salt and pepper to taste. Make the White Wine Sauce as given on page 60.

Cook the pasta in boiling salted water for 3–4 minutes. Drain the pasta well; then mix it with the White Wine Sauce. Spoon the mixture into one, large, warmed serving bowl or individual dishes. Top with the tomatoes and

basil, and garnish with sprigs of basil, if using. Serve at once, offering freshly grated Parmesan cheese with the pasta.

Beef Cannelloni

SERVES 4

FOR THE BEEF CANNELLONI

- 12 cannelloni tubes
- salt and freshly ground black pepper
- 2 tablespoons olive oil
- 1 onion, finely chopped
- 2 garlic cloves, crushed
- 1 tablespoon chopped fresh oregano
- 1¾ cups chopped chicken livers
- ⅔ cup finely chopped or ground, rindless bacon
- 12 ounces ground steak
- 6 black olives, stoned and chopped
- 3 tablespoons mushroom ketchup
- 1 cup fresh bread crumbs
- 4 tablespoons brandy
- 1 quantity Rich Tomato Sauce (see page 58)

FOR THE TOPPING

- 1¼ cups chopped mozzarella cheese
- 2 tablespoons freshly grated Parmesan cheese
- 4 tablespoons dried white bread crumbs

Cook the cannelloni in boiling salted water for 6 minutes, or until tender. Drain and rinse under cold running water to keep the tubes open; then drain and lay them out on a clean dish cloth to dry.

Preheat the oven to 320°F. Use a little of the oil to grease an ovenproof dish lightly.

Heat the remaining oil in a small saucepan. Add the onion and garlic; then cook, stirring, for 5 minutes. Stir in the oregano and chicken livers, and cook for 2 minutes; then remove from the heat.

Mix the bacon and steak with the olives, mushroom ketchup, bread crumbs and brandy. Add the chicken liver mixture, and salt and pepper to taste; then pound the ingredients together until they are thoroughly combined. Pipe or spoon the filling into the cannelloni tubes; then lay them in the prepared dish.

Pour the Rich Tomato Sauce over, cover with foil, and bake in the preheated oven for 45 minutes.

Meanwhile, mix the mozzarella, Parmesan and bread crumbs for the topping.

Remove the foil, and sprinkle the cheese mixture over the cannelloni. Return it to the oven, increase the temperature to 350°F, and bake for a further 40–45 minutes, or until the topping is crisp and golden, and the Beef Cannelloni are cooked through.

Turkey Cannelloni with Lemon Sauce

This is a good way in which to transform the leftovers of a roast turkey into a tempting meal. Instead of using bought tubes, try making fresh pasta, as here. Alternatively, for results of a similar standard, buy fresh lasagne, and use it to roll around the filling. The prepared cannelloni, coated in sauce, may be frozen for up to 3 months.

SERVES 6

- ½ quantity Rich Egg Pasta Dough flavoured with herbs (see pages 44–45)
- a little butter, for greasing
- 1 quantity Béchamel Sauce (see page 60)
- 4 cups finely chopped or ground, cooked turkey
- 1⅓ cups chopped button mushrooms
- 2 cups fresh white bread crumbs
- 3 tablespoons snipped chives
- 1 tablespoon chopped fresh tarragon
- 2 tablespoons chopped parsley
- grated rind of 1 lemon
- ½ cup grated mild Cheddar cheese

Make the pasta dough as given on page 44, and divide it in half. Roll out one half to form a square that is slightly larger than 12 inches. Trim the edges, and cut the pasta into nine 4-inch squares. Repeat with the remaining pasta dough; then cook the squares in plenty of boiling salted water for 3 minutes. Drain well, rinse under cold water, and lay out on a clean dish cloth.

Preheat the oven to 350°F, and grease an ovenproof dish with a little butter.

Make the Béchamel Sauce as given on page 60.

Mix the turkey with the mushrooms, half the bread crumbs, the chives, tarragon, parsley, and salt and pepper to taste. Stir in a little of the sauce – just enough to bind the ingredients into a firm mixture. Divide the

mixture in half. Roughly mold half the mixture into a cylinder shape on a plate, and mark it into nine equal portions.

Cut off a portion of stuffing, roll it into a sausage, and place it on a piece of pasta; then roll up the pasta to form cannelloni. Place in the prepared ovenproof dish. Repeat this process with the remaining sheets of pasta and portions of stuffing.

Stir the lemon rind into the remaining Béchamel Sauce, and taste it for seasoning before pouring it over the cannelloni. Mix the remaining bread crumbs with the cheese. Sprinkle this over the sauce, and bake in the oven for about 30 minutes, or until the topping is crisp, and the cannelloni have heated through.

Walnut Tortellini Tossed with Cucumber and Stilton

SERVES 4–6

- ½ quantity Rich Egg Pasta dough (see page 44)
- 1 quantity Walnut Stuffing (see page 197)
- 1 egg, beaten
- 2 tablespoons olive oil
- ¼ cup butter
- ½ English cucumber, very lightly peeled (see opposite) and diced

- 4 tablespoons snipped chives
- salt and freshly ground black pepper
- 4 tablespoons dry white vermouth or dry white wine
- 1½ cups crumbled blue Stilton cheese
- sprigs of tarragon, to garnish

Make the pasta and the stuffing as given on pages 44 and 197.

Cut the pasta dough in half. Roll out one portion to form a 12-inch square. Cut the dough into 2-inch wide strips. Then cut these across in the opposite direction to make 2-inch squares.

Work on about a quarter of the squares at a time, keeping the others covered loosely with plastic wrap to prevent the pasta drying out. Brush the squares with egg, and place a little of the filling in the middle – just

218

less than ½ teaspoon (not a measuring spoon, but a cutlery teaspoon) of filling is sufficient for each square. Fold the pasta diagonally over the filling, and pinch the edges together to make a triangle; then curl the long side around a finger tip, and pinch the points together to shape each tortellini (see page 191). Repeat using the remaining pasta to make a total of 72 tortellini.

Once the tortellini are shaped, prepare the Cucumber and Stilton dressing. Heat the olive oil and butter together. The cucumber should be so finely peeled that only the very outer layer of skin is removed, leaving the outside of the vegetable quite green. Add the cucumber to the butter and oil, and cook, stirring, for 5 minutes. Stir in the chives, salt and pepper to taste and vermouth or wine. Heat until the mixture is just simmering, then cover the pan, and leave it over the lowest heat until the pasta is ready.

Cook the tortellini in boiling salted water for 3–5 minutes. Drain well, and transfer to a heated serving dish. If you have to cook the pasta in batches, then spoon a little liquid from the cucumber over the first batch, and keep it covered and hot until successive batches are cooked.

Toss the cucumber and its liquid, and the Stilton with the cooked tortellini, and serve at once. Garnishing the tortellini with sprigs of tarragon indicates the flavor of the Walnut Stuffing.

A SALAD-STYLE STARTER
Prepare a half quantity of the tortellini, and serve them on a generous base of chicory and watercress salad with a little arugula if available. Then spoon over the Cucumber and Stilton dressing, and serve at once. The hot tortellini is delicious with the cold salad.

Baked Spinach and Ricotta Cannelloni

If you want to serve this as a first course, then halve the quantities or increase the number of portions to eight.

SERVES 4

- *double quantity Spinach and Ricotta Stuffing (see page 198)*
- *16 cannelloni tubes*
- *salt and freshly ground black pepper*
- *2 tablespoons olive oil*
- *1 large onion, chopped*
- *1 garlic clove, crushed*
- *2 × 14-ounce cans chopped tomatoes*
- *2 tablespoons tomato paste*
- *3 tablespoons chopped parsley*
- *1¼ cups chopped mozzarella cheese*
- *4 tablespoons freshly grated Parmesan cheese*

First, make the stuffing as given on page 198.

Cook the cannelloni in boiling salted water for 6 minutes; then drain well. Rinse the tubes under cold running water to open them; then set them out on a clean dish cloth to dry.

Preheat the oven at 350°F, and brush an ovenproof dish lightly with a little of the oil.

Heat the remaining oil in a saucepan, add the onion and garlic, and cook, stirring, for about 15 minutes, or until slightly softened.

Stir in the tomatoes, tomato paste, parsley and salt and pepper to taste. Bring to a boil, and simmer for 5 minutes.

Meanwhile, put the Spinach and Ricotta Stuffing into a piping bag fitted with a plain tip, and fill the cannelloni tubes, placing them in the prepared dish as you do so.

Pour the tomato sauce over the cannelloni. Mix the mozzarella and Parmesan, then sprinkle this over the top of the cannelloni, and bake in the preheated oven for 20–30 minutes, or until the sauce is bubbling, and the topping has browned and cooked through.

Feta Circles with Walnut Oil and Olives

These are just delicious! I have included a variety of alternative serving suggestions below as they are quite versatile.

SERVES 4

- *½ quantity Rich Egg Pasta dough (see page 44)*
- *5 ounces feta cheese*
- *1 egg, beaten*
- *salt and freshly ground black pepper*
- *2 tablespoons sunflower oil*
- *2 tablespoons butter*

- *6 scallions, finely chopped*
- *12 black olives, pitted and thinly sliced*
- *3 tablespoons walnut oil*
- *2 tablespoons chopped parsley*

First, make the pasta dough as given on page 44.

Cut the cheese into ¼-inch cubes.

Roll out half the pasta dough to form a 12-inch square. Stamp out 40 1½-inch circles, dipping the cutter in flour occasionally to prevent it sticking to the dough.

Place cubes of cheese on 20 of the circles. Brush the remaining circles with a little beaten egg. Then sandwich the cheese between the pasta circles, pinching their edges together neatly. Repeat with the remaining dough and cheese.

Cook the pasta circles in plenty of boiling salted water for 3 minutes.

Meanwhile, heat the sunflower oil and butter, add the scallions and olives, and stir over low heat for 2–3 minutes to cook the onions lightly.

Drain the cooked pasta, and turn it into a warmed serving dish. Stir the walnut oil and parsley into the scallion and olive mixture, and pour this dressing over the pasta, scraping every last drop from the pan. Toss well, and serve at once.

DIFFERENT CHEESE FILLINGS

Feta cheese may be replaced with a full-flavored alternative, such as a blue cheese (Maytag Blue, Dolcelatte, Gorgonzola, Stilton or Danish blue), or a garlic-flavored cheese. Many of the flavored cheeses made in Vermont also go well, provided the herbs or spices are fairly powerful.

ALTERNATIVE DRESSINGS AND SAUCES

FETA CIRCLES WITH TOMATO SAUCE
Toss the pasta with Light Tomato Sauce (see page 59) or Rich Tomato Sauce (see page 58)

FETA CIRCLES WITH PUTTANESCA SAUCE
Puttanesca Sauce (see page 173) complements the cheese.

BUTTERY FETA CIRCLES
Garlic Butter (see page 68) or Lemon Anchovy Butter (see page 69) are good with the pasta.

FETA CIRCLES WITH A LIGHT DRESSING
For a less-rich dressing, try Light Tomato Sauce (see page 59) or Greek Yogurt Topping (see page 71).

FETA CIRCLES WITH OLIVE DRESSINGS
Mixed Olive and Bell Pepper Topping (see page 77) or Anchovy and Olive Paste (see page 76) are ideal for coating the cheese pasta lightly.

Gratin of Mushroom Cappelletti

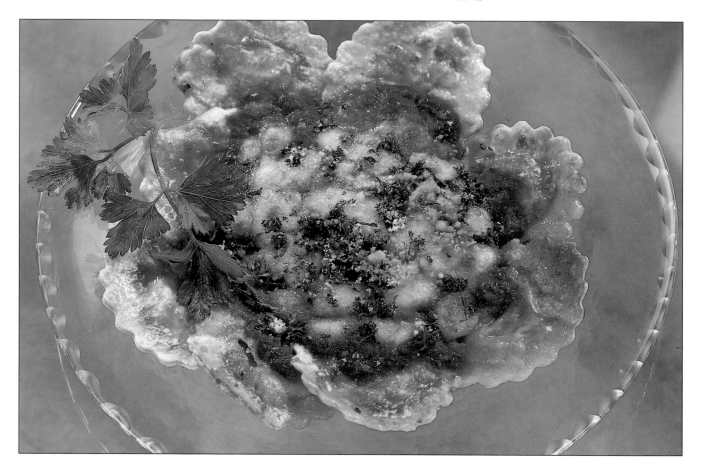

Cappelletti are also sometimes referred to as ravioli, and they can be square or circular. If you would prefer to make these square, then simply follow the instructions for ravioli at the beginning of the chapter.

SERVES 4–6

- ½ quantity Rich Egg Pasta Dough (see page 44) or ⅔ quantity Pasta Dough (also see page 44)
- 1 quantity Mushroom Stuffing (see page 194)
- 1 quantity Rich Tomato Sauce (see page 58)
- 1 egg, beaten
- 2 tablespoons–¼ cup melted butter
- 3–4 tablespoons chopped parsley
- 1 tablespoon chopped fresh oregano (optional)
- 1¼ cups finely diced mozzarella cheese
- 1 cup fresh white bread crumbs
- 4 tablespoons freshly grated Parmesan cheese

First, make the pasta, the Mushroom Stuffing and the Rich Tomato Sauce as given on pages 44, 194 and 58.

Roll out half the pasta dough to form a 12-inch square. Stamp out 40 1½-inch circles, dipping the cutter in flour occasionally to prevent it sticking.

Preheat the oven to 400°F. Use half the Mushroom Stuffing, placing a little on 20 of the circles. Brush the remaining circles with a little beaten egg. Then sandwich the stuffing between the pasta circles, pinching their edges together neatly. Repeat with the remaining dough and stuffing.

Cook the Mushroom Cappelletti in plenty of boiling salted water for 3 minutes. Brush a shallow, ovenproof dish, or individual dishes, with a little of the butter. Drain the Cappelletti; then transfer it into the dish, or divide it between individual dishes. Spoon the Rich Tomato Sauce over the pasta to cover.

Mix the parsley and oregano (you will probably need the larger quantity of parsley if you are using individual dishes), and sprinkle these herbs over the sauce. Top with the mozzarella cheese. Mix the bread crumbs and Parmesan, and sprinkle this over the top. Trickle the remaining butter over the bread crumbs and cheese; then bake the gratin in the preheated oven for 25–30 minutes, or until the mozzarella has melted, and the topping is crisp and golden. Serve at once.

Smoked Salmon Circles with Avocado Sauce

SERVES 4

FOR THE SMOKED SALMON CIRCLES

- *½ quantity Rich Egg Pasta Dough (see page 44)*
- *4 ounces smoked salmon (offcuts are fine)*
- *1 tablespoon snipped chives*
- *1 tablespoon chopped fresh dill*
- *2 tablespoons fresh white bread crumbs*
- *2 tablespoons ricotta cheese*
- *salt and freshly ground black pepper*
- *1 egg, beaten*
- *2 tablespoons melted butter*
- *4 tablespoons freshly grated Parmesan cheese*

- *2 tablespoons chopped fresh dill*

FOR THE AVOCADO SAUCE

- *2 tablespoons butter*
- *1 small onion, finely chopped*
- *2 tablespoons all-purpose flour*
- *1¼ cups dry white wine*
- *2 cups light cream*
- *2 avocados*

TO GARNISH (OPTIONAL)

- *1 avocado, halved, pitted, peeled and sliced*
- *juice of ½ a lemon*
- *sprigs of dill*

First, make the pasta dough as given on page 44; then set it aside to rest. To make the filling, finely chop the smoked salmon; then pound it to a coarse paste with the chives, dill and bread crumbs. Mix in the ricotta cheese, and salt and pepper to taste.

Roll out half the pasta dough until it is 12 inches square. Stamp out 40 1½-inch circles, dipping the cutter in flour occasionally to prevent it sticking to the dough. Use half the smoked salmon mixture on 20 of the circles. Brush the remaining circles with a little beaten egg. Then sandwich the stuffing between the pasta circles, pinching their edges together neatly. Repeat with the remaining dough and stuffing.

Next, make the base for the sauce before cooking the pasta. Melt the butter in a small saucepan, and add the onion. Stir well, then cover the pan, and cook for 15 minutes, or until the onion has softened well but not browned. Stir in the flour, then add the wine, and bring to a boil, stirring. Add salt and pepper to taste. Cover the pan, and set the sauce aside, off the heat, until the pasta has been cooked.

If you intend adding the garnish, then prepare the avocado, and sprinkle the lemon juice over the slices; cover them tightly; and set aside in the refrigerator.

Cook the pasta in plenty of boiling salted water for 3–4 minutes. Drain well, and toss with the butter; then place in a warmed dish, cover, and keep hot.

To finish the sauce, return the pan to the heat, and bring it to a boil. Then turn the heat to the lowest setting, or remove the pan from the heat to prevent the sauce boiling, and stir in the cream. While the cream is warming, but not simmering (or it will curdle), halve the avocados, and remove their pits. Scoop out all their flesh, and add to the sauce. Purée the sauce in a blender or food processor, or press it through a strainer. Add seasoning to taste.

To serve, arrange the pasta and sauce on plates or in shallow bowls, and add the garnish of avocado and dill.

Uszka

Uszka are small, tortellini-type pasta filled with a dried mushroom mixture. To be completely authentic, these Polish dumplings would need to be made slightly smaller than here, but they are a bit easier to make this size. They are a classic accompaniment for bortsch (beetroot soup) and, if you want to serve them in soup, cut the pasta into seven strips, then across into 49 squares and make tiny, filled pasta appropriate to soup.

DRIED MUSHROOMS

Polish dried wild mushrooms are threaded on long strings, and hung to dry. You will find the authentic ingredients hanging in Polish delis; however, dried porcini or ceps may be substituted. Do not use Chinese dried mushrooms (shiitake) as they have a quite different, strong flavor.

SERVES 4–6

- ½ quantity Rich Egg Pasta Dough (see page 44)
- 5 large dried mushrooms (see note)
- 2 tablespoons butter
- 1 onion, very finely chopped
- 1½ cups fresh white bread crumbs
- salt and freshly ground black pepper
- 1 egg, beaten
- ⅓ cup butter, to serve

First, make the pasta dough as given on page 44, and set aside while you prepare the filling.

Put the mushrooms into a small saucepan, and add enough water to cover them. Bring to a boil, then reduce the heat, and cover the pan. Simmer the mushrooms for about 5 minutes, or until they are tender. Drain the mushrooms, reserving the liquid. Rinse the pan out; then strain the liquid back into it through a strainer lined with cheesecloth (this removes any grit that has come from the mushrooms). Boil the liquid until it has reduced to about 2 tablespoons; then set it aside.

Chop the mushrooms finely, discarding any tough stalk ends. Melt the butter in a saucepan, add the onion, and cook, stirring often, for 10 minutes. Mix the mushrooms, onion and bread crumbs. Add salt and pepper to taste; then stir in the reduced cooking liquor.

Cut the pasta dough in half. Roll out one portion to form a 12-inch square. Cut the dough into 2-inch wide strips. Then cut these across in the opposite direction to make 2-inch squares.

Work on about a quarter of the squares at a time, keeping the others covered loosely with plastic wrap to prevent the pasta drying out. Brush the squares with beaten egg, and place a little of the filling in the middle. Fold the pasta diagonally over the filling, and pinch the edges together to make triangles; then curl the long side around a finger tip, and pinch the points together to shape each Uszka, as for tortellini (see page 191). Repeat, using the remaining pasta dough, to make a total of 72.

Cook the Uszka in boiling salted water for 3–4 minutes. Drain and toss with melted butter.

SERVING SUGGESTIONS

USZKA WITH CHIVES AND TARRAGON
Add 4 tablespoons snipped chives and 2 tablespoons chopped fresh tarragon to the melted butter for serving.

USZKA WITH HORSERADISH CREAM AND BEETS
Mix 2 tablespoons horseradish sauce into 1¼ cups sour cream. Add 3 tablespoons chopped fresh dill, and a little salt and pepper to taste. Toss the freshly cooked Uszka with a little melted butter and the horseradish cream. Top each portion with cooked beets cut into fine matchsticks, and serve at once.

USZKA WITH BEETS AND SCALLIONS
Coarsely grate ¾ cup cooked beets and finely chop 4 scallions. Cook the vegetables together in half the melted butter. Toss the Uszka in the remaining butter; then spoon the beetroot mixture on top.

CREAMY USZKA
Make a Béchamel Sauce (see page 60), and stir in 2–4 tablespoons horseradish sauce, to taste. Toss the Uszka with the sauce, adding 4 tablespoons chopped dill. Serve garnished with sprigs of dill, and offer a grated mild cheese with the Uszka.

Kreplach

226

Kreplach

These filled pastas are a traditional Jewish accompaniment for soup. Alternatively, they may be served with a meat gravy or tomato sauce, but the following recipe is the tastiest version I know.

MAKES 72

FOR THE KREPLACH
- *½ quantity Rich Egg Pasta Dough (see page 44)*
- *2 tablespoons beef drippings*
- *1 small onion, grated*
- *salt and freshly ground black pepper*
- *1½ cups ground, lean roast beef*

- *1 tablespoon finely chopped parsley*
- *1 tablespoon good beef gravy or the juices from underneath the drippings*
- *1 egg, beaten*

TO SERVE
- *Rich Tomato Sauce (see page 58) or soup or beef gravy*

First, make the pasta dough as given on page 44, and set it aside to rest while you make the filling.

Melt the drippings in a saucepan. Add the onion, and cook, stirring, for 5–8 minutes, or until some of the moisture has evaporated, and the onion has lost its raw taste. Remove from the heat, and stir in salt and pepper to taste. Then add the beef, parsley and gravy, which will bind the mixture. Taste for seasoning.

Cut the dough in half. Roll out one half to form a square slightly larger than 12 inches. Trim the edges; then cut the dough into 2-inch wide strips and across into 2-inch squares. Brush the squares with beaten egg. Place a little filling in the middle of each square until you have used half of the mixture; then fold one corner of the dough over to enclose the filling, forming a triangular-shaped piece of pasta. Pinch the edges of the dough together well. Repeat with the remaining dough and filling.

Cook the Kreplach in boiling salted water, or add them to clear soup. Cook for about 3 minutes, until tender. Drain or serve with the soup. Rich Tomato Sauce or gravy may be served with the Kreplach if they are not cooked in soup.

Fried Kreplach

Cooked Kreplach may be fried until crisp outside and golden. Here is a tasty filling, a variation on a favorite Jewish combination of chopped chicken livers and hard-cooked eggs.

MAKES 72

- *½ quantity Rich Egg Pasta Dough (see page 44)*
- *2 tablespoons butter*
- *1 small onion, grated*
- *1 garlic clove, crushed*
- *¾ cup finely chopped chicken livers*
- *1 egg, hard-cooked and finely chopped*

- *2 tablespoons chopped parsley*
- *salt and freshly ground black pepper*
- *flour, for coating*
- *oil, for frying*

First, make the pasta dough as given on page 44, and set it aside to rest while you make the filling.

Melt the butter in a small saucepan. Add the onion and garlic, and cook for 5 minutes, stirring. Then add the chicken livers, and continue to cook until they are firm and cooked. Remove the pan from the heat. Mix in the egg, parsley, and plenty of salt and pepper. Then leave until cold.

Roll out the dough, fill and cook the Kreplach as given on page 227. Drain them well, and toss in a little flour. Heat a thin layer of oil in a large skillet; then fry the Kreplach until they are crisp and golden underneath. Turn them over, and cook the second side; then drain them well on paper towels before serving.

Pierogi

These are the Polish equivalent of the Italian ravioli family of filled pasta. You can use any leftover cooked pork or beef as a filling instead of the smoked pork given in the ingredients below. Cottage cheese, stiffened with bread crumbs, is also suitable.

SERVES 4–6

FOR THE DOUGH
- 2 cups all-purpose flour
- ½ teaspoon salt
- 1 egg
- 5 tablespoons water
- 1 egg, beaten

FOR THE PORK AND
SAUERKRAUT FILLING
- 1 tablespoon oil
- 1 small onion, finely chopped
- 1 garlic clove, crushed

- ½ cup finely chopped sauerkraut
- 1½ cups ground smoked pork
- salt and freshly ground black pepper

TO SERVE
- ¼ cup butter
- 8 ounces rindless bacon

First, make the dough. Put the flour into a bowl. Mix in the salt, and make a well in the middle of the flour. Beat the egg with the water and pour it into the well in the flour; then gradually mix in the flour to make a firm dough. Knead the dough on a lightly floured surface until smooth. Wrap the dough in a plastic bag, and set it aside to rest while you prepare the filling.

Heat the oil in a small saucepan. Add the onion and garlic; then cook, stirring, for about 10 minutes, until the onion has softened, but not browned. Add the sauerkraut and pork. Remove the pan from the heat. Stir in salt and pepper to taste; then pound the mixture until it binds together.

Work with a quarter of the dough and a quarter of the filling at a time. Take the first quarter of dough, and roll it out thinly on a lightly floured counter, into a round measuring roughly 10–12 inches in diameter. Use a 2½-inch round cutter to stamp out circles.

Take the first quarter of the filling mixture, and spoon small amounts of it onto each of the circles. Brush the edges of the circles with beaten egg; then fold one side over the filling to make little pasty-like shapes. Pinch the edges to seal them together, and flute them attractively. Place the filled Pierogi on a floured platter. Repeat this process for each of the remaining quarters of dough and filling.

When the Pierogi are made, melt the butter, and fry the bacon. Add the Pierogi to boiling salted water, and cook at a steady, but not too fast, boil for about 4 minutes. Drain, and serve tossed with the butter and bacon.

COOK'S TIP

The Pierogi may be cooked in chicken stock, and a spoonful of stock may be spooned over them before serving for extra flavor.

Fruit Pierozki

MAKES ABOUT 32

FOR THE DOUGH
- 1½ cups all-purpose flour
- pinch of salt
- 1 egg, beaten
- 3 tablespoons water

FOR THE FILLING
- about 8 ounces fresh fruit, such as cherries, plums, apricots or blueberries
- confectioners' sugar, to dredge
- sour cream, to serve

Put the flour into a bowl, and mix in the salt. Make a well in the middle; then add the egg and water. Mix in the flour to form a dough; then knead well until smooth.

Prepare the fruit according to type: pit cherries, halve and pit plums and apricots, rinse and dry blueberries.

Roll out the dough into a circle on a lightly floured counter until it is roughly 16 inches across. Then stamp out 2½-inch rounds. Place a piece of fruit on each round, and brush the edges of the dough lightly with water. Then fold the dough around the fruit, and pinch the edges to seal them well.

Cook the Pierozki in boiling water for about 3 minutes, then drain well, and serve dredged with confectioners' sugar, with sour cream as an accompaniment.

Apricot and Almond Gems

I cannot decide how many of these should be served to make up a portion – I would find four an ample portion, but my partner will happily eat six . . . The almonds in the middle of the apricots were his idea.

MAKES 36

FOR THE APRICOT AND
ALMOND GEMS
- *½ quantity Rich Egg Pasta Dough (see page 44)*
- *36 blanched almonds*
- *36 ready-to-eat dried apricots*
- *1 egg, beaten*

- *flour, for dredging*
- *oil, for frying*
- *superfine sugar, for dredging*
- *whipped cream, to serve*

FOR THE SAUCE
- *¾ cup apricot preserve*
- *scant 1 cup dry sherry*

First, make the pasta dough as given on page 44.

Place an almond in the middle of each apricot.

Roll out half the dough until it is slightly larger than 12 inches square. Stamp out neat lines of 2-inch diameter circles, making 36 in all.

Place an almond-filled apricot on each of 18 of the circles. Brush the edges of the circles with egg; then cover with the remaining 18 circles. Pinch the dough neatly around the apricot to seal it in firmly. Repeat with the remaining apricots and dough.

Cook the pasta in boiling salted water for 3 minutes, then drain thoroughly, and dredge with flour.

Heat sufficient oil to deep-fry the pasta to 350°F, and fry the pasta for a few seconds until it is crisp and golden. Drain well on paper towels, and dredge at once with superfine sugar.

Now, make the sauce. Simply boil the apricot preserve with the sherry.

Serve the sauce with the Apricot Gems, spooning a little on the side of each plate, and offer whipped cream.

Blackcurrant Circles

SERVES 4–6

- *1½ cups fresh blackcurrants, topped and tailed*
- *¼ cup sugar*
- *crushed Amaretti biscuits*
- *½ quantity Rich Egg Pasta Dough (see page 44)*

- *1 egg, beaten*
- *confectioners' sugar, for dredging*
- *whipped cream, to serve*
- *bunches of blackcurrants, to decorate*

Put the blackcurrants into a saucepan with the sugar. Heat gently until the juice runs from the fruit; then simmer, stirring occasionally, until the fruit is soft. Remove from the heat, and stir in the crushed Amaretti biscuits. Let cool; then chill.

Meanwhile, make the pasta dough as given on page 44.

Roll out half the dough to form a square roughly 12 inches. Stamp out about 36 2-inch circles. Place a little blackcurrant filling on half the circles (about 18), using half the filling altogether. Brush the remaining circles with egg, and cover them with the blackcurrant filling. Pinch the edges to seal them well. Repeat with the remaining dough and filling.

Cook the pasta in boiling water for 3–4 minutes; then drain them well. Serve at once, on hot plates, dredged with confectioners' sugar, and topped with whipped cream. Decorate with bunches of blackcurrants.

Apricot and Almond Gems

BAKED PASTA DISHES

◆

$\mathcal{F}$ROM THE OLD FAVORITE LASAGNE TO A FEW WAYS TO VARY THE TRADITIONAL APPROACH TO STUFFING VEGETABLES, THIS CHAPTER INCLUDES DISHES THAT ARE PART OF EVERYONE'S REPERTOIRE, WITH OTHERS TO SURPRISE GUESTS OR ADD A NEW NOTE TO EVERYDAY MEALS.

AS WELL AS LAYERING AND BAKING LASAGNE, REMEMBER THAT ANY PASTA SHAPE WILL WORK IN THE SAME WAY. ❧ BOWS OR BUTTERFLIES MAKE EXCELLENT FLAT LAYERS BETWEEN SAUCES, FOR EXAMPLE, AND MACARONI AND SOUP PASTA ARE ALSO GOOD FOR MAKING SMOOTH LAYERS. TAGLIATELLE AND THE CHUNKIER OR ROUNDED SHAPES TEND TO MAKE UNEVEN LAYERS WITH BUBBLING-HOT TOPS AND GOLDEN-CRUSTED PEAKS.

SO, DO AS YOU WILL WITH THESE RECIPES, MIXING AND MATCHING THE SAUCES, PASTAS AND TOPPINGS FOR A VARIETY OF EFFECTS.

MAKING PERFECT LASAGNE

◆

The majority of the lasagne available in supermarkets is of the "no-need-to-precook" type. The quality of this type of pasta varies significantly. Some brands look suspect, the color of pale cardboard, with a textured, fibrous appearance and fork marks or holes all over. Then there are other types that look just like ordinary dried pasta.

I have tried a few types with very mixed results. One batch of pasta completely ruined what started out as a decent sauce, while another type was surprisingly okay, but not special. The result of my testing was that the dried pasta, which is boiled before being layered, and fresh lasagne were by far the best.

Here are some practical notes on the different types, and on constructing a good lasagne.

USING NO-NEED-TO-PRECOOK LASAGNE

Look for pasta that has the appearance of ordinary dried pasta; then experiment with different brands to see whether there is one you like.

I find that this type of lasagne is only suitable for layering with very moist sauces. Bolognese sauce is usually sufficiently liquid, but if you have reduced it to a thick richness, add more canned tomatoes as the pasta absorbs a significant amount of liquid. For comparatively dry fillings, such as a mixture of spinach and ricotta, the pasta should be boiled until tender first. Also, there must be plenty of room in your baking dish for a good covering of sauce on top of the pasta; otherwise the surface dries up quickly during cooking.

I obtained best results with this type of pasta by selecting a good brand, which looked like ordinary pasta, and boiling it for about 6–8 minutes in lightly salted water, until just tender. In essence, I treated it as "quick-cook" pasta rather than as a "ready-to-use" pasta.

Take care even so, because some of the cardboard-like types become extremely soft when layered with a moist sauce, even when they have not been pre-boiled, so you will have to get to know the product to insure success.

In terms of quantity, because the pasta is used dry, you do need more of this type of pasta than fresh.

DRIED LASAGNE

This is the next best alternative to fresh lasagne, but it is quite difficult to obtain because supermarkets stock the types that do not need precooking. Some delis or specialist

Italian grocery stores, however, keep a supply of dried pasta that has to be boiled before layering it with sauce.

The lasagne expands on boiling, so you do not need quite as much of this type as you do of the no-need-to-precook types.

FRESH LASAGNE

Readily available, this is the better choice. Cook the sheets in plenty of boiling salted water until just tender (about 3 minutes, or according to the instructions on the package); then drain and use with any sauce you like.

BOILING LASAGNE

Follow the steps below to precook lasagne successfully.

1 Lower the sheets, one at a time, into a large saucepan of boiling salted water. Stir them as soon as they are in the pan to prevent them sticking together.

2 Boil until tender (how long this will take varies according to type).

3 Lay out a couple of clean dish cloths. Drain the pasta in a colander; then rinse it with cold running water, separating the sheets.

4 Lay the sheets out on the dish cloths, and mop their tops with paper towels.

THE CHOICE OF DISH

I think this is the most difficult aspect of making lasagne! The large, rectangular gratin dishes that *look* ideal for lasagne are just not deep enough to hold three layers of pasta, the filling sauce and sufficient topping sauce without bubbling over around the edges and looking messy when cooked.

The answer is to look out for a straight-sided rectangular dish that is slightly deeper than the usual gratin dishes – independent potteries, some Spanish or Italian pottery and catering suppliers are likely sources. A good kitchen store will usually carry one or two suitable dishes. The other practical possibility is to use a traditional, deep-sided roasting pan. Avoid a plain metal pan, but the enamelled pans are an excellent choice – and some of them are attractive enough to serve from at the table, too.

Lasagne al Forno

Baked lasagne, layered with meat and topped with Béchamel Sauce is an international favorite. A Good Green Salad (see page 312) has to be the inseparable accompaniment for this dish.

SERVES 6–8

- *1 quantity Bolognese Sauce (see page 61)*
- *1½ quantities Béchamel Sauce (see page 60)*
- *about 8–10 sheets lasagne (see page 37)*
- *salt and freshly ground black pepper*
- *a little butter, for greasing*
- *½ cup fresh white bread crumbs*
- *4 tablespoons freshly grated Parmesan cheese*
- *½ cup finely chopped mozzarella cheese*

Preheat the oven to 350°F, and grease a large, rectangular ovenproof dish (about 12–15 × 8 inches).

Make the Bolognese and Béchamel Sauces as given on pages 61 and 60.

Cook the lasagne in plenty of boiling salted water according to the instructions on the package, or allow 3 minutes for fresh pasta. Drain well, and rinse it under cold water; then lay the sheets out on a clean dish cloth to dry.

Spread some of the Bolognese Sauce in the bottom of the prepared dish; then dot some of the Béchamel Sauce over it. Top with a layer of pasta. Continue layering the Bolognese Sauce, Béchamel Sauce and pasta, ending with a layer of pasta and with a good quantity of Béchamel Sauce left. Pour this over the top to coat the pasta completely.

Mix the bread crumbs, Parmesan and mozzarella, and sprinkle this over the top of the lasagne. Bake in the preheated oven for 45–50 minutes, or until the topping is crisp and golden, and the layers are bubbling hot.

Shrimp Lasagne Pots

Circles of lasagne conceal buttery garlic shrimp and mushrooms. The pasta absorbs the juices to make a well-balanced first course.

SERVES 4

- 4 sheets fresh lasagne
- salt and freshly ground black pepper
- ¼ cup butter
- 2 garlic cloves, finely chopped
- 2 cups peeled, cooked shrimp
- ⅔ cup thinly sliced button mushrooms
- 3 tablespoons chopped parsley
- 4 tablespoons freshly grated Parmesan cheese
- 4 tablespoons light cream
- 2 tablespoons dried white bread crumbs
- sprigs of parsley and lemon, quartered and sliced, to garnish

Preheat the oven to 400°C.

Cook the lasagne in boiling salted water for 4 minutes, or until tender. Drain and rinse under cold water; then lay the sheets on a clean dish cloth to dry. Using a ramekin dish as a guide, cut out two circles of pasta from each sheet.

Melt the butter in a small saucepan. Add the garlic cloves, and cook gently for 2 minutes. Remove the pan from the heat, and mix in the shrimp, mushrooms and parsley with salt and pepper to taste.

Place a spoonful of the shrimp mixture in the bottom of each of four ramekin dishes. Top with a circle of pasta; then share the remaining shrimp mixture among the ramekins. Cover with another circle of pasta, and press down firmly. Sprinkle the cheese over the pasta, then trickle the cream over, and finally sprinkle with bread crumbs.

Sit the ramekins on a baking sheet, and cook for 10–15 minutes, until browned on top and hot. Garnish with parsley and lemon, and serve at once.

Smoked Haddock Lasagne

SERVES 6

- a little butter, for greasing
- about 8–10 sheets lasagne (see page 37)
- double quantity Béchamel Sauce (see page 60)
- 1½ pounds smoked haddock fillets, skinned and cut into chunks
- 4 eggs, hard-cooked and roughly chopped
- 4 tablespoons chopped parsley
- grated rind of ½ a lemon
- salt and freshly ground black pepper
- ¾ cup grated, sharp Cheddar cheese
- 3 tablespoons dried white bread crumbs

Preheat the oven to 350°F. Grease a large, rectangular, ovenproof dish with butter.

Cook the lasagne in plenty of boiling salted water according to the instructions on the package, or allow 3 minutes for fresh pasta. Drain well, and rinse it under cold water; then lay the sheets out on a clean dish cloth.

Make the Béchamel Sauce as given on page 60.

Mix the haddock, eggs, parsley, lemon rind and a little salt and pepper together in a bowl. Place about a third of the fish mixture in the dish, then coat with some of the sauce (just under a quarter of the total volume), and top with lasagne. Layer the remaining fish, sauce and lasagne, ending with a layer of lasagne and reserving enough sauce to coat it.

Add ½ cup of the cheese to the remaining sauce; then pour it over the top of the lasagne. Mix the remaining cheese with the bread crumbs, and sprinkle the mixture over the top of the sauce. Bake in the preheated oven for about 45 minutes, or until the topping is golden-brown, and the sauce is bubbling hot.

Hidden Oysters

The browned topping of creamy pasta conceals lightly cooked oysters. Serve thin rye bread and butter with this first course.

SERVES 4

- 12 oysters
- 1 tablespoon lemon juice
- salt and freshly ground black pepper
- ¼ cup butter, melted and cooled
- ½ cup soup pasta

- scant 1 cup Béchamel Sauce (see page 60)
- 2 tablespoons freshly grated Parmesan cheese
- 2 tablespoons chopped parsley
- lemon slices and sprigs of parsley, to garnish (optional)

Shuck the oysters, saving their liquor (see page 133); then place both in a bowl. Add the lemon juice and a little salt and pepper. Divide the oysters between four ovenproof shell dishes or individual gratin dishes. Spoon the butter over, and set aside on a baking sheet.

Preheat the oven to 400°F.

Cook the pasta in plenty of boiling salted water for about 10 minutes, or until tender; then drain well.

Meanwhile, make the Béchamel Sauce as given on page 60.

Mix the pasta with the Béchamel Sauce; then add the Parmesan and parsley with salt and pepper if necessary. Spoon pasta mixture over the oysters, and bake in the preheated oven for about 20 minutes, or until the pasta mixture has browned, and the oysters cooked. Serve at once, garnished, if liked, with slices of lemon and sprigs of parsley.

Smoked Salmon Timbales with Spinach Sauce

The mixture can be baked in 8 ramekin dishes for a first course, or small ovenproof basins (disposable foil or glass) may be used instead of the soufflé dishes suggested below.

SERVES 4

FOR THE TIMBALES

- *1 cup soup pasta*
- *salt and freshly ground black pepper*
- *1 cup strained ricotta cheese*
- *1¼ cups chopped smoked salmon offcuts*
- *2 tablespoons snipped chives*
- *1 tablespoon finely chopped parsley*
- *1 large egg, beaten*
- *grated rind of ½ a lemon*

FOR THE SPINACH SAUCE

- *2 tablespoons butter*
- *1 small onion, finely chopped*
- *2 tablespoons all-purpose flour*
- *1¼ cups milk*
- *8 ounces fresh spinach leaves, washed*
- *freshly grated nutmeg*

Preheat the oven to 350°F. Base-line four individual soufflé dishes with non-stick baking parchment, and place them on a baking sheet.

Cook the soup pasta in boiling salted water for about 10 minutes, or until tender. Drain well.

Mix the ricotta, smoked salmon, pasta, chives, parsley, egg, lemon rind, and salt and pepper to taste. Spoon the mixture into the prepared dishes, pressing it down well. Cover with circles of non-stick baking parchment, and bake in the preheated oven for 30 minutes, or until the mixture has set.

Meanwhile, make the Spinach Sauce. Melt the butter in a saucepan. Add the onion, and cook for 10 minutes, stirring, until softened. Stir in the flour, then add the milk, and bring to a boil, stirring. Add the spinach, stir well, and cover the pan. Simmer gently for 5 minutes, stirring occasionally. Purée the sauce in a blender, and add salt, pepper and nutmeg to taste. Rinse out the saucepan, return the sauce to the pan, and reheat if necessary.

Pour some sauce onto each of four warmed serving plates. Remove the baking parchment from the tops, and slide a knife around the edge of the salmon and pasta mixture, to free the set mixture from the sides. Invert the timbales onto the sauce; then remove the remaining baking parchment before serving.

Cauliflower and Pasta Bake

Make a real meal of cauliflower cheese by adding cooked pasta. Any smallish pasta shapes can be used for this.

SERVES 4–6

- *8 ounces pasta shapes*
- *salt and freshly ground black pepper*
- *1 small cauliflower, divided into florets*
- *1 quantity Cheese Sauce (see page 58)*
- *1 teaspoon English mustard*
- *4 tablespoons snipped chives*
- *2 tablespoons freshly grated Parmesan cheese*
- *½ cup fresh white bread crumbs*

Preheat the oven to 400°F.

Cook the pasta in boiling salted water for 12–15 minutes, or until tender (check the instructions on the package). Add the cauliflower florets for the last 5 minutes of cooking time.

Drain the cauliflower and pasta together thoroughly. In fact, it is best to leave them sitting in the colander for 5 minutes, so that all the water drains away.

Turn the pasta mixture into an ovenproof dish.

Make the Cheese Sauce as given on page 58; then stir in the mustard and chives. Pour the sauce over the pasta and cauliflower. Mix the Parmesan and bread crumbs, and sprinkle the mixture over the top. Bake in the preheated oven for about 20 minutes, or until it has browned, and is bubbling hot; then serve at once.

Smoked Salmon Timbales with Spinach Sauce

Pork and Pasta Bell Peppers

SERVES 4

- *1 cup soup pasta*
- *salt and freshly ground black pepper*
- *4 red or green bell peppers*
- *2 tablespoons olive oil*
- *1 onion, finely chopped*
- *1 celery stalk, chopped*
- *1 garlic clove, crushed*

- *pork*
- *1 tablespoon chopped fresh oregano*
- *14-ounce can chopped tomatoes*
- *1 tablespoon tomato paste*
- *5 ounces mozzarella cheese, cut into four slices*

Preheat the oven to 350°F.

Cook the pasta in boiling salted water for about 7 minutes, or until tender. Drain well.

Meanwhile, cut the tops off the bell peppers and scoop out the seeds and core. Rinse and drain well, reserving the tops.

Heat the oil in a skillet. Add the onion, celery, garlic and pork. Cook, stirring, until the onion has softened, and the meat lightly browned. Stir in the oregano, tomatoes, tomato paste, and salt and pepper. Remove from the heat, and mix in the pasta.

Sit the peppers in an ovenproof dish, cutting the merest sliver off their bases, if necessary, to make them sit upright. Spoon the meat and pasta mixture into the peppers, cover the dish, and bake in the preheated oven for 40 minutes.

Place a slice of mozzarella on top of each pepper; then replace their tops. Cover loosely with foil, and bake for a further 20 minutes.

Soufflé-topped Pasta

This can also be cooked in individual soufflé or gratin dishes, when it actually looks better, but it tastes just as good when it is baked in one large dish.

SERVES 4

- *1½ cups orecchiette*
- *1 large leek, sliced (see Cook's Tip, page 116)*
- *salt and freshly ground black pepper*
- *2 zucchini, thinly sliced*
- *1⅓ cups sliced mushrooms*
- *½ quantity Rich Tomato Sauce (see page 58)*

- *8 tablespoons freshly grated Parmesan cheese*
- *3 eggs, separated*
- *¾ cup grated Cheddar cheese*
- *3 tablespoons plain flour*
- *3 tablespoons milk*

Preheat the oven to 375°F.

Cook the orecchiette and leek together in boiling salted water for about 15 minutes, or until tender. Add the zucchini for the last minute before draining the pasta, to blanch them lightly. Drain the pasta mixture well.

Meanwhile, make the Rich Tomato Sauce as given on page 58.

Transfer the pasta mixture to a casserole or deep, ovenproof dish. Mix in the mushrooms, Rich Tomato Sauce, salt and pepper, and half the Parmesan. Smooth the top of the pasta mixture level.

Mix the egg yolks, Cheddar, remaining Parmesan and flour; then beat in the milk. Pound the mixture thoroughly, and add a little salt and pepper. Whisk the egg whites until stiff, and fold them into the cheese mixture. Spread this over the top of the pasta, and bake for 30 minutes, or until the topping has risen and browned. Serve at once.

Pasta-filled Eggplants

The shells are not eaten, so be sure to scoop out all the soft middle of the eggplant. A side salad of tomatoes, olives and croûtons on a leafy base is ideal with this creamy pasta filling.

SERVES 4

- *2 large eggplants (about 1½ pounds in weight)*
- *salt and freshly ground black pepper*
- *1 cup soup pasta*
- *¼ cup butter*
- *1 onion, finely chopped*
- *⅓ cup chopped button mushrooms*

- *8 tablespoons light cream*
- *8 tablespoons grated Parmesan cheese*
- *2 tablespoons chopped parsley*
- *2 sliced mushrooms, a little lemon juice and a few sprigs of parsley, to garnish*

Cut the eggplants in half lengthwise, and scoop out the flesh. Reserve the shells, placing them in a gratin dish.

Cut the flesh into chunks, and put it into a colander, sprinkling the layers with salt. Set aside over a bowl for 20 minutes, then rinse well, and pat dry. Chop the eggplant flesh finely.

Cook the pasta in boiling salted water for about 7 minutes, or according to the instructions on the package until just tender. Melt the butter in a saucepan, and add the onion. Cook, stirring, for 5 minutes. Then add the chopped eggplant and mushrooms, and continue to cook for about 15–20 minutes, or until the vegetables are cooked.

Stir in the pasta, cream, Parmesan and parsley with salt and pepper to taste. Divide this mixture between the eggplant shells, spooning it into them neatly. Cook under a hot broiler until they are golden on top.

Quickly toss the mushroom slices in lemon juice, top the eggplants with the mushroom slices and sprigs of parsley, and serve at once.

Palmetto and Ricotta Bake

SERVES 8

- *¼ quantity Rich Egg Pasta Dough (see page 44)*
- *salt and freshly ground black pepper*
- *¼ cup butter*
- *1½ cups ricotta cheese*
- *1½ cups grated pecorino cheese*
- *grated nutmeg*
- *4 tablespoons chopped parsley*

- *8 ounces button mushrooms, wiped*
- *4 scallions, finely chopped*
- *1 egg, separated*
- *14-ounce can palmettos, drained*
- *4 tomatoes, peeled (see Cook's Tip, page 72), deseeded and roughly chopped*

Preheat the oven to 350°F.

Make the pasta dough as given on page 44. Then cut the pasta dough in half, and roll out each half to form a large round. Using a 10-inch round baking dish as a guide for cutting the pasta (you will need a fairly deep quiche or gratin dish in which to layer the cooked pasta and cheese), cut out a circle of pasta to fit the dish. Repeat with the remaining dough.

Cook both circles in a large saucepan of boiling salted water for 3–4 minutes. Drain the pasta, and rinse it under cold running water; then open out the circles, and lay them on a clean dish cloth to dry.

Grease the dish with a little of the butter; then melt the remainder. Mix it with the ricotta, three-quarters of the pecorino, a little grated nutmeg, salt, pepper and nutmeg to taste, and the parsley. Reserve six mushrooms, chop the remainder, and add them to the cheese mixture with the scallions and egg yolk. Mix well. Whisk the egg white until stiff; then fold it into the cheese mixture.

Lay one pasta circle in the base of the dish, and top it with half the cheese mixture. Add the second pasta circle, trimming off any excess with kitchen scissors; then spread the remaining cheese mixture over. Arrange the palmettos on top of the mixture like the spokes of a wheel. Halve the reserved mushrooms, and arrange them between the palmettos, with one mushroom half in the middle of the dish. Sprinkle with the reserved pecorino, and bake in the preheated oven for about 45 minutes, or until the top is golden. Spoon the tomatoes in between the palmettos, and serve at once.

Beef and Macaroni Bake

A taste of pasta served Greek style – this brings back a few holiday memories!

SERVES 4

- 2 tablespoons olive oil
- 1 onion, chopped
- 2 garlic cloves, crushed
- 4 cups ground beef
- 1⅓ cups sliced mushrooms
- 1¼ cups water
- 1¼ cups red wine
- 2 tablespoons tomato paste
- 1 tablespoon chopped fresh oregano
- 1 bay leaf
- 2 × 14-ounce cans chopped tomatoes
- salt and freshly ground black pepper
- 8 ounces quick-cook macaroni
- 1 tablespoon all-purpose flour
- 1 small egg
- 1¼ cups light cream
- 2 tablespoons freshly grated Parmesan cheese

Preheat the oven to 350°F.

Heat the olive oil in a flameproof, ovenproof casserole, and add the onion, garlic and beef. Cook, stirring, until the beef has browned lightly. Stir in the mushrooms, and cook for a further 5 minutes.

Pour the water and wine into the casserole. Stir in the tomato paste, oregano, bay leaf and tomatoes. Add plenty of salt and pepper, and bring to a boil. Stir in the macaroni, remove from the heat, and cover. Bake in the preheated oven for 15–20 minutes, or until the macaroni has absorbed much of the liquid to leave the mixture juicy, but not runny.

Meanwhile, put the flour into a bowl. Add the egg, and gradually whisk in the cream until smooth. Stir in the Parmesan and a little salt and pepper to taste. Press the macaroni down; then pour the cream mixture over the top. Return the casserole to the oven at once, and cook, uncovered, for a further 20–25 minutes, or until the topping has set, and is golden. Serve at once.

Seafood Lasagne

FOR THE LASAGNE

- a little butter, for greasing
- about 8–10 sheets lasagne (see page 37)
- 1 quantity White Wine Sauce (see page 60)
- 10 fresh scallops, shelled and sliced
- 8 ounces cooked, shelled mussels
- 2 cups peeled, cooked shrimp, defrosted and drained if frozen
- 1 pound salmon fillet, skinned and cut into chunks
- 2 tablespoons chopped parsley
- 2 tablespoons chopped fresh dill (optional)
- salt and freshly ground black pepper

FOR THE TOPPING

- 1 tablespoon all-purpose flour
- 2/3 cup milk
- 2 eggs
- 1 1/4 cups light cream
- 4 tablespoons freshly grated Parmesan cheese

Preheat the oven to 350°. Grease a large, rectangular, ovenproof dish with butter.

Cook the lasagne in plenty of boiling salted water according to the instructions on the package, or allow 3 minutes for fresh pasta. Drain well, and rinse it under cold water; then lay the sheets out on a clean dish cloth to dry.

Make the White Wine Sauce as given on page 60, and remove from the heat. Stir in the scallops, mussels, prawns, salmon, parsley, dill, and salt and pepper to taste. Layer the seafood mixture and lasagne in the dish, starting with seafood and ending with pasta.

To make the topping, put the flour in a large bowl and gradually whisk in the milk. Whisk in the eggs; when they are thoroughly combined, lightly whisk in the cream and Parmesan with a little salt and pepper to taste. Pour this mixture over the top of the lasagne, and bake in the preheated oven for about 40 minutes, or until it has set and browned.

COOK'S TIP

If you want to make a less rich topping, then use low-fat plain yogurt instead of the cream.

Turkey and Chestnut Lasagne

Look out for vacuum-packed canned chestnuts and shrink-wrapped packages of cooked chestnuts in supermarkets and delis. The shrink-wrapped packages are sometimes displayed near the fresh vegetables, and are usually available around Thanksgiving time, so it is worth stocking up as they have a long shelf-life.

- a little oil, for greasing
- about 8–10 sheets lasagne (see page 37)
- salt and freshly ground black pepper
- double quantity Béchamel Sauce (see page 60)
- 8 lean rindless bacon slices
- 6 scallions, chopped
- 3 cups diced, cooked turkey
- 1 1/2 cups cooked, peeled chestnuts (see left)
- 2 tablespoons chopped fresh sage
- 2 tablespoons chopped parsley
- 1/2 cup grated Cheddar cheese

Preheat the oven to 350°F. Grease a large, rectangular, ovenproof dish with a little oil.

Cook the lasagne in plenty of boiling salted water according to the instructions on the package, or allow 3 minutes for fresh pasta. Drain well, and rinse it under cold water; then lay the sheets out on a clean dish cloth.

Make the Béchamel Sauce as given on page 60.

Place the bacon in a large, heavy-bottomed saucepan, and cook gently until the fat runs; then stir in the scallions, and cook for 2 minutes.

Remove the pan from the heat, and pour in half the Béchamel Sauce. Stir in the turkey, chestnuts, sage and parsley. Taste for seasoning; then layer this sauce and the lasagne in the dish, starting with the sauce and ending with the pasta.

Stir the cheese into the remaining Béchamel Sauce, and pour it over the top of the lasagne. Bake the lasagne for about 45 minutes, until browned.

Mushroom Ring

SERVES 4–6

FOR THE PASTA
- 8 ounces lasagne verdi or half white lasagne
- salt and freshly ground black pepper
- 2 tablespoons olive oil
- 2 large onions, finely chopped
- 2 garlic cloves, crushed
- 6 cups chopped mushrooms
- 1 cup fresh bread crumbs
- 1½ cups strained ricotta cheese
- 2 tablespoons chopped fresh sage
- 2 tablespoons chopped parsley
- 1 egg

FOR THE FILLING
- ¼ cup butter or 2 tablespoons olive oil
- 12 ounces tomatoes, peeled, deseeded and quartered
- 2 tablespoons snipped chives

Preheat the oven to 350°F, and use a little of the oil to grease a 2-pint ring pan or mold.

First, cook the lasagne in plenty of boiling salted water according to the instructions on the package, or allow 3 minutes for fresh pasta. Drain and rinse under cold water; then lay the sheets out on a clean dish cloth to dry.

Heat the remaining oil in a large saucepan. Add the onions and garlic, and cook, stirring occasionally, for 10 minutes. Add the mushrooms, and cook for about 15 minutes, or until they are well reduced. Boil off the excess liquid; then remove the pan from the heat.

Stir in the bread crumbs, ricotta cheese, salt and pepper to taste, the sage, parsley and egg. Line the ring pan with pasta, using alternate pieces of green and white if you are using two colors. Leave the excess pasta overhanging the edge of the pan. Fill with the mushroom mixture; then fold the excess pasta over the top. Cover with greased foil, and bake in the preheated oven for 1 hour. Let sit for 15 minutes.

Meanwhile, melt the butter or heat the oil for the filling in a large skillet. Quickly sauté the tomatoes for a couple of minutes. Add salt and pepper to taste and the chives. Slide a knife between the pasta and the pan or mold to loosen it; then cover with a flat platter, and invert the ring. Remove the pan or mold, and fill the middle of the ring with the tomatoes. Serve at once.

Peperonata Pasta Round

SERVES 6–8

- ¼ quantity Rich Egg Pasta Dough (see page 44)
- salt and freshly ground black pepper
- 4 tablespoons olive oil
- 2 large onions, finely chopped
- 2 red bell peppers, deseeded and chopped
- 2 green bell peppers, deseeded and chopped
- 2 garlic cloves, crushed
- 1 quantity Béchamel Sauce (see page 60)
- 1 tablespoon chopped fresh oregano
- 1 pound tomatoes, peeled (see Cook's Tip, page 72) and sliced
- 4 tablespoons chopped parsley
- 10 ounces mozzarella cheese, thinly sliced
- 3 tablespoons freshly grated Parmesan cheese
- 3 tablespoons dried white bread crumbs

Make the pasta dough as given on page 44. Cut the pasta dough in half; then roll out each half to form a large round. Use a 10-inch round baking dish to cut out a circle of pasta to fit the dish. Repeat with the remaining dough.

Cook both circles in a large saucepan of boiling salted water for 3–4 minutes. Drain the pasta, and rinse it under cold running water; then open out the circles, and lay them on a clean dish cloth to dry.

Preheat the oven to 350°F.

Grease the dish with a little of the oil; then heat the remainder in a saucepan. Add the onions, bell peppers and garlic. Mix well, cover the pan, and cook gently for 20 minutes, or until the vegetables have softened but not browned.

Meanwhile, make the Béchamel Sauce as given on page 60.

Stir the oregano, and salt and pepper to taste into the vegetable mixture.

Lay the first pasta round in the dish. Spoon half the bell pepper mixture into the dish. Top with half the tomatoes; then sprinkle with half the parsley. Lay half the mozzarella slices on top, and dot with a little of the Béchamel Sauce, placing the occasional spoonful here and there on top of the cheese. Sprinkle with a little salt and pepper. Then lay the second pasta round on top.

Repeat the layers with the remaining mixture, reserving most of the Béchamel Sauce to cover the top of the lasagne. Stir the Parmesan cheese into the remaining Béchamel Sauce, and pour it over the lasagne. Then bake in the preheated oven for about 45 minutes, or until it has browned on top, and is bubbling hot throughout. Let sit for 10 minutes; then serve.

Spinach Lasagne

I have added sautéed leeks to the shredded spinach filling for this popular lasagne combination. It is great for vegetarians and confirmed carnivores alike.

SERVES 4

- about 8–10 sheets lasagne (see page 37)
- salt and freshly ground black pepper
- 2 tablespoons olive oil
- 2 cups thinly sliced leeks (see Cook's Tip, page 116)
- 2 garlic cloves, crushed
- 2½ cups Béchamel Sauce (see page 60)
- 2¼ pounds fresh baby spinach leaves, washed and shredded
- 2 cups strained ricotta cheese
- freshly grated nutmeg
- 6 tablespoons freshly grated Parmesan cheese

Preheat the oven to 350°F. Grease a large, rectangular, ovenproof dish with a little of the oil. Cook the lasagne in plenty of boiling salted water according to the instructions on the package, or allow 3 minutes for fresh pasta. Drain well, and rinse it under cold water; then lay the sheets out on a clean dish cloth to dry.

Heat the remaining oil in a large saucepan. Add the leeks and garlic; then cook, stirring often, for about 15 minutes, or until the leeks are tender.

Meanwhile, make the Béchamel Sauce as given on page 60.

Mix the spinach with the leeks and garlic, cover the pan tightly, and cook for about 5 minutes, or until the spinach has wilted, and is just tender. Remove the pan from the heat. Mix in the ricotta with salt and pepper to taste and a little nutmeg.

Layer the spinach mixture and lasagne in the dish, starting with spinach mixture and ending with lasagne. Stir the Parmesan into the Béchamel Sauce, and pour this over the lasagne. Bake in the preheated oven for about 45 minutes, or until the top has browned, and is bubbling.

Bacon and Artichoke Lasagne

This is rich and very tasty, with an unusual tarragon sauce for a topping.

SERVES 6

FOR THE LASAGNE

- 2 × 10-ounce jars seasoned artichokes in olive oil
- ⅔ cup diced, lean rindless bacon
- 1 onion, halved and sliced
- 1 red chili, deseeded and chopped (see Cook's Tip, page 90)
- 1 leek, sliced (see Cook's Tip, page 116)
- 2 garlic cloves, crushed
- 1 tablespoon all-purpose flour
- 14-ounce can chopped tomatoes
- 2-ounce can anchovy fillets, drained and chopped
- salt and freshly ground black pepper
- about 6 ounces lasagne (see page 37)

FOR THE TARRAGON SAUCE

- 2 tablespoons butter
- ¼ cup all-purpose flour
- 2 cups milk
- 1 tablespoon chopped fresh tarragon
- ½ cup grated, sharp Cheddar cheese

Preheat the oven to 350°F.

Now make the lasagne. Drain the oil from one of the jars of artichokes into a large saucepan. Drain the second jar, saving the oil, but it is not required for this recipe. Heat the oil in the saucepan; add the bacon, onion, chilli, leek and garlic. Stir well, then cover the pan, and cook for 15 minutes.

Stir in the flour; then add the tomatoes, anchovy fillets and the artichokes. Add salt and pepper to taste, and bring to a boil. Set aside.

Cook the lasagne in plenty of boiling salted water

according to the instructions on the package, or allow 3 minutes for fresh pasta. Drain and rinse under cold water; then lay out on a clean dish cloth to dry.

Layer the artichoke sauce and cooked lasagne in a large, rectangular, ovenproof dish, starting with the sauce and ending with lasagne.

Next, make the tarragon sauce. Melt the butter in a saucepan. Stir in the flour, then stir in the milk, and bring to a boil. Add the tarragon, cheese, and salt and pepper to taste, and stir over a low heat until the cheese has melted.

Pour the tarragon sauce over the lasagne, and bake in the preheated oven for about 45 minutes, or until it is bubbling hot and golden-brown.

Rutabaga Terrine

This was a slightly wild card idea that turned out to be a great success. The macaroni formed a lovely crusty base and top and the rutabaga mixture was light and well-flavored. You do need to use a good non-stick pan or non-stick baking parchment, though.

A crisp salad of frisée and very finely sliced carrot or Grated Zucchini and Basil Salad (see page 314) are ideal accompaniments.

SERVES 6

- 1 pound rutabaga, peeled and cubed
- salt and freshly ground black pepper
- ¼ cup butter
- 1 small onion, finely chopped
- 1 cup grated, sharp Cheddar cheese
- 1 cup slightly dry white bread crumbs
- 3 large eggs, beaten
- 6 ounces elbow macaroni
- ⅓ cup mascarpone cheese
- 3 tablespoons all-purpose flour
- 3 tablespoons freshly grated Parmesan cheese

Preheat the oven to 350°F. Grease a 2-lb loaf pan, using half of the butter. If the tin is not a good non-stick one, then line its base with non-stick baking parchment.

Cook the rutabaga in boiling salted water for about 10 minutes, or until tender.

Meanwhile, melt the remaining butter in a saucepan, and add the onion. Cook, stirring, for 5 minutes.

Drain the rutabaga and mash it thoroughly until smooth; then stir in the onion, cheese and bread crumbs with salt and pepper to taste. Cool slightly before mixing in 2 of the eggs.

Cook the macaroni in boiling salted water until tender – about 7 minutes, or according to the instructions on the package.

Drain the macaroni, and mix the mascarpone into it. Stir in the flour, Parmesan, and salt and pepper to taste. Spread half the macaroni mixture in the base of the pan. Top with the rutabaga mixture, smoothing this evenly over the macaroni; then spread the remaining macaroni mixture on top.

Bake the terrine in the preheated oven for 1 hour, or until it feels firm, and the top has browned lightly. Slide a flat-bladed knife between the mixture and the pan; then invert the pan onto a flat serving platter. Remove the lining paper, if used, and serve cut into thick slices.

Chicken and Vegetable Lasagne

SERVES 6

- 3 tablespoons olive oil
- about 8–10 sheets lasagne (see page 37)
- salt and freshly ground black pepper
- 1 garlic clove, crushed
- 1 large onion, chopped
- 4 celery stalks, sliced
- 1 carrot, diced
- 4 boneless chicken breasts, skinned and diced
- 1⅓ cups sliced mushrooms
- 2 × 14-ounce cans chopped tomatoes
- ⅔ cup water
- 1 bay leaf
- 2 tablespoons chopped fresh or 1 tablespoon dried oregano
- 4 ounces green beans, cut into short lengths
- ¾ cup frozen peas
- 1 quantity Béchamel Sauce (see page 60)
- 5 ounces mozzarella cheese, chopped

Preheat the oven to 350°F. Grease a large, rectangular, ovenproof dish with a little of the oil.

Cook the lasagne in plenty of boiling salted water according to the instructions on the package, or allow 3 minutes for fresh pasta. Drain well, and rinse them under cold water; then lay the sheets out on a clean dish cloth to dry.

Heat the remaining oil in a large saucepan. Add the garlic, onion, celery, carrot and chicken. Stir well, and fry the mixture until the onion has softened. Add the tomatoes, water, bay leaf, oregano, and plenty of salt and pepper. Heat until simmering, then cover the pan, and simmer for 15 minutes.

Meanwhile, make the Béchamel Sauce as given on page 60.

Stir the beans and peas into the vegetable and chicken mixture, and simmer, covered, for a further 5 minutes.

Layer the vegetable and chicken sauce and pasta in the prepared dish, starting with sauce and ending with lasagne. Cover with the Béchamel Sauce; then sprinkle the mozzarella over the top. Bake in the preheated oven for 40–50 minutes, or until the topping is golden, and the lasagne is bubbling hot.

ORIENTAL SPECIALTIES

◆

The Range of Pasta Products, Cooking Styles and Ingredients Used in the Orient is Enormous. ❦ There are, However, Similarities that run Through the Veins of Chinese, Japanese, Malaysian, Singaporean and Thai Cooking Which I have Included Here.

This Chapter Offers some Traditional Noodle Dishes Along with Interpretations of the Themes and Flavors that are Characteristic of the Countries. ❦ There are Occasional Specialist Ingredients, for Which you May have to Travel, but Only as Far as a Specialty Store in a

Large Town or City. Once You Have Made the Trip, Many of the Dried Ingredients Keep for Years, and Some Fresh Foods can be Frozen.

Dim sum are a Feature of this Chapter. ❦ These Chinese Snacks Date Back to the Tenth Century – Perhaps these are the Early Forms of Pasta that Marco Polo Found he Just Could Not

Leave Behind. ❦ Dim sum are Traditionally Served as Part of a Tea Meal, with Chinese tea Served as a Refresher Throughout. ❦ You Will be Able to Buy them Throughout the Day in an Authentic Chinese Café, and they are Ideal when Shopping gets to be Too Much and You Need a Little Reviver.

My Hong Kong Tourist Guide Tells me that Dim sum Literally means "To Touch the Heart," but it is a Light Snack in Modern Terms. ❦ They Certainly made a Lasting Impression on me – I hope You Enjoy Them, Too.

CHINESE DIM SUM

Dim sum are snacks, traditionally served in tea houses as a form of daytime refreshment and sustenance. Chinese restaurants usually serve dim sum from lunchtime through until the early evening; however, some specialize in these popular dishes, and make a feature of providing quite a number of dim sum throughout the day, including main meal times. These may include a wide variety of foods, such as barbecued spareribs and so on, served in small quantities, but it is the dumplings, won ton and spring rolls that have made dim sum internationally famous.

USING BAMBOO STEAMERS

Piping hot steamed dim sum are served directly from the bamboo steamers in which they are cooked. Bamboo steamers come in a variety of sizes, from as small as 4 inches in diameter to wide containers that fit over woks.

These large steamers are stacked on a wok, and a lid is placed over the top layer to keep in the steam. The lattice of bamboo slats inside the steamer is greased well, and the small dumplings or other dim sum are placed directly on it. However, it is more hygienic, and there is less danger of the dim sum sticking if the dim sum are placed on a flat, greased plate. The plate should fit inside the steamer with plenty of space to spare around the sides, so that the steam can rise through the layers. Alternatively, the perforated foil technique described below may be used.

USING A STEAMER ON A SAUCEPAN

Steamers that are graduated in size to fit on top of a saucepan do not afford as much space for cooking dim sum as the bamboo type. The dim sum can be placed directly on the greased steamer; however, when cooking a large batch, they are difficult to lift off.

A greased plate may be used, but this must allow space around the side for the steam to rise through the layers.

A practical method is to cut a double thickness of heavy cooking foil to fit in the base of the steamer. Puncture it all over to allow the steam through; then grease it well. Place the dim sum on the foil, and place them in the steamer. Another method used for larger steamed buns is to place a small square of non-stick paper under each bun. As the focus here is on pasta, you will not find recipes for these. This method can be adopted for the dim sum given here, but it is rather time-consuming, placing each dumpling on a tiny square of paper.

KEEP THE POT BOILING

Make sure the water is boiling vigorously, so that there is plenty of steam to cook the dim sum. There must also be sufficient water in the wok or pan to boil for the complete cooking time. If you are cooking dim sum in batches, you may need to keep a kettle of boiling water nearby to top up the pan under the steamer.

GARNISHING ORIENTAL STYLE

◆

Colorful vegetable garnishes are used in oriental cooking. You will need a small, fine-pointed knife with a sharp blade. Special knives with very small, narrow blades for intricate cutting are sold quite cheaply in hardware stores, or good-quality carving knives and tools are available from good kitchen stores and catering suppliers.

Remember that if you plan on cooking a range of dishes or selection of dim sum, then you really must prepare the garnishes well in advance – make them the day before, and chill them overnight. Spring onion curls are described on page 256, but here are a few additional ideas for presentation.

RADISH ROSES

Make small, crescent-shaped cuts down into the sides of the radish in a row around the base. The cuts should loosen a thin peeling of red skin. Then work around, making a second series of cuts above the first row, this time cutting the crescents, so that the first starts in the middle of one on the lower row, and ends in the middle of the next one. Continue cutting into the radish, building up the layers of petals all around the outside of the vegetable, right up to the top. Place in iced water until the "petals" separate from the radish to open out like a flower – the thinner the cuts, the quicker the flower opens, but it takes at least 30 minutes, and they should be left for about an hour – leaving them longer makes the flower open more fully!

STAMPING OUT CARROT SHAPES

Thinly slice large carrots, and cook in boiling water for 3–4 minutes; then drain well. Use aspic cutters to stamp out a shape from each slice.

CARROT FLOWERS

Use a canelle knife to pare strips off the length of a carrot, cutting evenly spaced channels around the vegetable. Slice the carrot, and blanch in boiling water for 2 minutes.

CHILI CURLS

To make chili curls, use a small, sharp knife to cut a fresh chili into fine strips lengthwise, working from the stalk end toward the point, and leaving all the strips attached at the stalk. Rinse out the seeds, and scrape out the middle of the chili as you work. Place the chili in a bowl of iced water for at least 30 minutes, or until the strips curl.

CUCUMBER CURLS

Cut 4-inch lengths of English cucumber. Peel the cucumber; then use a vegetable peeler to pare off thin slices down the length of the cucumber. Curl the long slices around loosely in an informal, ringlet-like arrangement.

CUCUMBER-SKIN SHAPES

Cut off thin lengths of English cucumber skin, and use aspic cutters to stamp out shapes. Alternatively, use a fine-pointed knife to cut out leaves freehand. Cut fine veins out of the skin.

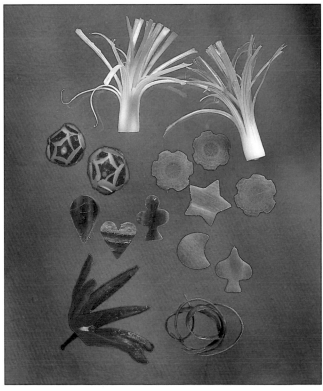

Radish roses, scallion curls, carrot flowers, cucumber shapes and curls and chili flowers.

Shrimp Har Kow

Once you get into the swing of shaping and filling these little dumplings, they are fun to prepare. If you become extremely adept at making them, then you may want to progress to making tiny, bite-sized dumplings, in which case the quantities given will make between 35 and 40 dumplings.

MAKES 24

FOR THE DUMPLINGS
- a little oil
- 1½ cups peeled, cooked shrimp
- 1 scallion, very finely chopped
- 2 tablespoons very finely chopped celery
- 2 tablespoons very finely chopped canned bamboo shoots
- 1 tablespoon light soy sauce
- 2 teaspoons cornstarch
- 1 egg, beaten
- 1 quantity Dim Sum Dough (see page 53)
- cornstarch, for rolling out

FOR THE DIPPING SAUCE
- 1 garlic clove, finely chopped
- 6 tablespoons soy sauce
- 2 tablespoons dry sherry

TO GARNISH
- scallion curls (see Cook's Tip)
- whole cooked shrimp

Prepare a steamer using a little oil (see page 254).

First, make the dumplings. Grind the shrimp, or chop them very finely in a food processor. Alternatively, chop them finely by hand; then pound them with the back of a mixing spoon or in a mortar with a pestle until they form a coarse paste. Add the scallion, celery, bamboo shoots, soy sauce and cornstarch. Mix the ingredients thoroughly, adding a teaspoon of the beaten egg if necessary to bind them together.

Make the Dim Sum Dough as given on page 53, then divide the dough in half, and mark each half into 12 equal portions. Cut off one portion, and keep the rest of the dough covered. Press out the dough into a circle; then roll it or press it out into a circle measuring about 2–3 inches in diameter on a counter lightly dusted with cornstarch.

Place a little of the shrimp mixture in the middle of the circle of dough, and brush the edge of the dough with a little egg. Fold the dough over the filling to form a shape like a miniature pasty. Pinch the edges of the dough together, fluting them decoratively. Place in the prepared steamer. Continue shaping and filling the Har Kow, using all the dough and filling.

Steam the Har Kow dumplings over boiling water for about 10 minutes, or until the dough is cooked, firm and glossy.

Meanwhile prepare the dipping sauce. Mix the garlic, soy sauce and sherry together; then divide it between four small dishes.

Serve the freshly cooked Har Kow garnished with scallion curls and whole cooked shrimp.

COOK'S TIP

To make scallion curls, cut the green part of the trimmed scallions into fine strips, leaving them attached at the root end. Place in a bowl of iced water for at least 30 minutes. The finely cut green part of the scallion will curl during soaking. Drain well before using.

Crispy Won Ton Noodles

SERVES 6–8

- 1 quantity Won Ton Dough, made with baking powder (see page 52)
- cornstarch, for rolling out
- oil, for frying

Cut the dough in half, and roll out one portion thinly on a counter dusted with cornstarch. Dust the top of the dough with cornstarch, then roll it up loosely. Cut the roll of dough into ¼-inch wide slices; then shake them out to make narrow noodles.

Heat sufficient oil to deep-fry the noodles to 375°F, or until a cube of day-old bread browns in about 30 seconds. Deep-fry the noodles, a handful at a time, until they have puffed up, and are crisp and golden. Drain well on paper towels.

Shrimp Har Kow

257

Sweet-and-Sour Pork Won Tons

These are delicious – one of my (many) favorite
Chinese dishes!

SERVES 4

- *about 6 ounces lean boneless pork*
- *pinch of five-spice powder*
- *1 teaspoon sesame oil*
- *1 garlic clove, finely chopped*
- *1 tablespoon soy sauce*

- *18 squares Won Ton Dough made with baking powder (see page 52), or ready-made wrappers*
- *1 egg, beaten*
- *1 quantity Sweet-and-sour Sauce (see page 63)*
- *oil, for deep frying*

Cut the pork into 18 small, neat pieces, no bigger than ½-inch cubes. Place the cubes of meat in a bowl, and sprinkle with a good pinch of five-spice powder, the sesame oil, garlic and soy sauce. Let marinate for a few hours or overnight, allowing plenty of time for the meat to become well-flavored with garlic and spice.

Brush the middle of a square of Won Ton Dough or a wrapper with a little egg, and place a piece of meat on it. Then gather the dough around the meat to make a tiny bundle with frilly edges. Fill and shape all the Won Tons in the same way; then make the Sweet-and-sour Sauce as given on page 63.

Heat sufficient oil to deep-fry the Won Tons to 375°F, or until a cube of day-old bread browns in about 30 seconds. Fry the Won Tons, a few at a time, until they have puffed up, are golden and cooked through. Drain well on paper towels. Transfer to a serving platter, and spoon the Sweet-and-sour Sauce over; then serve immediately.

Crispy Won Ton Packages

These are an adaptation of spring rolls.

MAKES 16

- 1 tablespoon oil
- 1 teaspoon sesame oil
- 1 garlic clove, finely chopped
- 2 scallions, finely chopped
- 2 tablespoons chopped vegetables (bamboo shoots, water chestnuts, carrot, celery or a mixture, according to availability)
- ¼ cup beansprouts
- 1¼ cups ground pork
- salt
- 1 quantity Won Ton Dough made with baking powder (see page 52)
- cornstarch, for dusting
- 1 egg white
- oil, for frying

Heat the oil and sesame oil in a small saucepan. Add the garlic, scallions and vegetables, and cook for 2 minutes. Add the beansprouts, and stir well; then remove the pan from the heat. Mix the vegetables with the pork, and add a little salt.

Make the Won Ton Dough as given on page 52; then cut it in half. Mark each half into eight portions. Cut off one portion of dough, and cover the rest. Roll out the portion of dough on a surface dusted with cornstarch to form a thin circle about 4 inches in diameter. Place a little of the meat mixture in the middle, pressing it together neatly. Brush the dough with a little lightly whisked egg white; then fold the side nearest you over the filling. Fold the sides of the dough in over the filling. Brush with egg white, and roll up neatly to make a miniature spring roll. Repeat with the remaining dough and filling.

Heat sufficient oil to deep-fry the packages to 375°F, or until a cube of day-old bread browns in about 30 seconds. Fry the packages until they are crisp and golden, turning them several times during cooking. Drain well on paper towels, and serve piping hot.

Pork and Shrimp Shiu My

MAKES 32

FOR THE SHIU MY
- *1½ cups lean ground pork*
- *1 cup cooked, peeled prawns, ground or very finely chopped*
- *1 tablespoon light soy sauce*
- *a few drops of sesame oil*
- *1 teaspoon cornstarch*
- *1 scallion, very finely chopped*
- *2 tablespoons finely chopped canned water chestnuts or celery*

- *1 quantity Dim Sum Dough (see page 53)*
- *cornstarch, for dusting*
- *32 small peeled, cooked shrimp, to garnish*

FOR THE DIPPING SAUCE
- *1 garlic clove, finely chopped*
- *6 tablespoons soy sauce*
- *4 tablespoons dry sherry*

Prepare a steamer (see page 254).

First, make the Shiu My. Mix the pork, shrimp, soy sauce, sesame oil, cornstarch, scallion and water chestnut or celery until well combined.

Make the Dim Sum Dough as given on page 53; then cut it in half. Roll one half of the dough into a cylinder shape, and mark it into 16 equal portions. Repeat this with the second half. Keep the dough covered with plastic wrap as you shape and fill the Shiu My.

Divide the meat mixture into quarters (when shaping the Shiu My, you should get eight portions from each quarter of the meat mixture).

Cut off a portion of dough, and knead it lightly in the palm of your hand; then flatten it on a counter lightly dusted with cornstarch, or roll it out thinly. Roll a small portion of the meat mixture into a ball, and place it on the dough. Fold the dough up around the meat to encase it on all sides, but leave the top uncovered. Pleat the sides of the dough neatly, and flatten the base. Flatten the top of the meat. The shaped Shiu My looks like a short cylinder with dough around the sides and underneath, and the neatly flattened meat filling showing on top. Repeat with the remaining portions of dough and meat mixture, placing the Shiu My in the prepared steamer as they are made. Top each Shiu My with a small shrimp; then steam them for 15–20 minutes, until the filling has cooked through.

Meanwhile, prepare the dipping sauce. Mix the garlic with the soy sauce and sherry. Divide the sauce between small dishes, one for each diner. Serve the Shiu My freshly steamed.

Pork Shiu My

MAKES 18

FOR THE SHIU MY
- *1 cup lean ground pork*
- *1 garlic clove, crushed and finely chopped*
- *2 scallions, finely chopped*
- *2 tablespoons finely chopped canned bamboo shoots*
- *2 tablespoons finely chopped celery*
- *2 tablespoons finely chopped cooked carrot*

- *1 teaspoon cornstarch*
- *2 tablespoons soy sauce*
- *1 egg, beaten*
- *1 teaspoon sesame oil*
- *1 quantity Won Ton Dough (see page 52), or 18 ready-made won ton wrappers*
- *cornstarch, for dusting*

FOR THE DIPPING SAUCE
- *6 tablespoons soy sauce*
- *4 tablespoons dry sherry*
- *1 scallion, finely chopped*

TO GARNISH
- *a little finely diced carrot*
- *18 frozen peas*
- *scallion curls (see Cook's Tip, page 256), optional*

Prepare a steamer (see page 254).

First, make the Shiu My. Mix the pork, garlic, scallions, bamboo shoots, celery, carrot and cornstarch. Pound the ingredients together until they are thoroughly combined. Then mix in the soy sauce and a little of the egg to bind the mixture.

Prepare and roll out the Won Ton Dough (see page 52). Use a cutter to stamp out 18 2½–3-inch circles from the dough. Ready-made wrappers may be left square, or the corners may be trimmed off to round their shape slightly.

To fill the Shiu My, brush the dough with a little egg; then place a small mound of the meat mixture in the middle. Gently gather the dough up around the sides of the meat filling, molding it into shape. If you are using

ready-made wrappers, which are still slightly square in shape, pinch the excess dough into two small wings at the side, and fold them flat in opposite directions. The shape can be neatened by placing the Shiu My on a counter lightly dusted with cornstarch, and gently rotating it between your hands so that the meat forms a neat, narrow cylinder shape, with the dough clinging to the outside and the top remaining open.

Place the Shiu My in the prepared steamer. Top each with a little diced carrot and a pea. Steam for about 20 minutes, or until the meat has cooked through.

While the Shiu My are cooking, make the dipping sauce. Mix the soy sauce, sherry and scallion, and place the sauce in small shallow saucers for each diner. Serve the Shiu My freshly steamed.

261

Beef Shiu My and Chili Dipping Sauce

These palate-awakening snacks really pep up a dim sum feast.

MAKES 32

FOR THE SHIU MY
- 2 cups ground steak
- 1 garlic clove, crushed and finely chopped
- 2 scallions, finely chopped
- 1 tablespoon finely chopped fresh ginger root
- 1 tablespoon soy sauce
- 1 teaspoon sesame oil
- 2 teaspoons cornstarch
- generous pinch of five-spice powder

- 1 quantity Dim Sum Dough (see page 53)
- cornstarch, for dusting
- 32 frozen peas, to garnish

FOR THE DIPPING SAUCE
- 1 red or green chili, deseeded and very thinly sliced (see Cook's Tip, page 90)
- 1 tablespoon hoisin sauce
- 2 tablespoons dry sherry
- 6 tablespoons soy sauce
- ½ teaspoon cider vinegar

Prepare a steamer (see page 254).

First, make the Shiu My. Mix the steak, garlic, scallions, ginger root, soy sauce, sesame oil, cornstarch and five-spice powder. Pound the mixture together until thoroughly and evenly combined.

Make the Dim Sum Dough as given on page 53; then cut it in half. Roll one half of the dough into a cylinder shape, and mark it into 16 equal pieces. Repeat with the second half. Keep the dough covered with plastic wrap as you shape and fill the Shiu My.

Divide the meat mixture into quarters (when shaping the Shiu My, you should get eight portions from each quarter of the meat mixture).

Cut off a portion of dough, and knead it lightly in the palm of your hand; then flatten it on a counter lightly dusted with cornstarch, or roll it out thinly. Roll a small portion of the meat mixture into a ball, and place it on the dough. Fold the dough up around the meat to encase it on all sides, but leave the top uncovered. Pleat the sides of the dough neatly, and flatten the base. Flatten the top of the meat. Repeat with the remaining portions of dough and meat mixture, placing the Shiu My in the prepared steamer as they are made. Top each Shiu My with a frozen pea; then steam them for 15–20 minutes, until the filling has cooked.

Meanwhile, prepare the dipping sauce. Mix the chili, hoisin sauce, sherry, soy sauce and vinegar. Divide the sauce between small dishes, one for each diner. Serve the Shiu My freshly steamed.

Chicken Chow Mein

SERVES 4

- 12 ounces fresh or dried Chinese egg noodles
- 2 boneless chicken breasts, skinned and cut into thin strips
- 1 tablespoon cornstarch
- 2 tablespoons oil
- 1 garlic clove, crushed
- 2-inch piece fresh ginger root, peeled and cut into thin strips

- 1 onion, halved and thinly sliced
- 1 green bell pepper, deseeded and cut into chunks
- 1 carrot, cut into fine matchstick strips
- 1 cup frozen peas
- 3 tablespoons soy sauce
- 1 cup chicken stock

Cook the noodles according to the instructions on the package, or add fresh noodles to boiling water, and bring back to a boil; then reduce the heat, and cook for 3 minutes. Drain well.

Toss the chicken with the cornstarch. Heat the oil in a large skillet or wok. Add the chicken, and stir-fry until it is lightly browned. Then add the garlic, ginger root, onion, bell pepper and carrot. Stir-fry for a further 3 minutes; then add the peas, soy sauce and chicken stock. Bring to a boil, stirring, and simmer for 5 minutes.

Add the noodles, heat through, and serve.

Braised Chicken with Rice Sticks

SERVES 4

- 2 dried Chinese mushrooms
- ⅔ cup hot water
- 2 boneless chicken breasts, skinned
- 1 carrot
- 1 tablespoon oil
- 1 teaspoon sesame oil
- 1 red bell pepper, deseeded and cut into 1-inch squares
- 4 scallions, finely shredded diagonally
- 1 garlic clove, chopped

- 1 piece of lemon grass
- 1-inch piece fresh ginger root, sliced
- 8-ounce can bamboo shoots, sliced into thin strips
- 3 tablespoons light soy sauce
- ¼ quantity Chinese-style Stock (see page 57)
- 8 ounces ribbon rice sticks
- 1 tablespoon cornstarch
- 3 tablespoons dry sherry

Put the mushrooms into a bowl or mug. Add the water, and cover; then leave to soak for 30 minutes. Drain the mushrooms, reserving the soaking liquid, and discard the stalks if they are tough; then slice the mushroom caps. Cut the chicken breasts across into fairly thick slices. Cut the carrot into 2-inch lengths; then slice them very thinly lengthwise into wide strips.

Heat the oil and sesame oil in a flameproof casserole. Add the pepper, carrot, scallions, garlic, lemon grass and ginger root. Stir-fry for 2 minutes; then add the bamboo shoots, soy sauce and stock. Strain the soaking water from the mushrooms, and add it to the pan with the mushroom slices. Heat until simmering; then add the chicken. Cover, and cook gently for 30 minutes.

Toward the end of this time, cook the rice sticks according to the instructions on the package, then drain and rinse them under cold water.

Blend the cornstarch with the sherry. Stir the cornstarch mixture into the sauce in the casserole, and bring to a boil, stirring. Add the rice sticks, and simmer for 2 minutes. Serve at once.

Spicy Duck with Mango and Rice Sticks

SERVES 4

- 4 boneless duck breasts, skinned
- 2 tablespoons soy sauce
- 2 garlic cloves, crushed
- 1 tablespoon sesame oil
- 2-inch piece fresh ginger root, peeled and cut into fine strips
- 2 tablespoons hoisin sauce
- 2 tablespoons dry sherry
- 12 ounces ribbon rice sticks

- 2 tablespoons oil
- 1 bunch of scallions, finely shredded diagonally
- 10-ounce can jelly mushrooms, drained
- 1 mango, peeled, pit removed and flesh cut into small pieces
- ½ cup roasted cashew nuts

Cut the duck breasts across into thin slices. Mix them with the soy sauce, garlic, sesame oil, ginger root, hoisin sauce and sherry. Let marinate for 3–4 hours.

Cook the rice sticks according to the instructions on the package.

Heat the oil in a large skillet or wok. Use a slotted spoon to add the duck pieces, removing as much of the marinade from them as possible. Stir-fry them briskly for 4–5 minutes; then add the remaining marinade with the jelly mushrooms. Heat through until the sauce is sizzling hot.

Drain the rice sticks, and put them into a dish. Mix the mango with the duck and sauce, and immediately add the mixture to the rice sticks. Serve at once.

Pork and Baby Corn Chow Mein

SERVES 4

- 8 ounces baby corn
- 8 ounces fresh or dried Chinese egg noodles
- 1 tablespoon oil
- 1 teaspoon sesame oil
- 6 ounces lean boneless pork, cut into fine strips
- 2-inch piece fresh ginger root, peeled and cut into very fine strips
- 1 red bell pepper, deseeded and cut into fine strips
- 6 scallions, shredded diagonally
- 1 teaspoon cornstarch
- 3 tablespoons dry sherry
- 2 tablespoons soy sauce
- ⅔ cup chicken stock

Blanch the corn in boiling water for 2 minutes; then drain well. Cook the noodles according to the instructions on the package, or add fresh noodles to boiling water, and bring back to a boil; then reduce the heat, and cook for 3 minutes. Drain well, and set aside.

Heat the oil and sesame oil in a large skillet or wok. Add the pork and ginger root, and stir-fry until the meat is lightly browned in parts, and just cooked.

Add the corn and red bell pepper, and continue to stir-fry for 2–3 minutes more. Then add the scallions, and cook for a further 1 minute.

Blend the cornstarch with the sherry, soy sauce and chicken stock, then stir the mixture into the pan, and bring to a boil, stirring all the time. Add the noodles, and toss them with the mixture for 2–3 minutes, until hot and well coated. Serve at once.

Spicy Beef Chow Mein

SERVES 4

- *1 pound rump steak or frying steak*
- *1 tablespoon cornstarch*
- *1 tablespoon fermented black beans*
- *3 tablespoons dry sherry*
- *2 tablespoons soy sauce*
- *½ teaspoon five-spice powder*
- *1 garlic clove, crushed*
- *1 teaspoon sesame oil*
- *1 green chili, deseeded and chopped (see Cook's Tip, page 90)*
- *12 ounces fresh or dried Chinese egg noodles*
- *2 tablespoons oil*
- *1 red bell pepper, deseeded and cut into small squares*
- *1 green bell pepper, deseeded and cut into small squares*
- *1 onion, quartered and cut across into small squares*
- *1¼ cups chicken stock*

Cut the beef across the grain into very thin slices (partially freezing the steak makes this easier). Place the meat in a non-metallic dish, add the cornstarch, and mix well. Then mix in the black beans, sherry, soy sauce, five-spice powder, garlic, sesame oil and chili. Cover and let marinate for 3–4 hours.

Cook the noodles according to the instructions on the package, or add fresh noodles to boiling water, bring back to a boil, then reduce the heat, and cook for 3 minutes. Drain well.

Heat the oil in a wok or skillet. Add the red and green peppers and onion. Stir-fry for 2 minutes, then use a slotted spoon to drain the marinating juices from the beef, and add the beef to the wok or skillet. Stir-fry until it is sealed and browned. Add the stock to the marinade, pour it into the wok or skillet, and bring to a boil, stirring. Add the noodles, and toss them with the meat, until they are thoroughly reheated. Transfer the Chow Mein to a serving dish, and serve at once.

Stir-fried Squid with Rice Vermicelli

Many fish vendors and supermarkets sell prepared squid sacs, but if you buy whole, fresh squid, read the Cook's Tip below for advice on how to prepare them.

SERVES 4

- *12 ounces rice vermicelli*
- *8 squid sacs (see Cook's Tip), thinly sliced*
- *salt and freshly ground black pepper*
- *2 tablespoons cornstarch*
- *4 tablespoons groundnut oil*
- *2 red chilis, deseeded and finely chopped (see Cook's Tip, page 90)*
- *4 garlic cloves, finely chopped*
- *6 scallions, finely shredded diagonally*
- *2 tablespoons light soy sauce*
- *2 tablespoons fish sauce (see note page 278)*

Soak the rice vermicelli in boiling water for about 3 minutes to soften the noodles; then drain well.

Toss the squid rings with salt, pepper and cornstarch.

Heat the oil in a large skillet or wok. Add the chilis and garlic, and cook for 1 minute. Then add the squid rings, and fry them briskly for a couple of minutes, until lightly browned. Use a slotted spoon to remove the squid rings from the skillet or wok, and set aside.

Add the scallions to the skillet or wok; then add the vermicelli. Continue to fry for 2–3 minutes, turning rather than stirring the vermicelli. Add the soy sauce and fish sauce. Return the squid to the skillet or wok, mix lightly, and serve at once.

COOK'S TIP

To clean whole squid, first pull the head and tentacle parts out of the sac (the tentacles may be cut off the head and these can be fried if wished). Remove the fine, opaque quill that runs down the length of the inside of the sac. Then wash the sac, rubbing off the mottled skin from the outside to leave the sac clean and white.

Crispy Shrimp Chow Mein

SERVES 4

- 8 ounces dried fine Chinese egg noodles
- 6 dried Chinese mushrooms
- 4 tablespoons oil
- 1 tablespoon sesame oil
- 1 large carrot, cut into fine matchstick strips
- 8 scallions, shredded diagonally
- 1 tablespoon cornstarch
- 6 tablespoons soy sauce
- 6 tablespoons dry sherry
- 3 cups peeled, cooked shrimp

Cook the egg noodles according to the instructions on the package; then drain well.

Soak the mushrooms in a small bowl in hot water to cover for 20 minutes; then drain, reserving and straining the liquid to remove any grit. Discard any tough stalks, and slice the mushrooms.

Heat 1 tablespoon of the oil and 1 teaspoon of the sesame oil in a large skillet. Tip in the noodles, and spread them out evenly, pressing them flat with the back of a spatula. Fry the noodles until they are crisp and golden underneath. Slide the noodles out onto a plate. Add another tablespoon of the oil and teaspoon of the sesame oil to the skillet. When the oil is hot, turn the noodles back into the skillet, uncooked side down. Brown the underneath of the noodles; then slide them out onto the plate. Transfer the noodles into a large serving dish, cover loosely with foil, and keep hot.

Add the remaining oil and sesame oil to the skillet. Stir-fry the carrot, scallions and mushrooms.

Blend the cornstarch with the soy sauce, sherry and liquid drained from the mushrooms in a measuring jug. Make up the mixture to 2 cups with water; then pour it into the skillet, and bring to a boil, stirring all the time. Boil the sauce for 2 minutes.

Reduce the heat, and stir in the shrimp. Heat, without boiling, for 2 minutes. Pour the shrimp and sauce over the noodles, and serve at once.

Pan Stickers

These are cooked by frying *and* braising – the results are very tasty! A good non-stick skillet with a lid is ideal for cooking these.

MAKES 24

FOR THE PAN STICKERS
- *1 dried Chinese mushroom*
- *1 cup ground pork*
- *1 cup ground steak*
- *2 scallions, finely chopped*
- *1 garlic clove, crushed*
- *1 tablespoons finely chopped tinned bamboo shoots*
- *1 tablespoon soy sauce*
- *1 teaspoon sesame oil*
- *2 teaspoons cornstarch*

- *1 quantity Dim Sum Dough (see page 53)*
- *cornstarch, for dusting*
- *1 egg, beaten*
- *oil, for frying*

FOR THE DIPPING SAUCE
- *6 tablespoons soy sauce*
- *4 tablespoons dry sherry*
- *1 scallion, finely chopped*

First, make the Pan Stickers. Put the mushroom into a small bowl or mug, add hot water to cover it, and let soak for 30 minutes. Drain well, reserving the soaking liquor, and remove the stalk if it is tough. Chop the mushroom finely, and mix it with the pork, steak, scallions, garlic, bamboo shoots, soy sauce, sesame oil and cornstarch. Pound the ingredients together well until thoroughly and evenly combined.

Make the Dim Sum Dough as given on page 53; then divide it in half. Mark each half into 12 equal portions.

Cut off one portion, and keep the rest of the dough covered. Press out the dough into a circle; then roll it or press it out further into a circle measuring about 2–3 inches in diameter on a counter lightly dusted with cornstarch.

Place a little of the meat mixture in the middle of the circle of dough, and brush the edge of the dough with a little egg. Fold the dough over the filling to form a shape like that of a miniature pasty. Pinch the edges of the dough together to seal in the filling. Continue shaping and filling the pan stickers, using all the dough and filling.

Pour a thin layer of oil into a large skillet (preferable one with a lid, or find a saucepan lid or plate that can be used to cover the pan later). Heat the oil, and fry the Pan Stickers until they are golden underneath; then turn them over. Strain the reserved soaking liquor from the mushroom, and add enough water to make it up to about 1 cup. Pour this into the skillet (you may have to add a little more water if the pan is large as the bottom of the pan needs to be completely covered).

Bring the water to a boil. Then reduce the heat, and cover the pan. Braise the Pan Stickers for 15 minutes. Remove the lid, and continue cooking until all the liquid has evaporated, and the Pan Stickers are again frying. Continue to cook until they are browned on this second side; then carefully lift them out of the skillet. Serve at once.

Wind-dried Sausage with Spinach

If you have not yet discovered Chinese sausages, then you have a real treat in store. They are sold in vacuum packages in oriental supermarkets, but, if you are not keen on offal or liver, check the ingredients and pay a little more for a package that does not have liver listed significantly high on the list.

SERVES 4

- *4 wind-dried Chinese sausages*
- *12 ounces fresh or dried Chinese egg noodles*
- *3 tablespoons oil*
- *1 tablespoon grated fresh ginger root*
- *8 ounces baby corn*
- *1 garlic clove*
- *1 bunch of scallions, finely shredded diagonally*

- *4 celery stalks, cut into fine matchstick strips*
- *2 cups shredded spinach*
- *4 ounces snow peas*
- *1 1/3 cups thinly sliced button mushrooms*
- *2 teaspoons cornstarch*
- *scant 1 cup chicken stock*
- *3 tablespoons dry sherry*
- *2 tablespoons light soy sauce*

Steam the sausages over boiling water for 20 minutes, or until tender. Cut the sausages diagonally into thin slices.

Meanwhile, cook the noodles according to the instructions on the package, or add fresh noodles to boiling water, and bring back to a boil; then reduce the heat, and cook for 3 minutes. Drain well.

Heat 1 tablespoon of the oil in a large skillet. Add the noodles, and press them down into the skillet. Cook until crisp and golden underneath; then slide the noodle cake out onto a large plate or platter. Add another tablespoon of the oil to the skillet. Invert the noodles into the skillet, press down, and cook as before. Transfer to a large plate, and keep hot.

Heat the remaining oil in a large skillet or wok. Add the ginger root, corn, sausage slices and garlic. Stir-fry for 2 minutes; then add the scallions, spinach, celery, snow peas and mushrooms. Blend the cornstarch with the stock, sherry and soy sauce, then pour the liquid into the skillet, and bring to a boil, stirring.

Pour the sausage and vegetable mixture over the crispy noodles, and serve at once. Cut the noodles into sections as you serve the mixture (if the noodles are sufficiently crisp when fried, they still retain some crunch after the sauce has been poured over them).

Fresh Shiitake and Snow Peas with Crispy Noodles

Homemade won ton noodles make a tempting topping for this flavorsome combination of vegetables.

SERVES 4

- ½ quantity Crispy Won Ton Noodles (see page 256)
- 2 teaspoons cornstarch
- ⅔ cup Chinese-style Stock (page 57) or Vegetable Stock (page 56)
- 2 tablespoons light soy sauce
- 2 tablespoons oil
- 1⅓ cups sliced, fresh shiitake mushrooms
- 8 ounces snow peas
- 4 scallions, finely sliced diagonally
- 2 bunches watercress, leaves only

Prepare and cook the noodles as given on page 256; then drain them well on paper towels.

Blend the cornstarch with the stock and soy sauce.

Heat the oil in a large skillet or wok. Add the mushrooms, snow peas and scallions; then stir-fry for 2 minutes.

Pour in the stock mixture, and bring to a boil, stirring all the time. Simmer for 2 minutes.

Stir in the watercress, and serve, topping with the Crispy Won Ton Noodles just before taking the dish to the table.

Vegetable Chow Mein with Deep-fried Bean Curd

SERVES 4

- 8 ounces firm bean curd
- 1 teaspoon sesame oil
- 2 tablespoons cornstarch
- salt and freshly ground black pepper
- pinch of chili powder
- oil, for frying
- 12 ounces fresh or dried Chinese egg noodles
- 2 tablespoons oil
- 2 leeks, thinly sliced
- 1 red or yellow bell pepper, halved, deseeded and cut into thin strips
- 8-ounce can bamboo shoots, drained and cut into thin strips
- 8-ounce can water chestnuts, drained and sliced
- 1 carrot, cut into fine matchstick strips
- ⅔ cup vegetable stock
- 4 tablespoons light soy sauce
- 4 tablespoons dry sherry
- 1 teaspoon cornstarch
- ¼ head of Chinese leaves, shredded

Cut the bean curd into small cubes (about ½-inch each side); then gently mix the sesame oil with them. Mix the cornstarch with plenty of salt and pepper, and a pinch of chili powder. When the sesame oil is well mixed with the bean curd, tip the cornstarch mixture over, and mix lightly to coat all the pieces. Heat sufficient oil to deep-fry the bean curd to 375°F, or until a cube of day-old bread browns in about 30 seconds. Deep-fry the bean curd until it is a pale golden color; then drain well on paper towels.

Cook the noodles according to the instructions on the package, or add fresh noodles to boiling water, and bring back to a boil; then reduce the heat, and cook for 3 minutes. Drain well, and set aside.

Heat the oil in a wok or large skillet. Add the leeks, bell pepper, bamboo shoots, water chestnuts and carrot. Stir-fry until the leeks and carrots have lost their raw texture without becoming soft (about 3–5 minutes).

Mix the stock, soy sauce and sherry into the cornstarch, then add to the skillet and bring to a boil stirring.

Add the Chinese leaves and noodles to the vegetable mixture. Mix well; then add the bean curd. Continue to mix the Chow Mein until it has thoroughly heated through (about 2 minutes). Serve at once.

Beef in Oyster Sauce with Rice Sticks

SERVES 4

- *1 pound rump steak or frying steak*
- *1 tablespoon cornstarch*
- *1 tablespoon soy sauce*
- *3 tablespoons oyster sauce*
- *4 tablespoons dry sherry*
- *4 tablespoons water*
- *12 ounces ribbon rice sticks*
- *2 tablespoons oil*
- *1 bunch of scallions, chopped*
- *½ an iceberg lettuce, shredded*

Cut the beef across the grain into very thin slices (partially freezing the steak makes this easier). Mix the steak with the cornstarch. When the meat is well coated, add the soy sauce, oyster sauce, sherry and water. Mix well, and set aside to marinate for 3–4 hours.

Cook the rice sticks according to the instructions on the package.

Meanwhile, heat the oil in a large skillet or wok. Drain the beef, reserving the marinade, and add it to the oil with the scallions. Stir-fry until the pieces of beef are lightly browned. Then add the marinade, and bring to a boil, stirring all the time. Simmer for 2 more minutes.

Drain the rice sticks, and transfer them to a warmed serving dish. Add the lettuce to the beef mixture, and stir well. Braise the lettuce for 2 minutes, then ladle the mixture over the rice sticks, and serve at once.

Yosenabe

This is the Japanese equivalent of a firepot meal, an oriental fondue, where diners select and cook their own food at the table by adding it to a pot of gently simmering broth. "Nabe" is the collective term for dishes cooked at the table, and this example is a seafood meal, where a selection of any fish and shellfish would be prepared. I have included a limited selection of seafood with broad appeal, but you may extend this according to your own tastes and availability.

SERVES 4

FOR THE YOSENABE
- *½ quantity Chicken Stock (see page 57)*
- *1 quantity Japanese-style Stock (also see page 57)*
- *2 carrots, cut into carrot flowers (see page 255)*
- *6 ounces harusame or soumen or rice vermicelli*
- *8 ounces firm bean curd*
- *1 bunch of scallions*
- *8 ounces button mushrooms*
- *16 large, uncooked shrimp, just defrosted if frozen*
- *16 fresh scallops*
- *1 pound fine-flavored thick fish fillet (for example grey mullet, monkfish, bream, hake or sea bass)*
- *16 cooked, shelled mussels*

FOR THE CONDIMENTS AND DIPPING SAUCE
- *1 white radish (daikon or mooli)*
- *½ English cucumber*
- *1 tablespoon Japanese rice vinegar*
- *wasabi (Japanese green mustard)*
- *6 tablespoons sake*
- *1 cup Japanese soy sauce*
- *1 teaspoon sugar*
- *1 tablespoon lemon juice*

First, prepare the Yosenabe. Make both types of stock as given on page 57. Cool and chill the Chicken Stock; then remove any grease from the surface. If you do not have time to do this, use a paper towel to skim the surface of the stock, and absorb any fat.

Heat the Japanese-style Stock until it is just simmering, then add the carrot flowers, and cook for 5 minutes. Use a slotted spoon to remove them from the pan, and drain well. Add the harusame, soumen or fine rice noodles to the simmering stock, and cook according to the instructions on the package, or remove from the heat, and let sit in the stock for about 15 minutes, until tender. Drain

the noodles over a bowl, reserving the stock.

Cut the bean curd into neat, diamond-shaped pieces. Trim the scallions, and cut them into 1½–2-inch lengths. Use a fine-pointed knife to cut evenly spaced narrow strips out of the tops of the mushrooms, working from the center and curving out down the side of each mushroom cap.

Uncooked shrimp are sold with shells on or peeled. If the shrimp are whole, then remove their heads, and peel them. Remove the dark vein that runs down the back of the shrimp with the tip of a sharp knife. Slice the scallops in half, or into three slices if they are large. Skin the fish fillet, and cut the fish into neat chunks, discarding any stray bones.

Arrange all the prepared ingredients on a serving platter, cutting the noodles up slightly (alternatively, they may be divided between individual plates, which can make the cooking process easier, and insures that everyone gets their fair share of the ingredients).

Next, prepare the condiments and dipping sauce. Coarsely grate the radish and cucumber, keeping them separate. Drain the cucumber well in a strainer; then mix it with the rice vinegar. Arrange small piles of the radish and cucumber on small plates.

Mix the wasabi with a little water to make a smooth, green paste. This mustard-like horseradish mixture is extremely hot, and must be taken in very small quantities, so warn unwary guests!

Heat the sake, soy sauce, sugar and lemon juice together in a saucepan until the sugar has dissolved. Boil the mixture; then remove it from the heat. Allow the dipping sauce to cool before pouring it into small dishes.

To serve the Yosenabe, heat the Chicken Stock and Japanese Stock together until boiling; then place the pan on a spirit burner to keep the stock only just simmering. Provide plates and chopsticks, and invite diners to cook pieces of food in the simmering stock. The cooked food is then dipped in the dipping sauce, or a little wasabi is eaten with it (especially the fish). The radish and cucumber are also eaten in small amounts to complement the hot ingredients.

Sukiyaki

This is another recipe that may be cooked at the table over a spirit burner. Shirataki noodles are sold ready cooked in cans (see page 20). Combining sugar in fairly significant quantities with savory foods is a distinctive feature of many Japanese dishes, and one that can seem very strange if the combination of savoury flavors and sweetness is not a familiar one. I use less sugar here than would be given in an authentic recipe, so you may want to increase the amount if you are familiar with the dish.

SERVES 4

- *1 pound lean rump steak*
- *8-ounce can shirataki noodles*
- *8 ounces bean curd*
- *½ cup Japanese soy sauce*
- *3 tablespoons sake*
- *1 tablespoon sugar*
- *⅔ cup Japanese-style Stock (see page 57)*
- *2 tablespoons beef drippings or 2 tablespoons oil*
- *1 large onion, halved and thinly sliced*
- *6 scallions, thinly sliced diagonally*
- *¼ head of Chinese leaves, shredded*
- *1⅓ cups sliced button mushrooms*

Cut the steak across the grain into very fine slices (partially freezing the steak makes this easier).

Drain the noodles, and add them to boiling water; bring back to a boil, and drain.

Cut the bean curd into small cubes; then mix them gently with the soy sauce, sake, sugar and stock.

Heat the beef drippings or oil in a large skillet. Add the steak, and stir-fry the pieces until they have browned. Then add the onion, scallions, Chinese leaves and mushrooms. Stir-fry for a couple of minutes. Pour in the bean curd and sauce, and bring to a boil. Add the noodles, cook for 1 minute, and serve at once.

Alternatively, the beef can be pushed to one side of the skillet, and the sauce and remaining ingredients added in individual portion quantities. Then, as each portion is cooked and served with some of the meat, the next can be added. This is a practical approach if you do not have a skillet large enough to take all the ingredients at once, or otherwise like this dish piping hot.

Udon with Chicken

This is a simple, Japanese-style dish of thin broth with noodles and vegetables – ideal for a light meal.

SERVES 4

- *3 boneless chicken breasts, skinned*
- *3 scallions, cut into short lengths*
- *1 small garlic clove, finely chopped (optional)*
- *3 tablespoons Japanese soy sauce*
- *4 tablespoons sake*
- *2 teaspoons sugar*
- *chicken stock*
- *12 ounces udon noodles*
- *2 cups baby spinach leaves*
- *salt and freshly ground black pepper*

Cut the chicken breasts across into thin slices; then put them into a bowl. Add the scallions and garlic, if using.

Heat the soy sauce, sake and sugar, stirring, until the sugar dissolves. Remove from the heat, and let cool before pouring over the chicken. When it has cooled, mix well with the chicken, then cover the bowl, and set aside to marinate for 2–3 hours before cooking.

Bring the stock to a boil, and add the udon noodles. Bring back to a boil, reduce the heat, and cook according to the instructions on the package, or for about 15 minutes, or until the noodles are tender.

Drain the noodles, reserving the stock, and divide them between individual dishes, or place in a serving dish. Cover, and keep hot.

Bring the stock back to a boil, then add the chicken with the marinade, and cook for 3 minutes. Then add the spinach, and cook for a further 2 minutes, or until the chicken is cooked. Taste for seasoning, and add a little salt and pepper if liked. Ladle the chicken, spinach and stock over the noodles, and serve at once.

Noodles with Japanese Fish Cake and Vegetables

Japanese fish cake bears no resemblance to the European product of the same name. Kamaboko, the Japanese name for it, is a smooth-textured loaf, sometimes with a red exterior, bought cooked and in slices. It is served as part of the celebratory New Year menu. I have taken the ingredients out of their authentic context in this recipe to make a light noodle dish.

SERVES 4

FOR THE NOODLES
- 2 slices Japanese fish cake
- 1 carrot
- 1 leek
- 4 ounces snow peas
- ¼ head of Chinese leaves
- 12 ounces udon noodles
- salt
- 1¼ cups chicken stock
- 12 large, cooked shrimp

FOR THE DIPPING SAUCE
- 6 tablespoons Japanese soy sauce
- 2 tablespoons sake
- 1 teaspoon sugar
- ⅔ cup Japanese-style Stock (see page 57)
- pinch of wasabi
- 1 scallion, finely chopped

First, prepare the dipping sauce. Heat the soy sauce, sake, sugar and stock, stirring until the sugar dissolves. Bring to a boil, then remove from the heat, and let cool. Add a small pinch of wasabi, and stir in the scallion; then pour the sauce into small dishes.

Now, prepare the noodles, fish cake and vegetables. Cut the fish cake into matchstick-sized strips. Cut the carrot and leek into matchstick-sized pieces also. Top and tail the snow peas, and shred the Chinese leaves.

Cook the noodles in boiling salted water for about 15 minutes, or following the instructions on the package, until tender. Meanwhile, bring the chicken stock to a boil. Add the carrot and leek, and simmer for 1 minute. Then add the snow peas, and cook for a further minute. Finally, add the Chinese leaves, and bring back to a boil. Add the shrimp, and remove the pan from the heat. Let sit for 2 minutes.

Drain the noodles, and divide them between four bowls. Carefully spoon the vegetables and shrimp over the noodles; then pour the stock over them. Top with the pieces of fish cake, and serve at once.

Fried Noodle Snack

Japanese fast-food stalls stir up quick dishes of Chinese-style egg noodles with vegetables and shrimp or meat like this. This recipe is ideal for making a quick, tasty meal.

SERVES 4

- *8 ounces fresh or dried Chinese egg noodles*
- *4 ounces green beans, cut into 2-in lengths*
- *3 tablespoons oil*
- *2 eggs, beaten*
- *1 bunch of scallions, finely shredded diagonally*

- *1 garlic clove, crushed*
- *1 large carrot, cut into fine matchstick strips*
- *1½ cups cooked, peeled shrimp*
- *4 tablespoons Japanese soy sauce*

Cook the noodles according to the instructions on the package, or add fresh noodles to boiling water, and bring back to a boil, then reduce the heat, and cook for 3 minutes. Drain well, and set aside.

Add the green beans to a pan of boiling water, bring back to a boil, and then drain the beans.

Heat a little of the oil in a large skillet. Add the eggs, and cook until they are beginning to set underneath. Then lift the edges of the omelet off the skillet, and let the unset egg on the top run onto the hot surface of the skillet. When the omelet has set completely, slide it out onto a plate, and cut it into small squares.

Heat the remaining oil in a large skillet or wok. Add the scallions, garlic, carrot and green beans. Stir-fry for 2 minutes; then stir in the shrimp and noodles. Stir-fry for a few minutes, until heated through, then sprinkle in the soy sauce, and add the omelet squares. Mix well, and serve at once.

Hiyamugi

This is a Japanese dish of cold noodles, hiyamugi being thin, white noodles of vermicelli thickness. To be authentic, ice cubes ought to be added to the noodles, and cold water is sometimes poured over them. Then the noodles and other ingredients are lifted from the water, and dipped into sauce before being eaten. I have not added water or ice directly to the noodles in this recipe, but you can do so if you wish.

SERVES 4

FOR THE NOODLES
- *2 eggs, beaten*
- *1 teaspoon Japanese soy sauce*
- *a little oil*
- *12 ounces hiyamugi*
- *salt*
- *4 scallions*
- *8 button mushrooms*
- *3-inch piece of English cucumber*
- *16 cooked, peeled shrimp*

FOR THE DIPPING SAUCE
- *1¼ cups Japanese-style Stock (see page 57)*
- *1–2 tablespoons dried bonito fish*
- *4 tablespoons Japanese soy sauce*
- *4 tablespoons sake*
- *1 teaspoon sugar*
- *1 teaspoon finely shredded fresh ginger root*

First, making the dipping sauce. Heat the stock with the bonito fish until boiling, then strain it into a clean saucepan, and stir in the soy sauce, sake and sugar. Bring to a boil, stirring; then remove from the heat. Add the ginger root, and let cool.

Meanwhile, prepare the noodles. Beat the eggs with the soy sauce. Heat a coating of oil in a skillet. Pour in the egg mixture, and cook until it is beginning to set; then lift the edge of the omelet, and let the raw egg on top run onto the hot surface of the skillet. When the omelet has set, slide it onto a plate.

Cook the hiyumagi in boiling salted water for 8–10 minutes, or according to the instructions on the package, until just tender. Drain, and rinse under cold water; then let drain.

Cut the scallions finely on the diagonal. Slice the mushrooms thinly, and cut the cucumber into fine matchstick strips. Cut the omelet into small squares.

To serve the hiyumagi, divide the noodles between four dishes. Top with the prepared ingredients, and serve with the dipping sauce. If liked, the dishes of noodles can be served on a bed of crushed ice.

277

Curried Shrimp with Green Beans and Noodles

SERVES 4

- 2 tablespoons oil
- 1 piece of lemon grass
- 1 onion, chopped
- 2 green chilis, deseeded and chopped (see Cook's Tip, page 90)
- 3 garlic cloves, crushed
- 2-inch piece fresh ginger root, grated
- 1 teaspoon turmeric
- 1 tablespoon ground coriander
- 1 tablespoon ground cumin
- 1¼ cups coconut milk

- juice of 2 limes
- ⅔ cup water
- 24 large, uncooked shrimp, defrosted and drained if frozen
- 8 ounces fine green or string beans
- 3 tablespoons light soy sauce
- 2 tablespoons fish sauce
- 12 ounces fresh or dried Chinese egg noodles
- chopped flat-leafed parsley, to garnish

Heat the oil in a large skillet or wok. Add the lemon grass, onion, chilis, garlic and ginger root. Stir-fry for 5 minutes, then add the turmeric, coriander and cumin, and cook, stirring, for a further 3 minutes. Pour in the coconut milk and lime juice, then add the water, and bring to a boil. Reduce the heat, cover, and simmer for 20 minutes.

Meanwhile, prepare the shrimp. If they are whole, remove their heads, and peel them. Remove the dark vein that runs down the back of each shrimp with the tip of a sharp knife. Then add the shrimp, green or string beans, soy sauce and fish sauce, and simmer gently for a further 15 minutes.

Cook the noodles according to the instructions on the package if dried, or, if fresh, boil them for 3 minutes when the shrimp are cooked; then drain them.

To serve, turn the drained noodles into a bowl, and pour the shrimp mixture over. Mix lightly, then sprinkle with the chopped parsley, and serve at once.

FISH SAUCE

A strongly flavored condiment, fish sauce or *nam pla* is widely used in Thai cooking, and it is readily available from Oriental delis.

Soba with Bean Curd and Nori

Soba are dark buckwheat noodles. You will find all the ingredients for this dish in some health food stores as they are popular vegetarian products.

SERVES 4

FOR THE NOODLES
- 1 pound firm bean curd
- 1 garlic clove, crushed
- 3 tablespoons Japanese soy sauce
- 1 teaspoon sesame oil
- 2 tablespoons sake or dry sherry
- 12 ounces soba
- salt

- 2 tablespoons oil
- 1 bunch of scallions, finely shredded diagonally
- 2 celery stalks, cut into fine matchstick strips
- 4 ounces snow peas

FOR THE NORI TOPPING
- ¼ cup dried, shredded nori
- 4 tablespoons Japanese soy sauce

- 1 teaspoon sugar
- 2 tablespoons sake or dry sherry

Cut the bean curd into 1-inch cubes, and put into a bowl. Mix the garlic, soy sauce, sesame oil and sake or sherry together; then pour this over the bean curd. Cover, and let marinate for 2–3 hours or longer (it can be left overnight).

Next, prepare the nori topping. Put the nori into a bowl, and pour on hot water to cover it generously. Allow plenty of room because it does increase in volume quite substantially. Let soak for 30 minutes, or according to the instructions on the package; then drain well.

Mix the soy sauce, sugar and sake or sherry in a small saucepan, and stir over a low heat until the sugar dissolves. Then add the nori, bring to a boil, reduce the heat, and cover the pan. Simmer for 5 minutes, then remove the lid, and continue to cook, stirring occasionally, until the liquid has dried up completely, and the nori is coated in a flavorsome glaze. Stir the mixture more frequently toward the end of cooking to prevent it burning. Set aside to cool.

Cook the soba in a saucepan of boiling salted water for about 10 minutes, until tender, or according to the instructions on the package.

While the noodles are cooking, heat the oil in a wok or large skillet. Add the scallions, celery and snow peas, and stir-fry for 2 minutes. Gently mix in the marinated bean curd, and cover the pan. Let cook gently for about 5 minutes, stirring occasionally, until the bean curd is hot.

Drain the noodles, and transfer to a serving dish. Top with the bean curd mixture, and garnish with small piles of the nori. Offer the remaining nori separately. Serve at once.

Marinated Beef with Noodles

The slightly sweet marinade with added chili powder used in this recipe tastes extremely good with this particular combination of vegetables and white noodles.

SERVES 4

- 6 tablespoons Japanese soy sauce
- 4 tablespoons sake
- 1 tablespoon sugar
- ½ teaspoon chili powder
- 2 tablespoons water
- 1 garlic clove, crushed
- 1 pound lean rump steak
- 12 ounces udon noodles
- 1 quantity Chicken Stock (see page 57)
- 2 tablespoons oil
- 1 teaspoon sesame oil
- 1 onion, halved and thinly sliced
- 1 red bell pepper, halved, deseeded and thinly sliced
- 8-ounce can bamboo shoots, drained and cut into thin strips
- 1 pound baby spinach leaves

Mix the soy sauce, sake, sugar, chili powder and water in a small saucepan. Heat, stirring, until the sugar dissolves; then bring to a boil. Remove from the heat, add the garlic, and let cool.

Meanwhile, cut the beef across the grain into very thin slices (partially freezing the steak makes this easier). Place the meat in a non-metallic dish, pour over the cooled soy sauce mixture, and mix well. Cover, and let marinate for 3–5 hours.

Cook the udon noodles in the stock for about 15 minutes, or according to the instructions on the package, until just tender.

Heat the oil and sesame oil in a large skillet or wok. Use a slotted spoon to add the beef, reserving the marinating juices; then stir-fry the beef for 2–3 minutes over a high heat until browned. Add the onion, bell pepper and bamboo shoots, and continue to stir-fry less vigorously, until the vegetables are just cooked. Add a spoonful of the stock from the noodles to the marinade; then cook gently for 5 minutes.

Drain the noodles, reserving the stock. Transfer the noodles to a serving dish, and keep hot. Return the stock to the pan, and bring to a boil. Add the spinach, and cook for 2 minutes, or until just wilted and tender. Drain the spinach, and arrange it on top of the noodles, ladling over a little of the stock to moisten the noodles.

Place the beef and vegetable mixture on top of the spinach, and serve at once.

Malaysian Fried Rice Sticks

A taste of the street food of Malaysia!

SERVES 4

- 12 ounces narrow rice sticks
- 2 tablespoons oil
- 1 piece of lemon grass
- 2 green chilis, deseeded and chopped (see Cook's Tip, page 90)
- 2 garlic cloves, crushed
- 6 ounces lean boneless pork, cut into thin strips
- 1 boneless chicken breast, skinned and cut into fine strips
- 4 squid sacs, thinly sliced (see Cook's Tip, page 266)
- 2 cups beansprouts
- 4 scallions, chopped
- 3 tablespoons soy sauce
- 2 cups peeled, cooked shrimp, defrosted and drained if frozen

Cook the rice sticks according to the instructions on the package. Drain, and set aside.

Heat the oil in a large skillet or wok. Add the lemon grass, chilis, garlic, pork, chicken and squid. Stir-fry until all the ingredients have cooked through, and are lightly browned.

Add the beansprouts and scallions, and cook for 2–3 minutes more before stirring in the soy sauce. Add the shrimp and rice sticks, and stir over a brisk heat until all the ingredients are hot. Serve at once.

Marinated Beef with Noodles

Mixed Rice Stick Stir-fry

SERVES 4

- 12 ounces sen lek rice noodles or rice sticks
- 1 small, boneless chicken breast, skinned and cut into very thin slices
- 2 garlic cloves, finely chopped
- 4 ounces rump or fillet steak, skinned and cut into very thin slices
- ¼ cup roasted peanuts

- ⅔ cup coconut milk
- 2 tablespoons light soy sauce
- 3 tablespoons groundnut oil
- 2 red chilis, deseeded and diced (see Cook's Tip, page 90)
- 6 scallions, finely shredded diagonally
- 1 cup peeled, cooked prawns
- 2 tablespoons fish sauce (see note page 278)

Soak the rice noodles or rice sticks in boiling water for 3 minutes, until softened. Drain well.

Mix the chicken with half the garlic. Add the remaining garlic to the steak.

Purée the peanuts with the coconut milk and soy sauce.

Heat the oil in a large skillet or wok. Fry the chilis for 1 minute, then add the chicken, and stir-fry for 3–4 minutes, until it has cooked, and is lightly browned.

Push the chicken to one side of the skillet, and stir-fry the steak until lightly browned. Add the scallions, and pour in the peanut and coconut milk mixture. Heat until it is bubbling hot.

Mix in the shrimp and fish sauce, then add the noodles or rice sticks, and cook for about 2 minutes to heat through. Serve at once.

Satay-style Pork with Egg Noodles

SERVES 4

- 1 pound lean, boneless pork, cut into thin strips
- 4 tablespoons groundnut oil
- 2 large onions, thinly sliced
- 2 garlic cloves, crushed
- 1 green chili, deseeded and chopped (see Cook's Tip, page 90)
- ½ cup roasted peanuts
- 4 tablespoons light soy sauce
- ⅔ cup coconut milk

- 2 teaspoons sesame oil
- 12 ounces fresh or dried Chinese egg noodles
- 6 scallions, finely shredded diagonally
- 8-ounce can bamboo shoots, cut into fine matchstick strips
- 1 red bell pepper, quartered, deseeded and cut into thin strips
- 2 cups beansprouts

Place the pork strips in a non-metallic dish.

Heat 1 tablespoon of the oil in a small saucepan. Add half the sliced onion, the garlic, chili and peanuts. Cook, stirring, for 10 minutes, then remove from the heat, and let cool slightly.

Purée the peanut mixture to a paste, adding the soy sauce and coconut milk. Pour this over the pork, and cover. Marinate for several hours or overnight.

Heat the remaining oil and sesame oil in a large skillet or wok. Add the remaining onion, and cook until browned. Then use a slotted spoon to remove the onion from the skillet or wok. Use a slotted spoon to remove the pork from any juices produced during marinating (reserving these), add the pork to the hot oil, and stir-fry until it has browned.

Meanwhile, cook the dried egg noodles according to the instructions on the package, or cook fresh egg noodles in boiling water for 3 minutes; then drain.

Add the scallions, bamboo shoots and bell pepper to the pork, and mix in any reserved marinade. Stir-fry for about 3 minutes; then add the noodles and beansprouts. Cook, stirring, for 2 minutes, or until the beansprouts are hot. Serve at once.

Spicy Meat with Wide Rice Noodles

SERVES 4

- 1½ cups ground steak
- 1½ cups ground pork
- 3 garlic cloves, finely chopped
- 1 green chili, deseeded and chopped (see Cook's Tip, page 90)
- 4 scallions, chopped
- 2-inch piece fresh ginger root, peeled and finely chopped
- 1 tablespoon ground coriander
- grated rind and juice of 1 lime
- 3 tablespoons groundnut oil
- 1 green bell pepper, deseeded, quartered lengthwise and cut into thin strips
- 2 cups beansprouts
- 2 tablespoons fish sauce (see note page 278)
- 4 tablespoons soy sauce
- 12 ounces sen yai (wide rice noodles)

Mix the steak, pork, garlic, chili, scallions, ginger root, coriander, lime rind and juice. Pound the ingredients together; then let them marinate for 2–3 hours before cooking.

Heat the oil in a large skillet or wok. Add the meat mixture, and stir-fry it briskly until it is beginning to brown. Add the bell pepper, and cook, stirring, for a further 5 minutes. Add the beansprouts, fish sauce and soy sauce. Reduce the heat, and cover the pan.

Add the noodles to boiling water. Bring back to a boil, then remove from the heat, and let sit for 2 minutes. Drain well, and transfer to a serving dish. Top with the meat mixture, and serve at once.

Curry Mee

Chicken curry with Chinese egg noodles was one of our successful vacation discoveries. Typical of Malaysian food, this brings together Indian curry spices with Chinese cooking techniques (and, of course, the noodles). Honestly, it is delicious!

SERVES 4

- 2 tablespoons oil
- 4 chicken thighs
- 3 garlic cloves
- 2-inch piece fresh ginger root, grated
- 1 large onion, finely chopped
- 2 green chilis, deseeded and chopped (see Cook's Tip, page 90)
- 1 teaspoon ground turmeric
- 1 tablespoon ground coriander
- 1 tablespoon ground cumin
- 1 teaspoon shrimp paste (optional)
- 1 piece of lemon grass
- grated rind and juice of 1 lime
- salt and freshly ground black pepper
- 2½ cups water
- 3 tablespoons instant coconut milk
- 4 ounces green beans, cut into short lengths
- 1 carrot, cut into fine matchstick strips
- 8-ounce can bamboo shoots, drained and cut into fine matchstick strips
- 12 ounces mee (Chinese egg noodles)
- 8 ounces firm bean curd, cut into 1-inch cubes
- 1 cup beansprouts
- 4 eggs, hard-cooked and quartered
- chopped fresh cilantro leaves
- lime wedges, to garnish (optional)

Heat the oil in a large, flameproof casserole, and brown the chicken thighs all over. Remove the chicken from the casserole, and set aside. Add the garlic, ginger root, onion and chilis to the casserole. Cook, stirring, for 5 minutes.

Stir in the turmeric, coriander, cumin, shrimp paste, if using, and lemon grass, and fry the spices, stirring to prevent them sticking, for 2–3 minutes. Then add the lime rind and juice, salt, pepper, and the water.

Bring the curry sauce to a boil, stirring; then return the chicken to the casserole. Reduce the heat, cover the casserole, and simmer the chicken curry very gently for 45 minutes. Taste for seasoning at this stage, and add more salt if required. Stir in the coconut milk, green beans, carrot and bamboo shoots, and continue to simmer for a further 15 minutes.

Cook the noodles according to the instructions on the package if dried, or cook fresh noodles in boiling salted water for 3 minutes. Drain well.

Add the bean curd to the curry, gently stirring it in. Sprinkle the beansprouts over the top, and heat through for 2 minutes.

Add the eggs just before serving the curry.

Put the noodles into a large serving dish or individual bowls, and ladle the curry over. Garnish with chopped fresh cilantro leaves and lime wedges.

Singapore-style Hokkien Noodles

Singaporean hokkien noodles are fundamentally the same as the fresh Chinese egg noodles.

SERVES 4

- 6 ounces lean boneless pork, cut into fine strips
- ½ teaspoon chili powder
- ½ teaspoon sesame oil
- 3 tablespoons soy sauce
- 2 dried Chinese mushrooms
- 6 tablespoons hot water
- 8 ounces fresh or dried hokkien or Chinese egg noodles
- 2 tablespoons oil
- 1 small onion, thinly sliced
- 1 green chili, deseeded and sliced (see Cook's Tip, page 90)
- coarsely grated rind of 1 lemon
- 1 tablespoon coriander seeds, crushed
- ½ cup frozen peas
- 1 teaspoon cornstarch

Mix the pork with the chili powder, sesame oil and 1 tablespoon of the soy sauce, and set aside.

Put the mushrooms into a bowl, and pour the hot water over them. Set aside to soak for 20 minutes.

Cook the hokkien or Chinese egg noodles according to the instructions on the package if dried, or cook fresh noodles in boiling salted water for 3 minutes. Drain well.

Drain the mushrooms, reserving the soaking liquid, and discard any tough stalks; then slice them thinly.

Heat the oil in a large skillet or wok. Add the onion, chili, lemon rind and coriander seeds. Stir-fry for 2 minutes. Add the pork, with all the flavoring ingredients, and the mushrooms, and stir-fry for 3–5 minutes, or until the meat is thoroughly cooked.

Add the frozen peas and noodles to the pork, and mix well. Blend the cornstarch with the remaining soy sauce, and strain in the reserved soaking liquid from the mushrooms. Pour this mixture over the noodles, and cook, stirring, until the juices boil to form a slightly thickened, glossy coating on the noodles. Serve at once.

PASTA SALADS

◆

$\mathcal{P}$ASTA IS GOOD COLD. ❧ IT TAKES A SALAD DRESSING WELL AND COMPLEMENTS FULL-FLAVORED INGREDIENTS BY PROVIDING THE BULK THEY NEED IF THEY ARE NOT TO BECOME OVERWHELMING.

UNFORTUNATELY, THE REPUTATION PASTA SALADS HAVE FOR BEING GAUDY IS A RESULT OF CONCOCTIONS THAT ARE SO OFTEN SERVED AT PARTIES – WHERE ANY OLD PASTA SHAPE WILL DO. ❧ TAKE A LOOK AT THE BETTER ALTERNATIVES IN THIS CHAPTER.

Pasta Platter

A pasta hors-d'oeuvre, this is an attractive first course that allows diners to opt for a light or satisfying starter, and it is easy to prepare ahead. Add to the ingredients according to your taste and pocket, and increasing the display turns this into an ample meal.

SERVES 6–8

- *8 ounces novelty pasta shapes or flavored pasta or one or two types (for example, try pasta flavored with porcini or three-colored pasta)*
- *salt and freshly ground black pepper*
- *½ quantity Pesto (see page 67)*
- *1¼ cups sour cream*
- *4 tablespoons snipped chives*
- *8 quails' eggs*
- *8 ounces mozzarella cheese, sliced*
- *1 cup chopped or finely crumbled pecorino cheese*
- *8 ounces salami (include a couple of different types)*
- *8 ounces tomatoes, peeled (see Cook's Tip, page 72) and sliced*
- *1 red onion, halved and thinly sliced*
- *1 cup black olives*
- *good-quality virgin olive oil*
- *warmed, fresh Italian bread, to serve*

Cook the pasta in boiling salted water for about 15 minutes, or according to the instructions on the package, until tender. Drain well, and rinse under cold water. Let drain.

Put the Pesto into a small bowl. Mix the sour cream and chives in another bowl.

Place the quails' eggs in a saucepan, and add cold water to cover. Bring to a boil; then cook for 3 minutes. Drain, rinse under cold water, and remove the shells.

Arrange these and all the remaining ingredients, except the oil, on a huge platter, overlapping the slices of mozzarella, piling up the pecorino, folding or overlapping the tomato slices. Sprinkle the onion in a small mound. Put the olives into a small bowl. Place the olive oil and a pepper mill on the table.

Diners help themselves to pasta, and dress it to taste with a little pesto or sour cream with chives, or trickle olive oil over. The other ingredients are eaten with the pasta. Plenty of warmed, fresh Italian bread is an essential accompaniment.

ALTERNATIVE OR ADDITIONAL INGREDIENTS

CANNED OR BOTTLED ARTICHOKE HEARTS
Dress them with olive oil and a squeeze of lemon juice, adding some chopped fresh marjoram if liked.

FENNEL OR GREEN BEANS
Cut the fennel into fine slices, or, if using beans, leave them whole. Blanch whichever vegetable you have chosen in boiling water for 1 minute. Drain and toss with a little lemon juice.

GARBANZO BEANS
Drain canned garbanzo beans, and mix them with chopped parsley, finely chopped garlic and some olive oil.

Salad of Pasta with Seafood

SERVES 4

- 1 pound mussels, prepared and cooked (see page 126)
- 12-ounce monkfish fillet
- 1¼ cups fish stock
- 12 large, uncooked shrimp
- 8 fresh scallops
- 6 ounces pasta shells
- salt and freshly ground black pepper
- 1 teaspoon superfine sugar
- juice of 2 lemons
- ⅔ cup olive oil
- 2 tablespoons chopped fresh dill
- 2 tablespoons chopped parsley
- 1 garlic clove, finely chopped
- 1 scallion, finely chopped
- grated rind of ½ a lemon
- lemon wedges, to garnish

Shell the mussels when they have been cooked, reserving a few in their shells to garnish the salad, if liked.

Place the monkfish fillet in a saucepan. Pour in the stock, and add the shrimp. Heat gently until just simmering, then cover the pan, and regulate the heat so that the stock just bubbles gently and occasionally. Poach the fish for 15 minutes.

Add the scallops, and cook for 2 minutes, or until firm. Remove from the heat, and let cool, covered.

Cook the pasta in boiling salted water for about 15 minutes, or according to the instructions on the package, until tender. Drain well.

While the pasta is cooking, whisk salt and pepper and the sugar into the lemon juice. When the sugar has dissolved, slowly whisk in the oil to make a thickened dressing. Stir in the dill, parsley, garlic, scallion and lemon, and pour this over the hot pasta in the bowl. Mix well, cover, and let cool.

Remove the seafood from the cooking liquor. Slice the monkfish and scallops, peel the shrimp, if necessary, and mix with the mussels. Lightly toss the seafood into the pasta and serve, garnished with a few whole mussels, if you have reserved them, and lemon wedges.

Salmon and Cucumber Salad

SERVES 4

- 8 ounces soup pasta shapes (do not use the smallest shapes, select slightly larger ones)
- salt and freshly ground black pepper
- ½ quantity Fish Stock (see page 56)
- 1 pound salmon fillet
- ⅔ cup Greek yogurt
- ⅔ cup mayonnaise
- 2 tablespoons snipped chives
- 2 tablespoons chopped fresh dill
- ½ English cucumber, peeled and diced
- 1 tablespoon lemon juice
- 2 tablespoons salad oil
- sprigs of dill, to garnish

Cook the pasta in boiling salted water for 5–10 minutes, or according to the instructions on the package, until tender; then drain.

Meanwhile, pour the stock over the salmon in a saucepan or skillet. Heat very gently, until just simmering, then cover, and cook for 3 minutes. Remove from the heat, and let the fish cool in the stock, during which time the thick part of the fillet will finish cooking.

Mix the yogurt with the mayonnaise, chives, dill, and salt and pepper to taste. When the pasta has cooled slightly, toss it with this dressing. Cover, and set aside to cool; then chill lightly.

Put the cucumber into a strainer, and sprinkle lightly with salt. Leave over a bowl for 30 minutes; then dry the cucumber with paper towels. Drain the salmon, and flake the fish in large pieces off the skin. Mix the salmon with the cucumber. Whisk the lemon juice with salt and pepper to taste. Whisk in the oil; then pour this dressing over the fish and cucumber.

Arranged the dressed pasta and salmon mixture together on a platter or individual plates, and garnish with sprigs of dill.

Avocado with Lime-dressed Pasta

An attractive and palate-refreshing pasta salad goes well with creamy avocado. Serve warmed plain crackers or Melba toast (see page 300) as a crunchy accompaniment.

SERVES 4

- ¾ cup soup pasta
- salt and freshly ground black pepper
- grated rind and juice of 1 lime
- ½ teaspoon superfine sugar
- 4 tablespoons olive oil
- 4 black olives, sliced
- 1 scallion, finely chopped
- ½ cup chopped pecorino cheese
- 3 sprigs of basil, shredded
- 2 ripe avocados
- sprigs of basil and lime slices, to garnish

Cook the pasta in boiling salted water for 5–10 minutes, or according to the instructions on the package, until tender. Drain well, and set aside to cool.

Whisk the lime rind and juice with the superfine sugar, and salt and pepper to taste. When the sugar has dissolved, whisk in the oil. Add the olives, scallion, pecorino and basil. Mix the pasta with the other ingredients until well coated in dressing.

Halve the avocados, remove their pits, and place in dishes. Fill with the pasta mixture, and garnish with sprigs of basil and lime slices. Serve at once.

Salad of Smoked Haddock with Lemon-dressed Tagliatelle

A strong, lemony dressing matches the robust flavor of the smoked fish.

SERVES 4

- *1½ pounds smoked haddock*
- *grated rind and juice of 2 lemons*
- *12 ounces fresh tagliatelle verde*
- *salt and freshly ground black pepper*
- *1¼ cups sour cream*
- *1 teaspoon Dijon mustard or other mild mustard*

- *4 tablespoons chopped parsley*
- *2 tablespoons chopped fresh dill*
- *8 ounces fresh, thin green beans, cut in half or shorter lengths*
- *1 red bell pepper, deseeded, quartered and cut across into thin slices*

Place the fish on a heatproof plate that fits over a large saucepan. Bring some water to a boil in the saucepan, sprinkle the fish with the lemon juice, and cover tightly with foil. Cook over the boiling water for 15 minutes, or until just cooked; then remove from the pan and let cool, covered. You may have to do this in two batches if you do not have a sufficiently large plate.

Cook the tagliatelle in boiling salted water for about 3 minutes, or until tender. Drain well, and rinse under cold water; then drain again.

Mix the lemon rind with the sour cream, mustard, parsley and dill. Add salt and pepper to taste; then toss this lemon dressing with the pasta. Transfer to a serving bowl or individual plates or dishes.

Add the green beans to a saucepan of boiling salted water. Bring back to a boil, and cook for 1 minute. Add the red bell pepper, and boil for a further 30–60 seconds; then drain well.

Flake the smoked haddock flesh off the skin in fairly large pieces, discarding any stray bones as you do so. Lightly mix the fish with the beans and bell pepper, taking care not to break up the flakes. Serve the fish mixture on the pasta base, so that it may be tossed with the pasta before being eaten.

Pasta Salad with Bacon and Pesto

SERVES 4

- 8 ounces short pasta spirals
- salt and freshly ground black pepper
- 2 large oranges
- 8 ounces baby spinach leaves, washed and shredded
- 4 scallions, finely chopped
- 1 bunch of watercress, leaves only
- 6 arugula leaves, shredded
- 4 large sprigs of parsley, roughly chopped
- 3 cups diced, rindless bacon
- ½ quantity Pesto (see page 67)

Cook the pasta in boiling salted water for about 15 minutes, or according to the instructions on the package, until just tender. Drain, and rinse briefly under cold water; then leave to drain completely.

Cut the top and bottom off each orange. Then sit the orange on a board, and cut off all the peel and pith, working down the side in overlapping strips. Holding the orange over a bowl to catch the juices, use a serrated knife to cut between the membranes dividing the segments, removing each section of orange.

Mix the spinach, scallions, watercress, arugula and parsley. Place this salad base in a bowl or on plates.

Dry-fry the bacon, stirring occasionally, until the pieces have browned, and are crisp. Drain on paper towels.

Toss the orange and bacon with the pasta, and add pepper to taste; then pile it on top of the salad leaf base. Top with Pesto, and serve (the Pesto is mixed with the pasta and leaves as the salad is eaten to act as a dressing).

Pasta in a Greek Salad

SERVES 4

- 8 ounces rigatoni or penne
- salt and freshly ground black pepper
- 1 red or white onion, thinly sliced
- ½ English cucumber, peeled, halved and thinly sliced
- 8 tomatoes, peeled (see Cook's Tip, page 72) and cut into eighths
- 12 ounces feta cheese, cut into cubes
- 2 cups pitted black olives
- virgin olive oil, to taste

Cook the pasta in boiling salted water for 15–20 minutes, or according to the instructions on the package, until tender. Drain, and rinse under cold water. Drain again.

Mix the onion, cucumber, tomatoes, feta cheese and olives in a large bowl. Add the pasta and plenty of pepper; then trickle over a little olive oil. Have more olive oil and a pepper mill at the table for diners to help themselves.

Whole Wheat Pasta Salad

SERVES 4

- 8 ounces whole wheat pasta
- salt and freshly ground black pepper
- 4 tablespoons cider vinegar
- 1 garlic clove, finely chopped
- ½ teaspoon superfine sugar
- ½ cup olive oil
- 4 tablespoons chopped parsley
- ½ cup finely chopped walnuts
- 4 scallions, chopped
- 2 avocados, quartered, pitted and cut across into slices
- 4 eggs, hard-cooked and roughly chopped

Cook the pasta in boiling salted water for about 20 minutes, or according to the instructions on the package.

Make the dressing while the pasta is cooking. Whisk the cider vinegar with salt and pepper to taste, then garlic and sugar. When the sugar has dissolved, whisk in the olive oil. Add the parsley, walnuts and scallions.

Drain the pasta, and toss it with the dressing; then cover, and let cool. Gently stir in the avocados and eggs before serving.

Cocktail Tomatoes

Yes, these are fiddly, but preparing impressive cocktail snacks always is, and these are just a bit different. It is essential to buy really tiny soup pasta – I use stelline, tiny stars – otherwise it is impossible to make a filling that is the right proportion to the tomatoes.

MAKES 30

- ½ cup tiny soup pasta
- salt and freshly ground black pepper
- 1 tablespoon walnut oil
- 2 cocktail gherkins, finely chopped
- 1 tablespoon finely chopped parsley
- 1 tablespoon finely snipped chives
- 30 cherry tomatoes
- coarse sea salt, to serve

Cook the pasta in boiling water for 5 minutes, or according to the instructions on the package, until just tender. Drain, and mix with the oil. Add salt and plenty of pepper, to taste. Mix in the gherkins, parsley and chives.

Cut the tops off the tomatoes, taking care not to cut off too much! Use an egg spoon and a fine-pointed knife to remove the middles of the tomatoes carefully; then turn them upside down on paper towels to drain.

Prepare a layer of sea salt on a serving platter – this will support the tomatoes, preventing them from tipping over when filled. Use an egg spoon or a spoon with a pointed bowl to fill each tomato with pasta. Nestle the tomatoes into the sea salt as they are filled.

COOK'S TIP

Pasta-filled tomatoes are also ideal for the first course of a meal. Use larger tomatoes instead of the tiny cherry variety, scooping them out in the same way. You can use the very tiny pasta or slightly larger soup pasta shapes. When plum tomatoes are available, halve them lengthwise, and scoop out their middles, then fill them – they are delicious served this way, with loosely folded slices of prosciutto.

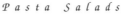

Spicy Chicken and Pasta Salad

SERVES 4

- 8 green cardamom pods
- 1 tablespoon ground coriander
- 1 teaspoon ground turmeric
- 1 tablespoon grated fresh ginger root
- ½ an onion, grated
- 2 garlic cloves, crushed
- 2 tablespoons oil
- grated rind and juice of 1 lemon
- salt and freshly ground black pepper
- 3 boneless chicken breasts, skinned
- 8 ounces pasta spirals or twists
- ⅔ cup mayonnaise
- ⅔ cup fromage frais
- 4 scallions, chopped
- 1 large ripe, but firm, mango
- ½ head of chicory
- 1 green bell pepper, deseeded, quartered and cut across into very fine slices
- a little chopped fresh cilantro

Preheat the oven to 400°F.

Split the cardamom pods over a mortar; then carefully scrape out the tiny black seeds from inside. Crush the seeds to a powder; then mix with the coriander, turmeric, ginger root, onion and garlic. Heat the oil in a small saucepan. Add the spice paste, and cook, stirring, for 5 minutes. Remove the pan from the heat, and add the lemon rind and juice with plenty of salt and pepper.

Place the chicken in an ovenproof dish, and spread with the spice paste. Cover, and bake in the preheated oven for 30–40 minutes, until cooked through. Let cool, covered, in the dish.

Cook the pasta in plenty of boiling salted water for about 15 minutes, or according to the instructions on the package. Drain, and rinse under cold water.

Mix the mayonnaise, fromage frais and scallions. Dice the chicken, and add it to the dressing with all the cooking juices and spice paste. Mix well, and taste for seasoning. Peel the mango, and cut the flesh off the pit in large slices. Then slice these across into small pieces. Shred the chicory, and toss it with the bell pepper; then place on a serving platter or in a large salad bowl.

Mix the pasta with the chicken until thoroughly combined. Add the mango to the pasta, and mix it in very lightly; then pile the salad on the bed of chicory. Sprinkle with a little chopped fresh cilantro, and serve promptly.

Endive with Spaghetti and Ham Salad

SERVES 4–6

- 8 ounces spaghetti, broken into short pieces
- salt and freshly ground black pepper
- 3 heads of endive
- 8 ounces smoked ham, cut into short strips
- 8 ounces tomatoes, peeled, deseeded and cut into strips
- 4 tablespoons snipped chives
- 6 black olives, pitted and roughly chopped
- 4 tablespoons chopped parsley
- 1 tablespoon chopped capers
- 3 tablespoons olive oil
- 1 lemon, cut into wedges

Cook the spaghetti in boiling salted water for about 15 minutes, or until tender. Drain well, and transfer to a bowl.

Meanwhile, separate the endive leaves, rinse, and dry them. Arrange the leaves on a platter.

Mix the ham, tomatoes, chives, olives, parsley, capers and oil with the hot spaghetti. Cover, and let cool. Stir the salad; then spoon it into and over the endive leaves. Arrange the lemon wedges around or on the salad, so that their juice can be squeezed over to taste on individual portions.

Shrimp and Pasta Cocktails

SERVES 4

FOR THE PASTA

- 1 cup soup pasta shapes, preferably shells
- salt and freshly ground black pepper
- 1 scallion, finely chopped
- 1½ cups peeled, cooked shrimp, defrosted and drained if frozen
- 2 tomatoes, peeled (see Cook's Tip, page 72), deseeded and diced

FOR THE DRESSING

- ½ teaspoon Dijon mustard or other mild mustard
- finely grated rind of ½ a lemon
- ½ teaspoon superfine sugar
- 3 tablespoons cider vinegar
- ⅔ cup olive oil
- 1 tablespoon finely chopped parsley
- 1 teaspoon chopped fresh tarragon

TO GARNISH AND SERVE

- 4 whole, cooked shrimp
- lemon slices
- Melba toast (see Cook's Tip below)

First, cook the pasta in boiling water for 5–10 minutes, or following the instructions on the package, until tender. Drain well.

Meanwhile, make the dressing. Whisk the mustard, lemon rind, superfine sugar, and a little salt and pepper with the vinegar in a bowl. When the sugar has dissolved, gradually whisk in the oil, trickling it in and whisking vigorously. Stir in the parsley and tarragon. Toss the dressing into the hot pasta, cover, and let cool. Then chill lightly for about 30 minutes in the bottom of the refrigerator. Stir the pasta when it has cooled and before putting it into the refrigerator, to make sure the dressing is covering it evenly.

Mix the shrimp and tomatoes into the pasta; then spoon the mixture into small glass dishes, stemmed glasses or shell dishes. Garnish with whole shrimp and lemon slices, and serve with fine, crisp Melba toast.

COOK'S TIP

To make Melba toast, toast medium-thick slices of white bread lightly on both sides. Work quickly with the hot, fresh toast for success as it is difficult to cut once it cools and becomes crisp. Use a large, serrated knife to cut off the crusts; then slice each piece through the middle into two thin layers. Toast the uncooked side of the bread under a broiler, keeping the broiler pan well away from the heat so that the toast begins to curl before it browns. Doing this also helps to prevent the corners and very thin areas burning before the rest of the slice has browned.

Winter Salad

SERVES 4–6

- 8 ounces elbows or *ditali* or small gnocchi
- salt and freshly ground black pepper
- 1¾ cups diced carrots
- ¾ cup diced rutabaga
- 2 celery stalks, sliced
- 1 leek, sliced
- 1 cup frozen peas
- 4 ounces cauliflower, divided into small florets
- 1¼ cups shredded white cabbage
- 1 small onion, finely chopped
- 1¼ cups mayonnaise
- 4 tablespoons plain yogurt

Cook the pasta in plenty of boiling salted water for about 15 minutes, or according to the instructions on the package, until tender. Drain, and rinse under cold water. Let drain.

Bring a large saucepan of water to a boil. Add the carrots, and boil for 1 minute; then add the rutabaga, and continue to boil for 2 minutes. Next add the celery, and cook for 2 minutes; then add the leek, frozen peas and cauliflower. Bring back to a boil, and cook for a further 2 minutes. By this time all the vegetables should be tender, and none should be too soft. Drain the cooked vegetables, and rinse them under cold water to prevent further softening; then drain well.

Mix the cabbage, onion and pasta in a large bowl. Add the mayonnaise, yogurt, and salt and pepper to taste. Toss the ingredients well until thoroughly combined; then lightly mix in the cooked vegetables.

Pasta with Crab Dressing

A couple of cans of inexpensive dressed crab make a good dressing for these simple first-course cocktails. Serve thinly sliced rye bread as an accompaniment, arranging black and light bread by overlapping slices of each color alternately on a platter.

SERVES 4

- *1½ cups soup pasta shells*
- *salt and freshly ground black pepper*
- *2 × 2-ounce cans dressed crab*
- *½ cup cream cheese*
- *4 tablespoons plain yogurt*
- *1 tablespoon snipped chives*
- *1 tablespoon chopped parsley*
- *6 tomatoes, peeled (see Cook's Tip, page 72) and sliced*
- *½ English cucumber, peeled and thinly sliced*
- *sprigs of parsley, to garnish*

Cook the pasta in boiling salted water for 5–10 minutes, or according to the instructions on the package, until tender. Drain, and let cool.

Mix the dressed crab with the cream cheese, yogurt, chives, parsley, and salt and pepper to taste. Toss this dressing into the cooled pasta.

To serve, arrange the tomato and cucumber slices on four plates or shallow dishes to form a border for the cocktail; then pile the pasta mixture into the middle. Garnish with sprigs of parsley, and serve.

298

Salad of Pasta with Roasted Bell Peppers

I used fusilli col buco (long spirals, which were available in a local supermarket) for this, but short spirals or twists can be substituted. I would not use spaghetti, tagliatelle, linguine or any of the longer pasta shapes — somehow they are not quite right.

SERVES 4

- 8 ounces fusilli col buco
- salt and freshly ground black pepper
- 2 red bell peppers
- 2 green bell peppers
- 2 yellow bell peppers
- 1 red or white salad onion, thinly sliced
- 4–6 large sprigs of basil, shredded
- 3 tablespoons balsamic vinegar
- 1 teaspoon superfine sugar
- 1 teaspoon mild, wholegrain mustard
- 1 tablespoon chopped fresh marjoram
- 2 tablespoons walnut oil
- ½ cup good virgin olive oil

Cook the pasta in boiling salted water for about 15 minutes, or according to the instructions on the package, until tender. Drain, and rinse under cold water; then let drain.

Peel the bell peppers by charring them individually over a gas flame, or place them all under a very hot broiler (see page 65). When the outside is blistered and blackened, rinse under cold water, and rub off the skin.

Cut out the stalk and core of the peppers from the top; then carefully remove any remaining seeds from inside. Rinse out, and dry the peppers on paper towels. Slice the peppers; then layer them in a wide, shallow dish, with the pasta, onion and basil (it is a good idea to start with a thin layer of peppers, then add half the pasta, then most of the remaining peppers, reserving a few rings to go on top of the last layer of pasta, but it is not essential to follow this pattern).

Whisk the balsamic vinegar with plenty of salt and pepper, the sugar, mustard and marjoram until the sugar has dissolved. Then whisk in the walnut and olive oils. Trickle the dressing over the salad, cover, and let sit for 1–2 hours before serving.

Pasta Salad Niçoise

This makes an excellent lunch or light meal.

SERVES 4

- 8 ounces penne
- salt and freshly ground black pepper
- 4 ounces fine green beans, halved
- 1 green bell pepper, deseeded and diced
- 1 pound tomatoes, peeled (see Cook's Tip, page 72), deseeded and quartered
- 8-ounce can tuna in oil
- 2-ounce can anchovy fillets
- 16 black olives, pitted
- 4 eggs, hard-cooked and quartered
- 1 garlic clove, finely chopped
- 3 tablespoons cider vinegar (or wine vinegar if preferred)
- 3 tablespoons olive oil
- croûtons (see Cook's Tip below)

Cook the penne in boiling salted water for about 15 minutes, or according to the instructions on the package, until tender. Drain, rinse in cold water, and let drain.

Add the green beans to boiling salted water, bring back to a boil, and cook for 1 minute; then drain, and rinse under cold water. Let the beans drain.

Mix the bell pepper and tomatoes in a large bowl. Drain, and reserve the oil from the tuna and anchovies. Flake the tuna, and add it to the pepper and tomatoes. Cut the anchovy fillets into short pieces, and add to the salad. Mix in the olives, penne, green beans and eggs.

Whisk the garlic and vinegar together with a little pepper (the oil from the anchovies and the fillets themselves will be sufficiently salty to season the salad). Then gradually whisk in the reserved oil from the cans and the olive oil. Pour this dressing over the salad, and mix well. Finally, toss in some croûtons, and serve.

> ### COOK'S TIP
>
> To make croûtons, trim the crusts off medium-thick slices of bread, and cut them into ½-inch squares. Heat a mixture of butter and olive oil in a large skillet. Add the bread cubes, and turn them in the hot oil with a slotted spoon. Fry the bread cubes, turning them regularly with the slotted spoon, until they are crisp and golden. Drain on paper towels.

Salami and Pasta Salads

These make a satisfying lunch, or they can be served in smaller portions and divided between shell dishes or glasses for a light first course. Serve with warmed crusty bread.

SERVES 4

- 8 ounces small pasta shapes, such as elbows or ditali
- salt and freshly ground black pepper
- 8 ounces good-quality Italian salami (see Cook's Tip below)
- 1 small zucchini, very lightly peeled, halved and thinly sliced
- 1 bunch watercress, leaves only
- 1 red onion or other mild salad onion, chopped
- 10 stuffed green olives, thickly sliced
- 4 tablespoons pine nuts
- 8 quails' eggs
- good olive oil
- 1 lemon, cut into large wedges

Cook the pasta in boiling salted water for about 10 minutes, or following the instructions on the package, until tender. Drain well.

Meanwhile, cut the salami into strips, and mix them with the zucchini, watercress, onion and olives.

Dry-roast the pine nuts in a small, heavy-bottomed saucepan over a low to medium heat, and shake it often so that they cook evenly until lightly browned.

Place the quails' eggs in a saucepan, and pour in cold water to cover them. Bring to a boil; then cook for 3 minutes. Drain, rinse under cold water, and remove the shells.

Toss the hot pine nuts with the freshly drained pasta, and trickle over a little olive oil. Mix well, and put into a bowl. Cover, and leave until warm. Lightly toss the salami mixture with the pasta, and divide it between four plates. Halve the quails' eggs, and arrange them on the salad. Garnish with lemon, and serve at once, offering extra olive oil to trickle over the salad to taste.

COOK'S TIP

To make this salad special, it is essential to buy good-quality salami from a good deli or Italian grocery store. If you do buy from a specialty store, you will find a fantastic range, including coarse-textured and extremely spicy types. If you are limited for choice to a poor selection at a small local supermarket, then have a look at the packed meats – you may find that either bresaola (cured beef) or prosciutto is a preferable alternative.

Salad of Warm Pasta with Spinach and Olives

SERVES 4

- 4 tablespoons pine nuts
- 1 garlic clove, finely chopped
- ⅓ cup golden raisins
- ⅔ cup robust red wine
- salt and freshly ground black pepper
- ⅔ cup olive oil
- 1 tablespoon chopped fresh marjoram
- 2 tablespoons chopped parsley
- 4 tablespoons snipped chives
- 8 ounces baby spinach leaves, washed and coarsely shredded
- 12 black olives, pitted and sliced
- 8 ounces fresh pasta shapes
- croûtons, to serve (see Cook's Tip, page 300)

Put the pine nuts into a small, heavy-bottomed saucepan, and dry-roast them over a low to medium heat, shaking the pan occasionally until they have browned lightly and evenly.

Add the garlic, golden raisins and wine, bring to a boil, and simmer gently for 5 minutes. Strain the mixture, pouring the wine into a large bowl, and reserving the dry ingredients.

Whisk salt and pepper to taste into the wine; then whisk in the oil. Return the dry ingredients to the liquid, add the marjoram, parsley and chives, and set aside.

Mix the spinach with the olives, and transfer the mixture to a serving bowl.

Cook the pasta in boiling salted water for 3 minutes, or until tender. Drain well, and add to the red wine dressing. Toss well; then mix with the spinach and olives. Toss in a generous sprinkling of croûtons, and serve at once.

Party Pasta

I feel as though I am doing pasta down by dropping in a salad specifically labeled for parties . . . would you want to make this one, I ask? Why not make multiple portions of any of the other salads? I suppose this is one of those "safe" recipes that everyone will enjoy, including the less adventurous diners. The other reason for setting this recipe aside specifically is because it can be doubled, trebled, quadrupled and so on without there being too much of one flavoring (like garlic or spice).

SERVES 8

- 8 ounces fresh green beans, cut into short lengths
- 1¾ cups diced carrots
- 4 celery stalks, sliced
- 1 red bell pepper, deseeded and diced
- 12 ounces pasta spirals or shells or bows or twists
- salt and freshly ground black pepper
- 1 bunch of scallions, finely chopped
- 13-ounce can corn kernels
- 1¼ cups mayonnaise
- 1¼ cups fromage frais
- plenty of chopped parsley

Cook the green beans and carrots in boiling water for 3 minutes, or until just cooked, but still with a bit of crunch. Add the celery and bell pepper, bring back to a boil, and drain. Rinse the vegetables under cold water to prevent them cooking further, and drain.

Cook the pasta in boiling salted water for about 15 minutes, or according to the instructions on the package, until tender. Drain well.

Mix the pasta, blanched vegetables, scallions, corn and some freshly ground black pepper in a bowl. Cover, and let cool.

Mix the mayonnaise, fromage frais and parsley into the salad; then taste for seasoning. Let sit for about an hour before serving, so that the flavors have time to develop.

Layered Tomato and Pasta Salad

This is a good recipe to remember if ever you find yourself on a self-catering vacation in a Mediterranean country, where there are ripe tomatoes bursting with flavor and wonderfully satisfying close-textured bread to mop up the juices.

SERVES 6

- 8 ounces pasta bows
- salt and freshly ground black pepper
- 2¼ pounds flavorsome tomatoes, peeled and sliced (see Cook's Tip, page 72)
- a little balsamic or cider vinegar
- 3 garlic cloves, finely chopped
- about 12 black olives, thinly sliced
- handful of sprigs of basil, shredded
- good-quality virgin olive oil
- croûtons, to serve (see Cook's Tip, page 300)

Cook the pasta in boiling salted water for about 15 minutes, or according to the instructions on the package, until tender. While the pasta is cooking, sprinkle the tomatoes with salt and a little vinegar (do not be too generous with the vinegar, a few drops from the cap of the bottle will do).

Drain the pasta, and layer it, while hot, with the tomatoes in a serving dish. Sprinkle each layer of tomatoes with garlic, freshly ground black pepper, olives and basil. Then trickle a little olive oil over the top (not as much as you would add to a salad), and cover the dish. Let marinate for 2–3 hours before serving.

To serve, trickle a little more oil over the salad, and sprinkle with croûtons.

Shredded Vegetable and Linguine Salad

This is the ideal accompaniment for broiled fish, poultry, meat or kebabs. Remember this recipe next time you plan a barbecue as it will make a complete meal with a steak, burger or some wonderful spicy sausages (try boiling coarse Italian sausages until tender, then cooking them on the barbecue).

SERVES 4–6

- *2 cups coarsely grated, young carrots*
- *salt and freshly ground black pepper*
- *juice of 1 orange*
- *1 tablespoon hazelnut or walnut oil*
- *8 ounces zucchini, very thinly peeled (see Cook's Tip, page 184) and coarsely grated*
- *juice of 1 lime*
- *3 tablespoons olive oil*
- *4 sprigs of basil, shredded*
- *12 ounces fresh linguine or paglia e fieno*
- *6 scallions, finely chopped*
- *sprigs of basil, to garnish*

Mix the carrots with a little salt and pepper. Toss with the orange juice and hazelnut or walnut oil; then let marinate for at least an hour before serving.

Toss the zucchini with the lime juice, 1 tablespoon of the olive oil and the basil. Cover, and let sit for 30 minutes or so (the zucchini should not be allowed to marinate for as long as the carrots).

Cook the linguine or paglia e fieno in plenty of boiling salted water for about 3 minutes, or until tender. Drain well, and toss with the remaining olive oil, the scallions and plenty of pepper.

Layer the pasta, carrots and zucchini in a serving dish, or arrange them on a large platter or shallow dish. Garnish with basil, and serve immediately.

Pasta Salad with Fresh Dates

SERVES 4

- 8 ounces pasta shapes (such as porcini-flavored, mushroom shapes, penne or rigatoni)
- salt and freshly ground black pepper
- 4 celery stalks, sliced
- 4 tablespoons pine nuts
- 1/2 cup roughly chopped walnuts or pecan nuts
- 8 ounces fresh dates, pitted and sliced
- 1 bunch of watercress, leaves only
- 4 tablespoons chopped parsley
- 1 tablespoon chopped mint
- handful of fresh basil leaves, shredded
- 3 tablespoons balsamic vinegar
- 1 garlic clove, crushed and chopped
- 1 tablespoon walnut oil
- 1/2 cup olive oil

Cook the pasta in boiling salted water for about 15 minutes, or according to the instructions on the package, until tender.

Blanch the celery in boiling salted water for 1 minute; then drain well.

Dry-roast the pine nuts in a small, heavy-bottomed saucepan over a low to medium heat, and shake it often or stir, so that they have browned lightly and evenly.

Mix the walnuts or pecans, pine nuts, dates, watercress, parsley, mint and basil in a large bowl.

Whisk the balsamic vinegar, garlic, and salt and pepper to taste in a bowl; then slowly whisk in the walnut and olive oils. Pour the dressing over the nut and date mixture.

Drain the cooked pasta, and add it to the bowl; toss well, and cover until cooled before serving.

BESIDES THE PASTA

◆

In essence, Pasta was Designed to be a Quick Food, a Light Meal or a Snack Course. ❧ Eaten Italian-style, it Can be a Little Something for Lunch or a Course to Curb your Hunger While You Anticipate the Meat Dish to Follow. ❧ In the Orient, Noodles, Dim sum or the Little Dumplings from Japanese Cuisine are Simply there as Fillers – In-Between-Meal Snacks or, Again in the Modern World, a Light Lunch or, even, Breakfast.

Move North to the Colder Climes and there are Parts of Europe Where this Kind of Food is Served Together with Substantial Main Dishes for Maximum Effect. Great Ladlefuls of Piping Hot Stew Crown Steaming Spatzle, or Bowls of Tiny Dumplings Will Form the Base for a Hearty Goulash. Even Here, Though, We Find Delicate, Filled Pasta with the Minimum of Dressing Being Served to Satisfy Midday Hunger Pangs.

You Do Not Have to Drown a Course with Pasta; It Can be a Subordinate Side Dish, and it Will Work with Other Accompaniments. ❧ Here are a Few Suggestions.

Olive Bread

MAKES 2 LOAVES

- 6 cups white bread flour
- 2 teaspoons salt
- 1 teaspoon dried oregano
- 1 teaspoon superfine sugar
- 2 envelopes easy-blend yeast
- ½ cup olive oil, plus extra for greasing and brushing
- 1 cup water
- ½ cup dry white wine
- 1 cup pitted black olives

Grease two baking sheets with a little oil.

Put the flour into a bowl. Mix in the salt, oregano, sugar and yeast. Make a well in the dry ingredients. Heat the olive oil, water and wine together in a saucepan, stirring, until just hand-hot.

Pour the liquid into the well in the dry ingredients. Gradually stir the flour mixture into the liquid; then use your hand to bring the mixture together into a dough. Transfer the dough to a floured counter, and knead thoroughly until it is smooth and elastic.

When the dough is thoroughly kneaded, gradually knead in the olives by pressing out the dough, adding some olives, then folding it over, and pressing it out again. Repeat this process until all the olives have been worked into the dough.

Cut the dough in half, and flatten the portions into round loaves. Place on the baking sheets, cover loosely with lightly oiled plastic wrap, and leave in a warm place until doubled in size. This may take several hours depending on room temperature.

Toward the end of this time, preheat the oven to 425°F.

Brush the tops of the loaves with a little olive oil, and bake for about 40 minutes, or until the loaves are well browned. To check whether or not the bread is cooked through, turn the loaf over, and tap its base: it will sound hollow when cooked. Let the loaves cool on a wire rack.

Lemon and Herb Rolls

A variation on the garlic bread theme, these are **excellent served with seafood pastas and pasta starters.**

SERVES 8

- ⅓ cup butter
- grated rind of 1 lemon
- 1 tablespoon chopped parsley
- 1 teaspoon chopped fresh thyme
- 1 tablespoon snipped chives
- 8 finger rolls

Preheat the oven to 400°F.

Cream the butter with the lemon rind, parsley, thyme and chives.

Cut the rolls in half lengthwise. Spread the cut sides with butter; then put them back together.

Wrap securely in foil, folding all the corners over neatly, and bake in the preheated oven for about 15 minutes, or until the rolls are crisp and hot, and the butter has melted. Serve at once.

Walnut and Olive Rolls

SERVES 8

- ½ cup butter
- 1 small garlic clove, crushed and chopped
- 12 black olives, pitted and chopped
- ¼ cup chopped walnuts
- 2 tablespoons chopped parsley
- 2 tablespoons snipped chives
- 4 large, soft, floury rolls

Preheat the oven to 400°F.

Cream the butter with the garlic; then add the olives, walnuts, parsley and chives. Slice the rolls in half; then spread both halves with the butter mixture. Place the baps, buttered sides up, on baking sheets, and bake for 5 –7 minutes, until the topping has melted, and the rolls are hot through. Serve at once.

Flat Breads with Herbs and Sunflower Seeds

The topping is optional on these breads, so make them plain if you prefer.

MAKES 12

FOR THE BREADS
- *4 cups white bread flour*
- *1 teaspoon salt*
- *2 envelopes easy-blend yeast*
- *4 tablespoons olive oil*
- *1 cup water*
- *3 tablespoons dry white wine*

FOR THE TOPPING
- *olive oil, for brushing*
- *6 tablespoons sunflower seeds*
- *2 tablespoons chopped fresh oregano*
- *1 tablespoon chopped fresh thyme*

You need four clean dish cloths on which to put the breads to rise, and to cover them.

Mix the flour, salt and yeast in a bowl. Make a well in the dry ingredients. Heat the olive oil, water and wine together in a saucepan, stirring, until just hand-hot.

Pour the liquid into the well in the dry ingredients. Gradually stir the flour mixture into the liquid; then use your hand to bring the mixture together into a dough.

Transfer the dough to a floured counter, and knead thoroughly until it is smooth and elastic. Cut the dough into 12 equal portions. Lay a clean dish cloth on a board or baking sheet, and dredge it with flour. Prepare another board or baking sheet in the same way.

Knead each piece of dough lightly, then roll it out thinly into an oval, and place on the floured dish cloth. When one baking sheet is full, dust the breads with a little flour, cover loosely with a dish cloth, and leave in a warm place until risen and puffy. This will take at least an hour.

Toward the end of this time, preheat the oven to 475°F, or the hottest setting on your oven. Heat two or three baking sheets for about 15 minutes. While the baking sheets are heating, brush each piece of bread with a little olive oil. Mix the sunflower seeds, oregano and thyme. Sprinkle the mixture over each of the breads.

Working quickly, transfer the breads to the heated baking sheets, and bake for about 10 minutes, or until the breads have puffed up, and are lightly browned. Serve freshly baked.

Avocado and Bell Pepper Salad

SERVES 4

FOR THE SALAD

- ¼ iceberg lettuce, shredded
- 1 large red bell pepper, peeled (see page 65), deseeded and sliced
- 1 large yellow bell pepper, peeled (also see page 65), deseeded and sliced
- 2 avocados, halved, pitted and cut across into slices

FOR THE DRESSING

- juice of 1 lemon
- salt and freshly ground black pepper
- 3 tablespoons olive oil
- 3 tablespoons sunflower oil
- 2 tablespoons chopped parsley
- 2 tablespoons snipped chives
- a little grated nutmeg

First, make the salad. Sprinkle the lettuce into a serving dish. Top with the bell peppers and avocado slices.

Next, make the dressing. Whisk the lemon juice with salt and pepper to taste; then whisk in the oils, parsley, chives and a little nutmeg to taste. Trickle the dressing over the salad, and serve.

Good Green Salad

THE INGREDIENTS

LETTUCE
A leaf lettuce really does not have much flavor, so select one with more character as the base for the salad. I like iceberg, which is sweet, crisp and flavorsome. Pomaine is another alternative . . . or experiment with the many other types now widely available.

CHICORY
A fine, curly salad green with pale green-yellow ends, this adds good texture to a green salad.

CORN SALAD
Small, oval leaves with a delicate, sweet flavor. Keep small leaves whole, or break up larger ones by hand as they bruise easily. An asset in a salad.

LOLLO BIONDO OR LOLLO ROSSO
The latter are tinged with red. These have soft, very wavy leaves. They look attractive in a salad, but they do not add a great deal of interest in terms of flavor.

CUCUMBER
Peel English cucumber for use in a green salad, and cut it finely, either into slices, dice or matchstick strips. Put the cucumber into a strainer, and sprinkle with salt; then leave for 15 minutes. Pat it dry with paper towels before adding it to the salad.

GREEN BELL PEPPER
Ideally, this should be peeled (see page 65), but it is not essential. However, a bell pepper should be very thinly cut, and prepared in small pieces.

WATERCRESS AND MUSTARD AND CRESS
Both add flavor to a green salad. Cut or pinch off the leaves from a bunch of watercress, or snip off the tops of mustard and cress.

ARUGULA
This has a strong, peppery flavor, and it is more of a herb than a salad vegetable. A few leaves add an excellent flavor contrast to a green salad.

SCALLIONS
I like scallions in a green salad as they are another ingre-dient to bring a zing of flavor to the mixture. The easiest and most satisfactory preparation is to snip them with a pair of scissors, or slice them finely with a sharp knife.

THE OIL AND VINEGAR DRESSING
This is all important, but it must be selected to complement the main dish as well as the salad. Here are a few ideas.

- Whisk the chosen seasonings with the lemon juice or vinegar before adding the oil. This allows substances such as salt and sugar to dissolve into the dressing, and flavor it rather than precipitate on the fringes of the mixture.
- The dressing must be a balanced mixture of tart ingredients with oil. The idea is to take away the rich oiliness of a dressing by balancing it with the right quantity of vinegar. Twice the volume of oil to vinegar makes a dressing with a tang, but up to four times the volume of oil to vinegar can be used depending on the ingredients, dish and personal taste.
- Use a light oil or one that has the required flavor. Olive oil is good, but sunflower and the even lighter grapeseed oil are alternatives. Walnut and hazelnut oils have distinctive flavors, but they are very strong, so add them in small proportions, alongside another oil.
- There are several types of vinegar. Malt vinegars (brown or distilled white) are not suitable for salad dressings as they are very harsh. Wine vinegars are quite harsh, but are suitable if you want a distinctly acidic taste coming through the dressing. I find this is so for white, red, champagne and sherry vinegars. Cider vinegar makes a smoother, more balanced dressing, and it can be used in larger amounts with better results. Balsamic vinegar is an aged vinegar that has a dark, rich flavor. Although it is strong and quite distinct, it is nothing like as harsh and penetrating as the wine vinegars, and does contribute a robust, rounded flavor to the dressing.

FLAVORING INGREDIENTS

Salt and pepper, sugar, mustard, garlic and herbs. Use them according to the main dish. Always taste the dressing – you should be able to enjoy the flavor of the dressing when taken on its own off a teaspoon; if it makes your face curl up, and you shrink away, then it will wreck the salad, and it probably has too much vinegar, or it was of the wrong type.

Pea Salad

SERVES 4

FOR THE SALAD

- 2 cups frozen petits pois
- 2 bunches of watercress, leaves only
- 4 scallions, finely sliced
- plenty of chopped parsley
- croûtons (see Cook's Tip, page 300)

FOR THE DRESSING

- 3 tablespoons cider vinegar
- salt and freshly ground black pepper
- 1 teaspoon wholegrain mustard
- ½ teaspoon sugar
- 6 tablespoons olive oil
- 1 tablespoon chopped mint (optional)
- 1 garlic clove, finely chopped (optional)

Make the dressing first. Whisk the vinegar with salt and pepper to taste, the mustard and sugar. When the sugar has dissolved, whisk in the oil. Add mint and garlic if liked.

Now, prepare the salad. Add the petits pois to boiling water, and bring back to a boil; then cook for 3 minutes. Drain, and mix with the dressing; then let cool.

Add the watercress, scallions and parsley. Toss in the croûtons just before serving.

Zucchini and Basil Salad

A simple summer salad that goes well with most pasta dishes.

SERVES 4

- 12 ounces young courgettes, very thinly peeled (see Cook's Tip, page 184)
- 1 small scallion, finely chopped
- salt and freshly ground black pepper
- a little lemon juice
- olive oil
- 4 fresh sprigs of basil, shredded

Coarsely grate the zucchini, then mix them with the onion, and add salt and pepper to taste. Squeeze a little lemon juice over the zucchini, and trickle olive oil over to taste. Mix in the basil, and taste for seasoning, lemon and oil before serving (do not make this salad more than 30 minutes before serving it).

Leeks with Spinach

SERVES 4–6

- ¼ cup butter
- 1 bay leaf
- 4 cups thinly sliced leeks (see Cook's Tip, page 116)
- 1¼ pounds fresh spinach, washed and shredded
- salt and freshly ground black pepper

Melt the butter in a large saucepan. Add the bay leaf, and cook it for 1 minute, pressing it with a spoon so that it flavors the butter well.

Add the leeks, and stir well. Cover, and cook gently for about 15 minutes, or until the leeks are tender, stirring occasionally. Add the spinach to the pan, and stir as best you can; then cover the pan tightly. Cook the spinach for about 10 minutes, stirring once or twice, and replacing the lid each time. Taste for seasoning, adding salt and pepper as necessary, and discard the bay leaf before serving.

Braised Fennel

SERVES 4

- ¼ cup butter
- 1 onion, finely chopped
- 1 carrot, diced
- 1 bay leaf
- salt and freshly ground black pepper
- ⅔ cup dry white wine
- ⅔ cup chicken or vegetable stock
- 4 large fennel bulbs
- 1 tablespoon all-purpose flour

Preheat the oven to 350°F.

Melt half the butter in a flameproof, ovenproof casserole. Add the onion, carrot and bay leaf with salt and pepper to taste. Cook, stirring, for 5 minutes, then add the wine and stock, and bring just to a boil. Remove from the heat.

Cut the fennel bulbs in half, and trim out any tough parts of the bases. Place the fennel in the casserole, and baste with the juices. Cover tightly, and bake in the preheated oven for 1¼–1½ hours, or until the fennel is completely tender.

Cream the flour with the remaining butter. Use a slotted spoon to transfer the fennel to a warmed serving dish, cover the vegetable, and keep hot. Discard the bay leaf from the cooking juices, then bring them to a boil, and whisk in the butter and flour mixture. Continue whisking until the juices have boiled, and thickened slightly. Boil hard for 1–2 minutes. Taste for seasoning, then pour the sauce over the fennel, and serve at once.

Stuffed Baby Eggplants

These make a fitting accompaniment for a wide variety
of pasta dishes, adding interest to an otherwise one-
dish main course without making the meal too bulky or
competing with the sauce.

SERVES 4

- *½ cup fresh light rye bread crumbs*
- *2 tablespoons pine nuts*
- *3 fresh sage leaves, chopped*
- *1 scallion, chopped*
- *2 sprigs of basil, finely shredded*
- *2 tablespoons sour cream*
- *salt and freshly ground black pepper*
- *8 baby eggplants*
- *3 tablespoons butter*

Preheat the oven to 350°F.

Mix the bread crumbs, pine nuts, sage, scallion and
basil. Stir in the sour cream, to bind the ingredients
together, and season the stuffing with salt and pepper to
taste.

Slice the eggplants, leaving the slices attached at the
stalk end. Carefully spread a little of the stuffing between
the slices, and press the eggplants back together. Grease
a baking dish with a little of the butter, place the eggplants on it, and dot them with the remaining butter.
Bake in the preheated oven for 30–35 minutes, or until
the flesh is just tender. Serve at once.

Crusted Tomatoes with Basil Filling

SERVES 4

- 1/3 cup butter, softened
- salt and freshly ground black pepper
- 8 basil leaves, shredded
- 8 firm, ripe tomatoes, peeled (see Cook's Tip, page 72)
- all-purpose flour, for coating
- 2 large eggs, beaten
- 1 cup dried, very lightly browned breadcrumbs
- 8 small basil leaves, to garnish

Preheat the oven to 475°F, or the hottest setting.

Cream the butter with salt and pepper; then lightly mix in the basil. Carefully cut the stalk out from the top of each tomato, using a fine-pointed knife. Take care not to damage the shell of the tomato. Mop the cavity left by the stalk with a paper towel; then place a little of the basil butter in each tomato, pushing it down gently as far as possible.

Coat the tomatoes in flour, then in egg and bread crumbs. Repeat this coating a second time, so that they are thoroughly coated all over. Then chill the tomatoes well.

Place the tomatoes on a greased baking sheet, and bake them in the preheated oven for about 5 minutes, or until the coating has browned lightly and is crisp (do not leave the tomatoes for too long or they will collapse into a mess). Garnish each tomato with a basil leaf, and serve at once.

Chicory with Dates and Olives

A distinctive salad that goes well with simple pastas — macaroni cheese, carbonara, pasta with oil and garlic, butter-tossed fresh pasta and so on.

SERVES 4–6

FOR THE SALAD
- 1 head of chicory, shredded
- 1 cup pitted and thinly sliced fresh dates
- 12 green olives, pitted and thinly sliced
- 1 red or white onion, finely chopped
- handful of parsley, stalks removed, roughly chopped

FOR THE DRESSING
- 1 garlic clove, crushed (optional)
- 2 tablespoons cider vinegar
- 1/2 teaspoon salt
- salt and freshly ground black pepper
- 6 tablespoons olive oil

First, make the salad. Mix the chicory, dates, olives, onion and parsley in a bowl.

For the dressing, mix the garlic, if using, with the vinegar, sugar, and salt and pepper to taste. When the sugar and salt have dissolved, gradually whisk in the oil. Trickle the dressing over the salad just before serving, and toss well.

INDEX